The Lark Ascending

by the same author

ORIGINAL ROCKERS

HOW SOON IS NOW?

The Lark Ascending

The Music of the
British Landscape

Richard King

FABER & FABER

First published in the UK in 2019
by Faber & Faber Ltd
Bloomsbury House
74–77 Great Russell Street
London WC1B 3DA

First published in the USA in 2019

Typeset by Faber & Faber Ltd
Printed and bound by CPI Group (UK) Ltd, Croydon CR0 4YY

A CIP record for this book
is available from the British Library

ISBN 978-0-571-33879-5

Extract from *Undersea* by Rachel Carson reprinted by permission of Pollinger Limited
(www.pollingerlimited.com) on behalf of the Estate of Rachel Carson

Extract from *Under Milk Wood* © Dylan Thomas, 1952. Reprinted by permission of New Directions
Publishing Corp and The Dylan Thomas Trust

Author note:
In 2018, a House of Commons briefing paper stated:

'The term "Gypsies and Travellers" is difficult to define as it does not constitute
a single, homogenous group, but encompasses a range of groups with different
histories, cultures and beliefs including: Romany Gypsies, Irish Travellers, and
Scottish Gypsy Travellers. There are also Traveller groups which are generally
regarded as "cultural" rather than "ethnic" Travellers. These include "New" (Age)
Travellers and occupational travellers, such as showmen and waterway travellers.'

While respectfully acknowledging the various definitions of the term
'Travellers', in the context of this book 'Traveller(s)' refers to the community
colloquially known as New Age Travellers throughout the 1980s and 1990s.

2 4 6 8 10 9 7 5 3

To the memory of my father,
Edgar Hayden King

Contents

'No One Can Own A River'. Sign near the banks of the River Wye at Llyswen, Powys. (Nick Hand)

Prologue

'When we have first-hand knowledge of the land on
which we live, then we can re-shape it according to
our ideals.'

'Ken-ea' (Mabel Barker), *The Nomad, Kibbo-Kift Newsletter*, 1924

The landscape is never truly ours. A mile away from my home in
Mid Wales there is a notice attached to a fence in the corner of
a secluded field. The notice states that the path beneath it leads
to a designated access and egress point on the bank of the River
Wye, which has been provided for the use of canoeists wishing to
navigate the water. Entrance is permitted each October to March
but under strict conditions. The notice then lists the set of rules
regarding the various rights granted by the five organisations
that have agreed this location as an access point to the river: the
Countryside Council for Wales, Environment Agency Wales, the
Welsh Assembly Government, the Wye & Usk Foundation, BOPA
(the British Outdoor Professional's Association).

Three of these organisations whose insignia run along the bottom of the notice no longer exist, so it is uncertain whether the
permissions stated on the notice are still upheld. During summer
the area around the notice is overgrown with bracken and ferns
that protect its colour from fading but ensure that the information

is barely visible. In this sparsely populated rural area, where farming remains the principal economic activity and canoeists are seldom seen even outside the fishing season, graffiti is rare. It is therefore a surprise to see that someone has scratched a message in neat letters onto this metal notice that rejects its designations and instructions. The statement they have left is straightforward: 'No one can own a river'.

The presence of the Wye & Usk Foundation on the sign, a still-thriving local charity that issues day tickets and permits for fishing, attests to the fact a river may be subject to environmental jurisdictions. Nevertheless, the assertion made by the graffiti artist – technically their message is a work of sgraffito, the scratching away of a top layer of paint – is undeniable. A river is a movement of energy that cannot be halted, only controlled or dredged by complicated processes of engineering. Unlike the land that surrounds this quiet stretch of the River Wye on which the notice stands, no one can lay claim to free-flowing water.

Conventions and laws that have endured for centuries dictate the relationship we have with the countryside, whether on land or in water. Despite these jurisdictions our sense of union with the landscape feels equally durable. In our lifetime very few of us will ever own a physical piece of the landscape, yet it continues to define our national identity: the White Cliffs of Dover, England's Mountains Green and the meadow, mill, cottage and shallow water depicted in Constable's *The Hay Wain*. These images, now all but anodyne in their familiarity, are embedded in our national psyche to such a degree they sustain the belief that the landscape is timeless and ours to commune with. Rural Britain remains the panorama onto which we project the idea of our best selves.

According to the 2011 census over 90 per cent of the population live in urban areas, but urban Britain represents no more than 10 per cent of our country's landmass. The identity of those to whom the majority of the land of Great Britain belongs remains vague, if not opaque. A survey in *Country Life* magazine, held four years after the census, estimated that 36,000 people, roughly half a percentage point of the population, owned more than half of rural England and Wales. In Scotland, the devolved government similarly estimated that in their country a mere 432 individuals owned a similar amount of land. Yet to many of us, including the writer of the neat sgraffito on the sign near the River Wye, the depth of feeling we have for nature transcends the rule of law and the ownership of property or acreage. When contemplating the landscape our emotional response is often one that cannot be defined merely as nostalgia or patriotism. It is instead the realisation that something in our consciousness remains undiscovered beneath the soil. The attachment we experience is elemental, an act of identification of such strength it directs us back to inhabit the countryside, however temporarily, despite the regulations that inhibit us from doing so. Music has a rare ability to articulate this sense of yearning and few compositions capture our affinity with the natural world so affectingly as The Lark Ascending, the fifteen-minute 'romance' begun by the composer Ralph Vaughan Williams at the outbreak of the Great War and completed in 1920.

The Lark Ascending was premiered as an arrangement for violin and piano in a concert at Shirehampton, near Bristol, in December of that year where the violinist Marie Hall, to whom Vaughan Williams dedicated the work, performed it. Six months later, on a June evening in London when Hall was accompanied by the British Symphony Orchestra under the baton of Adrian Boult, *The Lark Ascending* received its premiere as the 'romance for violin and orchestra' beloved by millions of listeners.

The significance of *The Lark Ascending* in British life is hard to overstate. It is the most requested piece of music on the radio programme *Desert Island Discs*, is often awarded first place in polls of the country's favourite piece of music and is regularly heard at funerals, particularly, though by no means exclusively, in rural areas. A review of its London premiere in *The Times* suggested that the music of *The Lark* 'dreams itself along'. Vaughan Williams's evocation of a bird flying free from earthbound realities, crossing a perfectly imagined landscape, has resonated deeply with anyone who has found themselves dreaming along with *The Lark Ascending*. It is an experience as intimate, if not spiritual, as music can create.

Vaughan Williams regularly included place names with which he felt a great affinity in his compositions. The composer's sense of *genius loci* was acute. 'Down Ampney', the tune he composed for the hymn 'Come Down, O Love Divine', takes its name from the Gloucestershire village of his birth. Vaughan Williams was similarly assiduous in cataloguing the locations of the many traditional songs he collected throughout his life, ensuring they would always be identified with the site of their discovery and the place in which they had traditionally been sung. In 1932 he gave a series of lectures at Bryn Mawr College, Pennsylvania, titled 'National

Music'. 'Folk song,' the composer told his audience, 'is not a cause of national music, it is a manifestation of it.'

Throughout his life, the principle that a country's music was made by its people, rather than for them, was one Vaughan Williams adhered to. He recognised the ability to understand, enjoy and immerse oneself in music in everyone.

According to the composer music was 'the art of the humble' but also the art form with the greatest capacity to transform the everyday, even if only by celebrating it, such is the function of many folk songs. His friend and musical biographer Michael Kennedy later wrote of Vaughan Williams: 'His nationalism was avowedly conscious; never was it self-conscious. There never was a less typical "typical Englishman". Vaughan Williams believed music was a latent force in all people – "the only means of artistic expression which is natural to everybody".'

In contrast to many of his works, the physical setting of *The Lark Ascending* is anonymous. The open land over which the lark launches itself ever upwards remains unspecified. The imagination of the listener, who travels to their own mental destination when experiencing the music, decides its location, a place known only to them, in the countryside of the mind. Vaughan Williams wrote, 'I believe that every community and every mental state should have its artistic equivalent.' In his most popular composition he created the musical equivalent of a British landscape open to 'every community'.

To realise the ideal of a countryside of the mind in the living landscape of the United Kingdom is an almost impossible task. In the animated section of *The Lark* the bird witnesses activity taking place on the ground below. Throughout the twentieth century, despite the restriction of access experienced by the majority of people in Britain, attempts were made to reinvent the countryside. These experiments in rural reconfiguration were made with the same energy and celebration that the lark observed from on high during its flight. And as Vaughan Williams anticipated, wherever there is congregation in the countryside it achieves its fullest expression in music, the art form that so uniquely renders the mysterious connection we feel with the ground beneath our feet.

This book is an exploration of how the landscape was re-imagined; from the psychologically altered green fields of England Vaughan Williams and the generation returning from the trenches encountered after the armistice; to the agrarian revivalists and idealists of the 1920s and 1930s; to the position of rural Britain in the nation that was rebuilt after the Second World War; to the 'Back to the Land' movement of the 1960s; to the changing countryside of the 1980s, which witnessed the Women's Peace Camp at Greenham Common and New Age Travellers congregating every year at Stonehenge; and to the 1990s ravers who assembled for one final free party at Castlemorton in 1992. From the song written to commemorate the mass trespass of Kinder Scout to the moment before the sound systems of the free festivals finally ran out of charge, music was the thread of this activity and flowed through the century with the authority of a river.

Ralph Vaughan Williams concluded the first of his lectures on 'National Music' by stating: '. . . if the roots of your art are firmly planted in your own soil and that soil has anything individual to give you, you may still gain the whole world and not lose your own souls.'

This is a history of how music, 'the art of the humble', lies at the roots of such individuality. And it is a story of those who attempted to gain the whole world in the soil of the fields and hills of this country, and the effect it had on their souls.

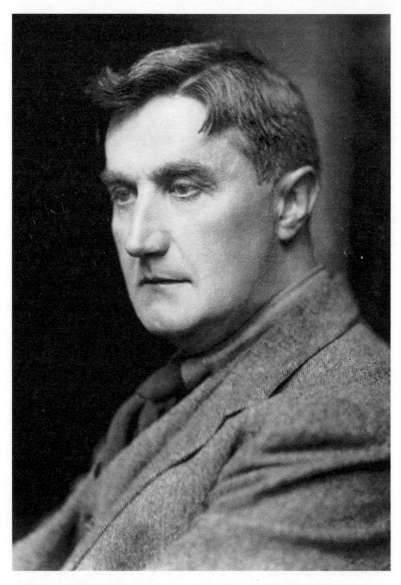

'The art of music above all other arts is the expression of the soul of a nation.'
Ralph Vaughan Williams, 1872–1958. (Getty)

1 : The Landscape of the Lark

There is a familiar moment on any walk of reasonable length. Our sense of time undergoes an almost imperceptible transformation; the distance to our destination no longer concerns us, our point of departure is located in the past and we feel vividly but gracefully alive in the present. Our footsteps have a natural rhythm over which we neither need, nor feel capable of, control. The momentum of our feet silences the inner dialogue of our thoughts, as our physical and subconscious selves coalesce in therapeutic and forgiving harmony. The journey continues in a manner that now feels effortless, restorative, and reminds us of our own vitality.

Although gratifying, experience tells us such moments are far from assured during our time spent outdoors. Often the chatter in our head, the very anxieties and everyday strains of life for which we have prescribed ourselves a long walk, resurface to distract us.

For this reason, many years ago, I made certain any walk I undertook of reasonable length had recourse to being accompanied, or perhaps more accurately, salvaged, by music. The ability of music to dull and placate the thoughts, conversations and memories we are prone to dwell on when walking is incomparable, as is the manner in which a soundtrack brokers the view. The advances in technology were such that, for myself, to listen while walking became reflexive, almost habitual.

My choice of listening material was always instrumental music. I had come to the conclusion that if one is attempting to silence the voices in one's head, it is preferable to abandon the voice altogether. Instead, my walks were conducted to meditative sounds that weaved in and out of one's consciousness: minimalism, the composers Laurie Spiegel and Steve Reich in particular, the mid-nineties electronica of Boards of Canada, Jim O'Rourke and Aphex Twin and the long guitar ragas of 1960s primitives such as John Fahey and Robbie Basho.

Occasionally the effect of walking alone in open country while listening closely to a piece of music overwhelmed me. I felt as though I was demanding too much of my senses, which could quickly grow resistant to such a concentrated form of transcendence. I nevertheless experienced regular moments of complete immersion in my surroundings. When heard with the appropriate musical accompaniment, the sight of minor, everyday details seen on a walk such as a recently fallen branch revealed themselves with a momentary and magical clarity. A familiar view, such as the one that presented itself by looking downwards along the footpath I had followed to the top of a hill, was now a scene of great, instinctive drama.

On another occasion I found myself staring, entranced, for almost twenty minutes at two young buzzards overhead, as their endless circling serendipitously fell into rhythm with the music in my headphones. At the end of this reverie, when the birds flew on and I brought my gaze back to ground level, I was greeted by disorientating stares from a flock of ewes standing stock still at the hedgerow of a neighbouring field. I had been unaware of the sheep as they crossed the field towards me. Now, as I emerged from my own mental enclosure we exchanged long glances with each other, occupying our territory in silence.

Despite the experience of these raptures I was also aware that music cancels out the sound of the landscape. I was never at ease with this compromise, one I was reminded of each time I removed my headphones as every activity taking place around me, even the merest suggestion of a breeze, registered in my ears with breathtaking intensity. The trill of birdsong sounded so radiant it was as if I were hearing it for the first time. As I traipsed though a thick bed of leaves the volume of their crunch underfoot was more suited to the noise made by wading through a river in full spate.

At its purest the relationship between music and landscape feels almost divine, an eternal association that resists analysis. The relationship between music and the land itself is often more exasperating and conflicted than the contemplative beauty of pastoral compositions suggests. In honour of the composer who was born in the village of Broadheath, in the Malvern Hills near Worcester, the area is frequently given the name 'Elgar Country' by the National Trust, the Council for the Preservation of Rural England and similar organisations. The conjecture being that the landscape of 'Elgar Country', the rolling hills and open green pasture redolent of Albion, is reflected in the music of the composer Edward Elgar: the *Pomp and Circumstance Marches* that include 'Land of Hope and Glory', *The Enigma Variations*, and lesser known works such as *Pageant of Empire* and the composer's setting for Rudyard Kipling's musical booklet *The Fringes of the Fleet.* Throughout the twentieth century 'Elgar Country' thus represented a heartland that provided a rousing and proud chorus, particularly in times of war or national celebration, a locus for an easily defined and easily sung patriotism, a rural embodiment of the Last Night of the Proms.

In 1992 an estimated twenty to forty thousand people attended a four-day rave at Castlemorton Common in the Malvern Hills. For its inhabitants and the self-appointed custodians of 'Elgar Country', the ninety-six hours of continuous dance music relayed and distorted by the sound systems occupying the Common were not merely a source of irritation or noise pollution. This invasion of ravers and libertarians also represented a psychological intrusion, a momentary rupture in the hitherto assured character of the landscape, one so extreme as to temporarily question its identity.

My own memories of attending Castlemorton are suitably vague and fractured, although I vividly recall my friends and me sitting in stoned anticipation that we would move further along the narrow road on which an endless line of traffic had ground to a halt. Our reasons for attending were prosaic. We were inexperienced and irregular ravers who lived little over an hour away in Bristol, and as the party was held towards the end of May, we assumed there would be serial opportunities to experience an early summer sunrise. As we sat together in a cheap car with the mute anticipation of youth, we gradually realised the music playing around us on car stereos was being danced to energetically by our neighbours, and the vehicles in the queue had been absorbed into the rave. It became clear that no one at Castlemorton was in any position of authority, nor indeed did anyone appear to want to be; the sense of free will encircling us was extraordinarily powerful. The festival had no discernible centre of activity, each sound system had established their own area, one or two of which included a tent. There were no stages or focal points to direct our attention. It was the relentless dancing, a continuous circulation of energy lasting for days, which represented the festival's nucleus.

Despite the widespread euphoria, a tension circulated in the air, as though it was being broadcast across the sound systems' remorseless bass lines. To the hedonistic visitors Castlemorton Common represented one of the few accessible central areas in rural England where music might be experienced outdoors, through the visceral and unfettered pleasures of dancing under open skies. To the onlooking residents of its neighbouring villages, the free festival represented a deconsecration of the unchanging set of values in our national past with which the Common was synonymous. The perceived wisdom, that the Common should be experienced as a site to be gazed upon for its historic beauty and as a source for a very British form of reassurance and contemplation, had been shattered.

Due to its legal status as common land and to the frustration of the authorities the rave at Castlemorton was able to continue uninterrupted until the generators and the spirits and energy of those attending had worn out. The police presence at Castlemorton, such as it was, was inadequate to curtail the festival and questions were subsequently asked as to whether sufficient powers were in place to prevent such an event taking place in the future. These questions were answered by the introduction of a new set of laws.

Arguments over to whom it belongs and to what uses it should be ascribed are as old as the land itself, and the four-day free party at Castlemorton was a further incidence of an ongoing rural conflict that predates the Enclosure Act of 1773. The darkened atmosphere at Castlemorton, accentuated by sleeplessness and narcotic disorientation, felt as ancient as the mist that rose over the Common at daybreak.

Before the outbreak of war in 1939, the right to walk through the more remote parts of Britain was an often debated issue. In 1932 around five hundred people, mainly young men, a handful of whom were known to have Communist sympathies, participated in the mass trespass of Kinder Scout, the highest point in the Peak District and an area of several hundred acres of moorland managed privately for grouse shooting. This was a form of hunting that was popular with landowners as it provided a higher income than the poor returns received from farming. There was consequently a significant presence of gamekeepers on Kinder Scout, with whom the trespassers came into confrontation. Arrests were made and the incident, which had consisted of little more than pushing and shoving, during which a gamekeeper had suffered a sprained ankle, was declared a 'riotous assembly'.

The trespass drew great media interest, as did the severity of the punishment dispensed to the organisers, one of whom, the twenty-year-old organiser Benny Rothman, was gaoled for four months. In his summing-up the judge made reference to the fact Rothman was both a member of the Young Communist League and Jewish. As trespass was a civil rather than a criminal offence, the sentences and the fact the defendants were charged for the crime of 'riotous assembly' were considered vindictive and harsh. Rather than suppress the burgeoning interest in exploring the country's open spaces, the furore over the Kinder Scout trespass emboldened members of the public with an interest in the outdoors throughout the country. The popularity of rambling grew further, and the Ramblers' Association, founded in 1935, began a successful campaign for the right to be granted access to the countryside. After the conclusion of the Second World War the National Parks and Access to the Countryside Act of 1949 included the right of legal trespass.

The Act stated the creation of a network of National Parks in Britain was a result of the need to promote 'opportunities for the understanding and enjoyment of the special qualities of those areas by the public'. Landowners in these designated areas were now obliged by law to agree to grant the general public right of way, in order that they might enjoy these opportunities.

The creation of National Parks, the accreditation of legal trespass and the ability to roam carefree, if only through designated areas of countryside, engendered a sense of common kinship with the natural environment. In the decades to come Parliament would herald the Kinder Scout mass trespass as a powerful symbol of the ability for mild civil disobedience to lead to the advancement and democratisation of society.

In the spring of 1994, over sixty years after Kinder Scout and two years after the rave at Castlemorton, the Criminal Justice and

Public Order Act was introduced to the House of Commons. The Act, which experienced a protracted and often fractious passage through Parliament before receiving Royal Assent towards the year's end, contained a broad swathe of measures aimed at reducing what the ailing Conservative government, in an attempt at populism, described as 'Anti Social Behaviour'.

The length and scale of the events at Castlemorton ensured any distinction between raving, free festivals and any other form of casual hedonism had been deemed irrelevant by the authorities.

The Criminal Justice Bill, as it was referred to in news bulletins and became known in the popular imagination, was widely regarded as a draconian piece of legislation. One of the Bill's most lasting effects was to curtail several of the marginal social movements that had grown in the previous decade, such as the phenomenon of New Age Travellers, and to discourage entrepreneurial promoters in the black economy who hosted outdoor raves and free twenty-four-hour parties in Britain's countryside. These events were unlicensed, both in the legal sense and also in their formlessness and lack of hierarchy or structure. Their organisers' principal motivation, aside from the revenue generated by the buying and selling of drugs, was to provide an open space for anyone present to dance to the sound systems on site.

The life of quiet contemplation symbolised by 'Elgar Country' existed for barely a few fleeting moments, if at all, in the average working day of anyone whose living was derived from the land. Yet a sentimentality and nostalgia for an apparently fictitious pastoral idyll has continually dominated our view of rural life. Whatever definition we use, the countryside remains a contradiction: a place of survival still, for many who make their living there, but a source of recuperation and rapture to its visitors. To walk through much of rural Britain is to walk through our past. Our landscape may stimulate our subconscious and prompt in us thoughts of airy self-reflection, but the ground itself is as laden with history as any ancient city and the beauty of the view often conceals the anxieties and arguments that characterise this history.

In 1921, the year in which *The Lark Ascending* received its orchestral premiere, significant areas of the British countryside were undergoing a period of substantive change. The lark flies over terrain whose character had started to alter towards the end of the previous century, when agriculture in England and Wales experienced consecutive years of heavy rainfall followed by inevitably poor harvests. Such conditions only exacerbated the already diminishing returns of farming and the precariousness of the antiquated methods still popular on large country estates. These various misfortunes consolidated and developed into a depression. The steep decline in ocean freight rates and the invention and proliferation of refrigeration allowed cheap imports of staple goods such as cereal, meat and butter from the United States, Argentina and other distant countries to dominate the market. The result was a fall in domestic prices and stagnating levels of yield. Between 1875 and 1895 the prices of wheat and wool halved while the value of livestock depreciated by almost a third. For the half-century between the 1860s and the outbreak of the First World War there was little demonstrable increase in the material health of British farming; the soil and its crops were weakening.

Despite protracted opposition for over a year from a House of Lords populated by wealthy landowners, David Lloyd George's Liberal government finally passed its People's Budget in 1910. As a consequence of the continuing agricultural depression the country's landowners had already suffered a decline in income from the tenancies charged to the farmers who worked their land. The passing of the People's Budget ensured they were now expected to shoulder the further burden of taxation. The original legislation had included the aggressively contested measure of a land tax, but this controversial proposal was dropped in return for others being accepted, such as an increase in death duties and the taxation of profits made from the sale and ownership of property.

This change in the fortunes of the great estates inaugurated a gradual transformation of the character of the countryside in the twentieth century. Many landowners reluctantly accepted they had no choice but to sell off their assets, and a new class of farmer, the owner-occupier, was created.

The rural population underwent a similar realignment in the years that followed the armistice and witnessed an exodus from domestic service to the cities; having encountered a less restricted life away from the country house, few people were minded to return, even if the work had compared favourably to agricultural labour, an industry which yoked boys as young as eight to remorseless fourteen-hour working days under gruelling and harsh conditions. A depleted post-war public was reluctant to provide the workforce needed to maintain the running of an estate.

The aristocracy and gentry had experienced suffering equally and were coming to terms with the loss of a generation of heirs. The reduced revenue of farming rents, the introduction of taxation and the societal shift away from the rigidity of the Edwardian Age, a rigidity that had especially prevailed in the countryside, made the perpetuation of the English country house an impossible task for all but the very wealthy.

Before giving consideration to the overtures of property developers eager to participate in the expansion of house building of the 1920s (overtures that were regularly accepted), many estates attempted to realise an income by converting parts of their lands for increasingly popular field sports. It was for the fashionable activities of hunting, shooting and fishing that Britain's landowners employed gamekeepers such as those who skirmished with the trespassers at Kinder Scout.

The confidence with which those ramblers defied their authority demonstrated that the certainties of the previous era no longer prevailed.

———————————————

Perhaps more than any other piece of British, or specifically English, music Vaughan Williams's composition *The Lark Ascending* epitomises an idea of place. Due to the absence of a lyric, The Lark is immune to the corruption of interpretation that befell Blake's short verse 'And didst those feet in ancient time' as it transmuted into the green and pleasant lands of 'Jerusalem'. *The Lark Ascending* is a meditation of less than fifteen minutes, during which one experiences a reverie initiated by birdsong.

As listeners to *The Lark Ascending* we might exchange mental notes of our interpretation of this music and its location, one with which we feel a deep sense of recognition. A country dance observed by a bird in flight; the flight itself, a lyrical expression of grace and freedom; a sense of being perfectly alone in a perfect landscape so powerful it renders us almost inarticulate, suspended in its daydream. Memories and emotions are stirred from our subconscious as we follow the bird on our inner journey through its pentatonic score.

We might remind ourselves that however forcefully the music stirs in us nostalgia or wistfulness of our own, Vaughan Williams was, with good reason, himself nostalgic for a prelapsarian landscape, an idea of a pastoral idyll of Albion which the Great War had nullified permanently.

There are unsubstantiated stories regarding the piece's inspiration, later dismissed by his second wife Ursula as apocryphal. One involves the composer being mistakenly arrested as a spy, while idly observing troop manoeuvres during a holiday the couple were taking in Margate, at the outbreak of the war.

What is certain is that within weeks Vaughan Williams volunteered as a private for the Royal Ambulance Corps. At the age of forty-two the composer was almost twenty years older than the average soldier and legally exempt from active service. Vaughan Williams initially served for two years as a medical orderly, a post that included tending to the dying, before receiving a commission to the Royal Garrison Artillery in 1917. The war had as considerable an influence on Vaughan Williams as on any of his contemporaries, its emotional and physical effects enduring throughout the composer's life.

Ursula Vaughan Williams later suggested her husband would have found it difficult to identify a lark, but as a student of traditional English music and a former editor of *The English Hymnal* and as a collector of regional carols, Vaughan Williams drew on his instinctual temperament for the cadences of the past to create the sense of agelessness that is one of *The Lark Ascending*'s principal characteristics. His lack of familiarity with its call notwithstanding, in the delicacy and intensity of Williams's score the language of birdsong has an undeniable emotional charge.

The dream state recognised by the reviewer in *The Times* is established by the piece's opening modal chords, before a solo violin played in high register recreates the lark's call to create a sense of weightlessness and of growing becalmed, as though time were being suspended. For the listener this is often experienced as the sensation of feeling physically rested but awake in one's imagination.

The playfulness of this soaring bird is then heard in dialogue with the orchestra. In the central orchestral section echoes of folk song, harvest dances and hymns are played with a liveliness evoking country weddings or the libidinal exhilaration of a morning in May. These are Arcadian rhythms, the steps of the 'Earth feet, loam feet' of T. S. Eliot's 'East Coker' bounding together across the land, passed around by the orchestra as though it were a dance partner.

Vaughan Williams achieves a synthesis of air and earth as the skylark shares in the merrymaking taking place below, and the intoxicating sense of euphoria is absolute.

The orchestra slowly fades as the solo violin returns to prominence; we are left alone once more with the trills of the lark, now played at the top of the instrument's range as the notes gradually die away. The lark's final song of the day bids us farewell, a conclusion that even in the mildest encounter with this composition can produce a feeling of catharsis, or in certain moods, a poignancy accompanied by tears.

Vaughan Williams had drawn his inspiration from the poem 'The Lark Ascending' by the Victorian novelist George Meredith and prefaced the original score with twelve of its lines:

> He rises and begins to round,
> He drops the silver chain of sound
> Of many links without a break,
> In chirrup, whistle, slur and shake . . .
> For singing till his heaven fills,
> 'Tis love of earth that he instils,
> And ever winging up and up,
> Our valley is his golden cup
> And he the wine which overflows
> To lift us with him as he goes . . .
> Till lost on his aërial rings
> In light . . . and then the fancy sings.

Vaughan Williams subsequently deleted this epigraph; the following lines, which occur in the central section of Meredith's poem, perhaps better describe the effect Williams's composition has on the listener:

The song seraphically free
Of taint of personality,
So pure that it salutes the suns
The voice of one for millions,
In whom the millions rejoice
For giving their one spirit voice.

The listener quietly rejoices while listening to *The Lark*, an activity that recognises a shared sense of reverie that may be particular to this contemplative piece of music and gives their spirit a voice. Music above all else and music 'free of taint of personality', such as the music I heard on the sound systems at Castlemorton where the presence of the DJs was purely technical and almost entirely un-egotistical, bestows us with a sense of direction with which to wander our mental pathways; *The Lark Ascending* grants us access to ramble through our mind's own wild places.

Vaughan Williams rarely spoke of his time at the Western Front. This was a trait common among many veterans who were aware that, while serving, they had witnessed a fracture in human nature so profound its character may have been permanently altered. If

The Lark Ascending is imbued with nostalgia, it is a nostalgia that recognises the depth of this rupture, and the landscape it evokes is one of a more innocent age. The composer wrote that 'The art of music above all other arts is the expression of the soul of a nation – any community of people who are spiritually bound together by language, environment, history and common ideals, and, above all, a continuity with the past.' The break with the past experienced by his generation was so severe any sense of continuity would struggle to be apparent. A significant element of The Lark's emotional range lies in Vaughan Williams's ability to evoke the spiritual bond connecting 'the soul of a nation', despite what he had witnessed while serving at the front.

This is a geography similar to that described in one of the most celebrated passages from *Memoirs of a Fox-Hunting Man*, the anonymously written novel by Siegfried Sassoon, a contemporary of Vaughan Williams who served in the Royal Welch Fusiliers and was decorated for his bravery. George Sherston, the narrator and titular fox-hunter, recalls riding before the war when 'The air was Elysian with early summer and the shadows of steep white clouds were chasing over the orchards and meadows; sunlight sparkled on green hedgerows that had been drenched by early morning showers . . . For it was my own countryside, and I loved it with an intimate feeling, though all its associations were crude and incoherent. I cannot think of it now without a sense of heartache, as if it contained something which I have never quite been able to discover.' The 'something', which George was unable to discover, lay buried within the landscape of his memory. Sassoon's use of the word 'discover', rather than recover or rediscover is notable; it suggests a source of impenetrable emotional energy made all the more overwhelming by his inability to locate it, an inability he is carrying as if it were a wound from the battlefield.

In a later passage Sassoon describes George's relationship with the landscape of the trenches in terms of intimacy, where despite the enduring horror he still recognises the song of the lark: 'Now and again a leisurely five-nine shell passes overhead in the blue air where the larks are singing. The sound of the shell is like water trickling into a can. The curve of its trajectory sounds peaceful until the culminating crash.'

It is the sounds made by another bird, an earthbound partridge, which dissipate these momentary distractions. George's thoughts lead instead to the more immediate past and the death of his friend Dick, with whom he had recently ridden in the French woods and, the novel suggests, fallen in love: 'Somewhere on the slope behind me a partridge makes its unmilitary noise – down there where Dick was buried a few weeks ago. Dick's father was a very good man with a gun, so Dick used to say.' In his grief George recognises that the youthful life of contemplation and country pursuits he enjoyed before the war has been extinguished in him, that even if its hills might look and feel familiar should he be lucky enough to survive the war, the landscape through which he rode no longer exists.

The war similarly intrudes into, then provides the conclusion for Virginia Woolf's contemporaneous novel *Jacob's Room*. Its innovative structure is resolved in a scene of great catharsis. Jacob's mother enters her son's room and casts her eye over his belongings, which now have a new significance as Jacob has died on the Western Front. A lark is heard and sighted in an earlier section of the book that takes place before the outbreak of war: 'Yes, yes, when the lark soars; when the sheep, moving a step or two onwards, crop the turf, and at the same time set their bells tinkling . . . when there are distant concussions in the air and phantom horsemen galloping, ceasing; when the horizon swims blue, green, emotional.'

The fractured narrative of *Jacob's Room* represented a significant break with the traditional and linear storytelling of *Memoirs of a Fox-Hunting Man*. Woolf's restructuring of time, voice and character acknowledge the change in awareness that had occurred during the war. These experiments established a means with which that change might be recognised and processed. Jacob had died in battle, but in her following novel, *Mrs Dalloway*, Woolf explores the mental suffering endured by those who returned from the front. One of the main characters, the veteran Septimus Warren Smith, suffers terrible hallucinations, struggles to distinguish between the living and the dead and occupies a state of near-perpetual hysteria. For long periods he is haunted by Evans, a friend killed in the trenches. As the severity of his condition increases, his suffering grows so great he throws himself through a window onto the Fitzrovia pavement.

The delayed symptoms of extreme post-traumatic stress disorder that were diagnosed as 'shell shock' are present throughout the literature written in the aftermath of the war. Siegfried Sassoon developed an acute nervous condition for which he was granted convalescent leave. During his stay in hospital he concluded he was unwilling to return to the Front and wrote an open letter to his commanding officer that was then widely published in national and local newspapers. He had written the letter as 'an act of wilful defiance of military authority because I believe that the war is being deliberately prolonged by those who have the power to end it'. Sassoon considered he had 'seen and endured the sufferings of the troops and I can no longer be a party to prolonging these sufferings, for ends which I believe to be evil and unjust'. In conclusion Sassoon stated he was taking this course of action 'on behalf of those who are suffering now, I make this protest against the deception which is being practised upon them.'

Prior to his convalescent leave Sassoon had been previously decorated with the Military Cross for his valour. That he chose to communicate his decision not to return to the battlefield in such strong terms put him at risk of great censure. In all likelihood a highly commended officer who embarrassed his superiors so publicly would face court martial. In his memoir *Goodbye to All That*, Sassoon's friend and regimental comrade in the Royal Welch Fusiliers, Robert Graves, claims he intervened on Sassoon's behalf and informed the military authorities of his colleague's nervous problems and pleaded clemency. 'Much against my will, I had to appear in the role of a patriot distressed by the mental collapse of a brother-in-arms – a collapse directly due to his magnificent exploits in the trenches. I mentioned Siegfried's "hallucinations" of corpses strewn along on Piccadilly. The irony of having to argue to these mad old men that Siegfried was not sane!' Graves and Sassoon would later fall out, their shattered emotions outlasting their friendship.

A condition as acute as post-traumatic stress is experienced by degree; there is no record of Vaughan Williams exhibiting its symptoms, although Ursula Vaughan Williams noted her husband experienced survivor's remorse. The composer suffered in other ways, enduring the loss of hearing in one ear, a consequence of his nightly proximity to 18-pounder cannon while serving in the Royal Artillery. The first major work Vaughan Williams completed after the war was *A Pastoral Symphony*, his third, in 1922. Several contemporary critics made assumptions about the composer's use of the word 'pastoral' in the title and in so doing misunderstood the work and the composer's intention. Although it habitually evokes the bucolic imagery and rural gentleness associated with his compositions, Vaughan Williams weighted this pastoral with a less obvious meaning.

In a letter to Ursula written before their marriage the composer defined its usage: 'It's not really lambkins frisking at all, as most people take for granted,' he wrote. Earlier in the correspondence he had indicated that the landscape the symphony evoked was the condemned battlefields of the trenches. 'It's really wartime music – a great deal of it incubated when I used to go up night after night in the ambulance wagon at Ecoivres and we went up a steep hill and there was a wonderful Corot-like landscape in the sunset.' Such scenes are more usually the subject of requiems; their evocation by Vaughan Williams as 'pastoral' is a recognition of the need for forms of composition and narrative to undergo an adjustment equivalent to those who had witnessed the war's horrors, to proceed with ambiguity and hesitancy through the uncertainty of its remains.

The hills and sunsets in *A Pastoral Symphony* are drawn from memories of war, locations that despite their outward beauty are now associated with death and futility, not the vitality of nature, a paradox that provides an unresolved air of tension throughout the work. From the opening of the First Movement, as the harmonic idiom shifts from one tonal centre to another, the listener is aware only of the ephemeral and indistinct, creating an atmosphere where little seems fixed or certain, other than the need for reflective concentration.

At the start of the Second Movement a lone trumpet is heard, a sound immediately evocative of the Last Post; there is a remoteness to the instrument, as though we might be hearing the tune being played through a fog. In the same letter to Ursula, Vaughan Williams wrote, 'A bugler used to practise and this sound became part of that evening landscape and is the genesis of the long trumpet cadenza in the second movement of the symphony.' Later in the movement the stillness of the orchestra around the trumpet grows unsettling and there is a brief impression of incapacity, as though the trumpeter were missing notes or playing them incorrectly; that reaching the end of the tune, although familiar from repeated practice, is a struggle.

Surges of sudden energy frequently interrupt the sense of insubstantiality that continues throughout the symphony, which the listener now recognises as the signature Vaughan Williams chose for this work. The Fourth and final Movement introduces a wordless soprano, a voice without the power of speech. In the score this is marked 'distant' and in performance the soprano is often off stage, disembodied from the orchestra and alone. *A Pastoral Symphony* concludes with the uncertain climax of a final, disconcerting tonal shift, before the lamenting soprano is once more heard, now even further in the distance, now a ghost. In his use of a fluctuating tonal structure and his refusal to allow the listener to settle, Vaughan Williams suggests received ideas such as victory or defeat are of little consequence. This is the sound of absence made temporarily and temporally present, music assembled from memories of lost lives, a pastoral for a landscape in which the lark's voice would struggle to be heard.

It is inarguable that volunteering for the front line at an age when he was not legally required to do so was an act of great patriotism by Vaughan Williams. His sense of national duty was profound and unhesitating. During the Second World War, now in his late sixties, the composer contributed to the Home Front by growing food in a field he had dug specifically. He also organised the collection of spare household aluminium that might be put to use in the construction of aircraft. When calling on houses in his hometown of Dorking to enquire of any spare pots or pans the composer was occasionally mistaken for a tramp. In later life he was often regarded as a teddy-bear like figure, and his rumpled tweeds and patrician nature were mistaken for a fustiness. This was an opinion that misunderstood the passion in his music, which provided a country known for its stiff upper lip with a means of experiencing the emotion it so frequently buried within the rigidity of its society. Throughout his compositions and during *The Lark Ascending* in particular, Ralph Vaughan Williams offered every listener the opportunity of a heightened consciousness.

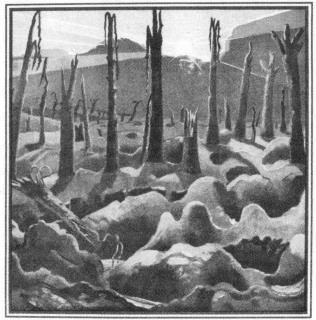

CONTINUATION OF *THE WESTERN FRONT*   PART THREE

BRITISH ARTISTS AT THE FRONT

PAUL NASH

PUBLISHED FROM THE OFFICES OF "COUNTRY LIFE," LTD.,
20, TAVISTOCK STREET, COVENT GARDEN, LONDON
AND
GEORGE NEWNES, LTD., 8-11, SOUTHAMPTON STREET, STRAND,
LONDON. W C. 2

PRICE

5/-

British Artists at the Front by Paul Nash. The third in the four-volume series *British Artists at the Front*, a publication series created in 1918 at Wellington House, the cover name of the War Propaganda Bureau, later known as the Ministry of Information. In order to maintain discretion over the activities of Wellington House the series was published by *Country Life*. (Bridgeman Images)

2 : Genius Loci

'Where the grey rocks lie ragged and steep
I've seen the white hare in the gullys
And the curlew fly high overhead
And sooner than part from the mountains
I think I would rather be dead.'

Ewan MacColl, 'The Manchester Rambler'

The battlefield landscapes Paul Nash painted as an Official War Artist offer a visual equivalent to the internalisations of the experience of the Great War that stimulated Vaughan Williams to write A Pastoral Symphony. Nash applied for the role when recovering from an injury he had suffered while stationed at the Ypres Salient in the Artists Rifles in the spring of 1917. On first arriving at the Western Front Nash had found the flora and fauna of the battlefield unsettling but stimulating. Just as Vaughan Williams had written of the 'Corot-like' landscape of the trenches, Nash spoke of the unexpected joy he experienced in seeing the 'bright gold' dandelions that grew among the parapets. Upon his return to duty as a war artist later that year these brief moments of transcendence were nullified as he witnessed the bombardment of the Ypres Salient at the battle of Passchendaele. The reaction Nash felt to the horror he witnessed was so strong he titled a painting made from sketches taken there 'Void'. It is a study in the dark symbolism of misery: a falling biplane; relentless rain; sodden fragments of clothing; an abandoned vehicle; random shards of battle among denuded tree stumps and the effluent gush of a flooded trench. The idea of redemption offered by seasonal change and the flowering of spring is no longer plausible.

The sense of only partially understood forces at work in the landscape is dominant throughout Nash's life, in the paintings made before the outbreak of war and those produced afterwards, even as they exhibit the evident trauma of his battlefield experiences. The work he made during the war is all the more harrowing for this perceptible belief the artist had in the unaccountable energies of nature. Although Nash failed to complete the autobiography he worked on throughout his life, he had intended to give the book the title *Genius Loci*, the spirit of place (it was published posthumously, in fragmentary form as *Outline*). At an early age Nash had felt a fracturing between the material and spirit worlds. He developed a strong attachment to the trees around his family home in Iver Heath in rural Buckinghamshire and it is trees, not people, that populate his landscapes. Nash met his wife Margaret Odeh while studying at the Slade, where she modelled in life drawing classes. Margaret was a prepossessing figure with an active role in the suffragette movement, one that she balanced with an equally strong interest in Christian Science and the mystical tenets of Theosophy. As a founder of the Committee for Social Investigations and Reform she pioneered the creation of rural communes as retreats for inner city prostitutes, who, once removed from their urban deprivations, she anticipated, might find rehabilitation through a nature cure. After the Nashes married in 1914 Margaret nurtured the mystical impulses in her husband and set great faith in their mutual sense of a power located in the hills, fields and trees that define the horizon.

The couple's belief in the spiritual authority of the landscape is evident in Nash's war paintings; on his official visit to the Ypres Salient Nash composed 'fifty drawings of muddy places', battlefield sketches he later developed into oils and lithographs modified by his shattered nerves and hallucinations. They share a topography of suffering that is partially healed by a faith in the mystic shafts of artificial starburst, eerie pyramids and grids that constitute the fearful symmetry which would increasingly inhabit and give structure to his landscapes after the war.

We are Making a New World, Nash's most celebrated war painting, was a source of anger for the military authorities, who considered the title a comment on the futility of the war. The image of a desolate battlefield is bereft of any life save for clusters of Nash's characteristic trees. Nevertheless there is a sun, whose presence suggests that the spirit world Nash instinctively retreated to may be a more powerful habitat than the material world of the battlefield; the thin rays of light have the power to illuminate and cast shadows across a scene of hopelessness. But if Nash is suggesting the ground will return to a new world of growth, the psychological condition of those who survive, including the now traumatised painter, ensures that such prospects of vitality are limited.

Throughout his career Nash painted little else but the landscape. His geography of rolling fields under open skies might appear pastoral yet there are other elements: moons, equinoxes, symmetrical tides and hatched trees, incongruous shapes and objects, which resist our desire to settle on the order of the natural world's beauty. A fundamental presence of life inhabits Nash's landscapes, yet it is accompanied by an inescapable feeling of anxiousness, the condition that is a constant presence in his work. His predecessors had depicted similar locations as sources of serenity, but for Nash these were territories on which he felt the need to force the stricture of a grid, to order their geography in a manner his nerves might tolerate.

In the year *The Lark Ascending* was premiered Nash started experiencing black outs that would endure for the remainder of his life. There is a tormented quality to all his work that the war exacerbated, but his relationship to the landscape, however vividly its form overwhelmed him, helped him to survive. The lark flew here as well, over his suffering.

———————————————

Trade routes across the Atlantic were successfully targeted and blockaded during the First World War to the point where the country began experiencing food shortages. The government duly accepted that if the country was to feed itself, some aspects of food production required intervention, and for the first time in almost a century it made a handful of agricultural subsidies available to farmers. Wheat growers benefited from 'deficiency' payments and a subsidy was awarded to producers of domestic sugar. Both these initiatives continued well into the 1920s, although as they favoured regions where particular crops could be grown successfully such an arrangement was by nature selective. These and similar schemes partially stabilised the overall decline in agriculture prices that had accelerated before the outbreak of war. After the armistice they started to fall once more, reaching their lowest point in 1932, by which time many areas of rural Britain had descended into rack and ruin. Farms lay abandoned then collapsed, to leave an expanse of the countryside with the aura of failure.

Akenfield by Ronald Blythe is an oral history of an East Anglian village, set in the first decades of the twentieth century, and a masterpiece of reportage; Blythe's interviews with many of the village's older inhabitants cover the period between the wars and create an unsentimental image of rural life with a notable absence of nostalgia. In *Akenfield* the instances in which the past is dwelled on with any fondness are a product of the instinctive grace notes of memory, rather than as examples of how better things may have once been. Blythe has a natural empathy with the rhythms of work and pleasure that the villagers describe. He has perhaps an even greater understanding of the need to give his subjects a voice and the opportunity to reflect on their lives, often of profound hardship, spent working in the countryside. Many years later, Blythe wrote *The Time by the Sea*, his memoir of living near the Suffolk town of Aldeburgh during the 1950s, where his work included collaborating with Benjamin Britten on preparing and editing the festival programme for the Aldeburgh Festival, and where his friends and neighbours included John Nash, the brother of Paul (and to whom *Akenfield* is dedicated), and his wife Christine.

In a passage from *The Time by the Sea* Blythe describes the condition of the River Stour in the mid-1930s that serves as an apt metaphor for much of rural Britain during the height of its decline:

> Once the local boys challenged them [John Nash and his
> friend Adrian Bell] to bring a canoe down the Stour from
> Sudbury to Bures, the state of the river, due to the farming
> depression, the collapse of barge transport and neglect

generally, making it virtually invisible here and there in mid-summer, so dense were the weeds, so overgrown the trees on its banks. Some of the now unwanted barges which John Constable had painted had been scuttled at Ballingdon, and lay just below the surface of the water like vast black motionless fish.

The serenity of rural Albion suggested in Constable's paintings such as *The Hay Wain* or *Dedham Vale* relies on the idea of a timeless rural tradition. A national desire for such an idyll may be powerful enough to sustain the idea in the public memory, but the past is rarely immune from decay. Objects featured in the work of Britain's favourite landscape painter that had signified pastoral reverie now lay discarded and submerged. Nature had taken its course.

A further contributing factor to the increasing decline of rural Britain was the establishment in 1919 of a Forestry Commission. The nation's woodland trees, oak in particular, had been requisitioned then felled during the war for the manufacture of rifles and ammunition boxes, a situation aggravated by the fact Britain had already been a heavy importer of timber in the early years of the twentieth century. As the government had accepted the country's requirement to grow its own food it recognised a similar need for a domestic supply of wood. The Commission was charged with the replacement of the country's greatly diminished woodland stock, and to maintain a 'strategic reserve of timber' it duly began a mass-planting programme of spruce conifers imported from Scandinavia. Financial stringency was imposed from the beginning because of high post-war inflation, but as agriculture was a depressed industry the Commission was able to buy land cheaply. By September 1929 its holdings included 600,000 acres in 152 forests, a figure that grew to almost a million by the outbreak of war a decade later.

The species was only partially suited to the British climate, which had previously only produced three successful varieties of native conifers: Common Juniper, Yew, and Scots Pine. Under damp, British conditions the newly imported Scandinavian saplings grew into spindly trees that were a meagre substitute for oak or other broad-leaf trees. The planting of a single variety on such a scale also risked the creation of a monoculture susceptible to infestations and disease. The Forestry Commission continued to acquire increasing amounts of acreage and issued grants and tax incentives for forestation to private landowners. Over the ensuing decades, monotonous rectangular blocks of pine and spruce would become a feature of the country's hillsides, as the scale of the Forestry Commission's planting increased to the point where the institution – officially a non-ministerial government department – was the nation's largest landowner, a position it retains today.

As the countryside fell into dilapidation and the drift from the land to towns and cities continued throughout the 1920s, the nation's population grew, with the attendant need to house them. Over four million homes were built between the wars, a third of the number recorded by Register in 1939. In many cases the land for their construction was purchased from farms and estates that were finally prepared to sell up rather than endure an agricultural depression that had now, ten years after the First World War, become acute. The majority were houses built by ribbon development. The phrase became synonymous with a rapid rise in unplanned construction that permanently altered the landscape:

the semi-detached villas that appeared almost instantly alongside arterial roads across rural areas, in tandem with the sudden proliferation of bungalows beside the coastline of much of southern England.

The villas of the new, energetically promoted suburbia of Metroland were built on land owned by the Metropolitan Railway, which was in the unusual position of having been permitted to keep its considerable stock of surplus land. By the early 1920s the railway had created a bespoke property development company, Metropolitan Railway Country Estates Ltd, to develop and market its new homes. The success of its nostalgic branding schemes ensured that within a decade the former rural counties of Middlesex, Buckinghamshire and Hertfordshire became largely suburban. Much of the change in character of the Home Counties between the wars took place on rich soil; some of the finest acreage for market gardening in Britain was ploughed up for new homes. Prosperous farms in receipt of government subsidy that neighboured Metroland and remained unaffected by the agricultural depression found the prices offered by speculative developers too high to resist. The volume of food produced within the United Kingdom fell into further decline.

The alterations to the character of the landscape in the years that followed the Great War occurred with unpredicted speed. They were met with intense opposition by a group of new organisations whose aim was to prevent any further destruction to rural Britain and which appointed themselves custodians of its scenery. In 1926 the Council for the Preservation of Rural England (CPRE) was established in order to draw attention to the changes taking place in the countryside and, when possible, to legally challenge and resist them. Its membership was largely drawn from serving and former military officers and landowners. This was a constituency characterised by an interest in assuring the future of huntin', shootin' and fishin', and until the 1960s its reputation ensured that conservation was associated – perhaps unfairly – with conservatism. Although easily caricatured as a pressure group founded to ensure the survival of field sports, from its inception the Council established the future of the environment as a growing concern.

In 1927 the CPRE's activities were complemented by Ferguson's Gang, a group who undertook a policy of direct action. The Gang were a secretive collective of environmental activists comprised of five or six women. The encroachment of ribbon development into the countryside had inspired them to take a stand to save rural buildings such as the old mill seen in *The Hay Wain*. The Gang's members remained anonymous, but drew attention to themselves and their activities through the use of memorable aliases such as Red Biddy, Bill Stickers, Bludy Beershop and Sister Agatha. The actions of Ferguson's Gang often consisted of well-heeled tomfoolery and unsurprisingly gained them notoriety and publicity. These included delivering donations to the National Trust in the form of liqueur bottles packed tightly with fifty-pound notes. On another occasion a substantial amount of Victorian coins were elaborately sewn into the carcass of a goose. Their successful efforts to save and restore an abandoned mill at Shalford, near Guildford in Surrey, included an invented ritual, which the Gang sang in Latin as they processed around the property at dawn; the mill was later appropriated as their headquarters. Locals were made aware of their activities by the regular arrival of grocery vans from London, although their provenance varies. In the histories of Ferguson's Gang the vehicles are usually attributed to Fortnum & Mason, but occasionally to Harrods. The stories of their adventures have given them a reputation for eccentricity worthy of P.G. Wodehouse or Lord Berners. Given that the Gang's members were drawn from the aristocracy and more bohemian Establishment families, this is perhaps unsurprising. The scale of their commitment to the preservation of rural buildings and to fundraising is indisputable. The Gang endowed Shalford Mill to the National Trust in 1932. Within four years they had also donated almost five thousand pounds to the organisation and significantly raised the National Trust's membership through their skilled and well-connected attention seeking.

The National Trust had been founded some thirty years earlier towards the end of the nineteenth century when ecological and socialist concerns at living conditions in urban industrial Britain gathered momentum and were given voice by polemicists such as William Morris and John Ruskin. The National Trust was one of several concerns founded in response; others included the Commons Preservation Society (a forerunner of The Council for the Preservation of Rural England), the Kyrle Society 'for the diffusion of beauty' which planted inner cities with trees, shrubs and flowers, and the Guild of St George, conceived by Ruskin to 'provide a National Store' for the benefit of all England.

The fact that of these contemporary voices and societies only the National Trust endured was largely due to the pragmatism, ideology and experience of its founder, Octavia Hill, the daughter of a wealthy family of corn merchants. James Hill, Octavia's father, held strong convictions of the need for social reform, suffered bankruptcy and was subsequently diagnosed with the late-Victorian illness of insanity and committed to an asylum. Octavia was brought up by her mother in the Christian Socialist Tradition and began her work in London, where she sought to purchase green spaces in the city for the use of the urban poor. This included the acquisition of Paradise Place, three near-derelict cottages in Marylebone which were bought with financial assistance from John Ruskin.

There, tenants were encouraged and expected to participate in the restoration of the properties and to live communally, healthily and parsimoniously, as any arrears in rent led to evictions. Due to the success of the scheme Hill was able to raise further finance with which to purchase sufficient housing for over three thousand people. Canon Hardwicke Rawnsley, a Lake District clergyman and friend of Beatrix Potter, collected the rents from these properties. In 1883 Rawnsley, Hill and a lawyer, Robert Hunter, worked together to raise public awareness of plans proposed to develop a railway that would run across the Lake District. Their campaign was successful in halting its development and the collaboration between Hill, Rawnsley and Hunter eventually led to the foundation of The National Trust for the Preservation of Historic Buildings and Natural Beauty, whose principal aim was to hold land and buildings in perpetuity 'for ever, for everyone'.

The original founders of the National Trust were liberal reformers with a strong belief in the right of all, including the poor, to have access to and experience the countryside. Hill's achievements in social housing and her first-hand experience of conditions in the inner cities led her to regard the behaviour and motives of the majority of landlords with a degree of scepticism. This was especially the case if landlordism included the draconian use of trespass laws or policing of rights of way that inhibited free access to the countryside.

By the 1920s the National Trust had itself become a landlord, having acquired properties and open spaces considered to be representative of British rural life, including castles, post offices and entire villages, in order to safeguard a sense of identity that the Trust considered to be under threat from the expansion of towns and suburbia. In 1937, the year after the abdication crisis, Parliament passed the National Trust Act, permitting the organisation to acquire and hold land or investments and act as an endowment on behalf of the large estates and country houses that would otherwise be forced into the position of selling to property developers. In exchange for the donation of their property and chattels, country house and estate-owning families were no longer liable to pay death duties or other taxes and could remain in their homes, even though the Edwardian society their occupants had once been accustomed to had long ended and the landscape they looked out upon was transformed. The Act of 1937 ensured that the decline of rural Britain was arrested; it also formalised an idea of preservation and heritage that would increasingly determine the narrative with which the countryside was experienced and understood as the century progressed.

The National Trust was at the forefront of creating this new identity. It sought to preserve aspects of the landscape it considered to be of historical significance and was abetted by the activities of the Council for the Preservation of Rural England, Ferguson's Gang and other self-determining organisations. The Trust also helped produce a change in public opinion, as through the purchase of houses, estates and lands it promoted the idea that the nation's natural beauty should be protected and the countryside could now be considered a national asset that might be enjoyed by 'everyone'.

The rambling clubs of the North of England and similar upland regions had increased during the 1920s and long held such views. A significant number of them had members who were drawn from the proletariat left and considered their hobby an inherently political activity. Other ramblers, especially in the South East, merely saw the health benefits of walking in the fresh air. Despite its increase in popularity, or in all likelihood because of it, rambling remained unrecognised in law and was considered to be an activity without rights. In 1931 a National Council of Ramblers Federations was founded in recognition of the need of a co-ordinating association for the estimated half a million people who took to the countryside in their leisure time.

In the case of the many unemployed ramblers, walking in the open air was a means to recharge their spirits. In the same year the country's first generation of Youth Hostels opened, providing accommodation and a destination for walkers. The constitution of the Youth Hostels Association stated its founding principles were: 'To help all, especially young people of limited means, to a greater knowledge, love and care of the countryside, particularly by providing hostels or other simple accommodation for them in their travels, and thus to promote their health, rest and education.'

The mass trespass of Kinder Scout that followed was in part a consequence of this changing perception of rural Britain; those who owned the land no longer solely defined the countryside. These shifts in attitude occurred during a time of high national unemployment and rural desolation. The gamekeepers with whom the trespassers on Kinder Scout scuffled were not only denying the ramblers access, but defending a precious commercial interest. The ramblers' act of walking in open country in order to enjoy the invigorating experience of clean air was to ask for what purpose, and in whose interests, the landscape was maintained. Such a question had rarely been asked so energetically and with the support of differing public groups whose numbers were growing. On New Year's Day, 1935, the Ramblers' Association was founded and proved to be an effective unitary voice. As the country faced the threat of another war, the Association felt confident that there was sufficient momentum and popular approval for a change in the laws of access.

Many of those participating in the trespass of Kinder Scout considered the Ramblers' Association too cautious in their approach. The Salford folk singer and songwriter Ewan MacColl, born James Henry Miller, was a sporadically employed seventeen-year-old school leaver when he participated in the trespass. Like Benny Rothman, the organiser of the hike, he too was a member of the Young Communist League and believed in direct action.

MacColl wrote 'The Manchester Rambler' to record and celebrate the achievement of the trespass. The song's final verse evokes the new sense of assertiveness and identification his generation felt with our country's natural world:

> So I'll walk where I will over mountain and hill
> And I'll lie where the bracken is deep
> I belong to the mountains, the clear running fountains
> Where the grey rocks lie ragged and steep
> I've seen the white hare in the gullys
> And the curlew fly high overhead

And sooner than part from the mountains
I think I would rather be dead.

Vaughan Williams wrote that he considered a folk song to be 'an individual flowering on a common stem'. In his young adulthood, as he collected the songs that would influence his compositions, including *The Lark Ascending*, Vaughan Williams was greatly concerned about whether folk music might survive as a widely heard form of music. Ewan MacColl would be in the vanguard of the generation that produced the second great revival in folk song, which gained momentum during the 1950s; by writing new songs such as 'The Manchester Rambler' he ensured the continuation of the tradition's 'common stem'. To express his longing to feel harmony with the landscape MacColl chose the image of a high-flying, sharp-beaked curlew, a bird that breeds in the moorland habitat of the Pennines and one still seen by ramblers on Kinder Scout today. Their sighting is a victory for the declaration MacColl made in the 'individual flowering' of 'The Manchester Rambler'. It is no longer necessary to part from the mountains.

To observe a bird overhead, whether a curlew or lark, is to be made aware of our earthbound limitations. In its distinctive song and flight, there is rarely a more uplifting sight than the familiar lark as it loops through the air, encouraging us to follow its trajectory. As Vaughan Williams read the lines in George Meredith's poem he identified the call of the skylark as a summons to free ourselves. MacColl and his fellow ramblers on Kinder Scout justified their trespass in similar terms, as an expression of fellowship and the right to communion with our own landscape.

The South Downs, Your Britain Fight For It Now, 1942. One of a series of posters produced by Frank Newbould, assistant designer to Abram Games at the War Office Public Relations Department. Such forceful use of nostalgia for an idealised landscape represented an anomaly among the material produced during wartime by governmental bodies. (Imperial War Museum)

3 : Spring Morning, Larked and Crowed and Belling

'Oh Tom, Dick and Harry were three fine men
And I'll never have such loving again
But Little Willy Wee who took me on his knee
Little Willie Weasel is the man for me'

Dylan Thomas, 'Polly Garter's Song', *Under Milk Wood*

The notion that only certain initiates are privileged to know the true mystery of the landscape is a constant feature in literature concerning nature and the countryside, as is the assumption that as a consequence of its age, rural Britain is sanctified with atavistic properties. The question of how and with whom its secrets are to be shared is addressed with less frequency. The libidinal freedom Dylan Thomas celebrated in the pastoral of *Under Milk Wood* is itself an ideal, but, in the spirit of the age in which it was written which saw Britain build itself anew, the inhabitants of the small town of Llareggub are certain in the belief that the woods and hills that surround them are theirs to enjoy in the moonlight.

Polly Garter's song occurs in the second half of the day, as Dylan Thomas's 'play for voices', set over the course of twenty-four hours, begins its slow return to night and the dreams and interrupted sleep patterns of its characters. Polly sings her lament for a dead lover during the 'sunlit sleepy afternoon . . . the meadows still as Sunday', as 'the dumb duck ponds snooze'.

In his notes on the play's characters Thomas described Polly Garter as 'Midwife. Loves children, loves loving, is loose and thoughtless, therefore has children.' Her song is an accompaniment to that day's chore of washing the floors of the Welfare Hall in preparation for the Mothers' Union Social Dance that will take place in the evening. In contrast, Polly will spend the night in the forest near Milk Wood in the arms of the drunk Mr Waldo.

Although Polly may have a reputation among some of her neighbours, her self-possession is resolute and her promiscuity is never denounced. *Under Milk Wood* was broadcast in 1954, the year in which rationing ended, and the sexual liberation Polly Garter expresses provided audiences with a sense of release that is complemented by the sense of abandon running through the play.

In classical tradition pastoral literature is concerned with the lives of shepherds, who often narrate the story, although the writers of pastoral literature were seldom shepherds themselves. The shepherds rarely work, the weather is fair, and life is simplified and spent at leisure and to the intermittent accompaniment of music; theirs is a way of life surrounded in a protective air of innocence. *Under Milk Wood* is an example of pastoral modernism. The contained topography of the town of Llareggub may be imaginary, but its character and landscape are one with which contemporary listeners would have been familiar. The instruction in the play's text indicates that its description of the town should be spoken in the 'Voice of a Guide Book':

Less than five hundred souls inhabit the three quaint streets and the few narrow bylanes and scattered farmsteads that constitute this small, decaying, watering place which may indeed, be called 'a backwater of life' without disrespect to its natives who possess, to this day, a salty individuality of their own.

The absence of narrative structure is also a feature of pastoral literature. Thomas had become adept at writing for radio, and rather than create the arc of a story he introduces his characters in a sequence of transmissions. The individuality of each character is revealed by the inner monologues through which they communicate with the audience. The population of Llareggub either spend their hours in the solitude of sleep, or broadcast and echo their thoughts as signals to one another, often via their memories. The voices of two narrators, the shepherds of this modern pastoral, describe the activities and whereabouts of the town's population; according to the play's First Narrator it is a place of animated contentment: 'our green hill . . . spring morning larked and crowed and belling.'

Thomas's evocation of the chaotic and improvisatory nature of Llareggub's townspeople is rendered through their collective subconscious. The idea of 1950s Britain adjusting to post-war austerity and the construction of a new form of planned society is abandoned entirely to what Seamus Heaney termed *Under Milk Wood*'s 'genial dream scape'.

These are dreamers for whom death is also a presence. As the play commences, its characters wake from a night of conversations with the deceased and their memories. In *Under Milk Wood*, where every character is a recognisable archetype – 'the farmers, the fishers, the tradesmen and pensioners, cobbler, schoolteacher, postman and publican, the undertaker and the fancy woman, drunkard, dressmaker, preacher, policeman, the webfoot cocklewomen and the tidy wives' – Thomas was offering his listeners an awakening from the aftermath of war that suggested there is a beatific potential within everyone.

In addition, the sexual honesty heard in Polly Garter's song creates an aura of what Heaney also memorably characterised as 'an idyllic romp, as if *The Joy of Sex* were dreamt under the canvas at a Welsh Eisteddfod'; or, as Thomas describes Llareggub in the text, 'a place of love':

> Now men from every parish 'round
> Run after me and roll me on the ground
> But whenever I love another man back
> Johnny from the hill, or sailing Jack
>
> I always think as they do what they please
> Of Tom, Dick and Harry who are tall as trees
> But most I think when I'm by their side
> Of little Willie Wee who downed and died
>
> Oh Tom, Dick and Harry were three fine men
> And I'll never have such loving again
> But Little Willy Wee who took me on his knee
> Little Willie Weasel is the man for me

The town's figure of social authority is Reverend Eli Jenkins. Instead of reproaching Polly for her behaviour he rejoices in hearing her sing and remarks: 'Praise the lord, we are a musical nation.'

Dylan Thomas first wrote for the BBC at the age of twenty-two and thereafter wrote regularly for the broadcaster; the commission for the play that would, after several years of protracted delays and excuses, be delivered as *Under Milk Wood* was developed from an earlier work. In 1944 Thomas had recorded a reading of his short story *Quite Early One Morning* for the BBC Welsh Home Service, a piece set in a 'sun-lit sea town . . . not yet awake'. He finally completed *Under Milk Wood* just days before its debut performance; some accounts claim it was finished only hours before the curtain, where it was read on stage at the Poetry Center in New York in 1953.

The hour-long duration of the play befitted the format of radio, which throughout the Second World War radio had been a tool for patriotism and the voice of the public realm, and through which Thomas delivered a very different message of communal sanctity and personal liberation. The state, government and national interest of post-war Britain are absent from *Under Milk Wood*. The population of Llareggub embody the post-war desire for a new, fairer society, but one whose behaviour is blessed by saintly grace, which in the play includes sensuality, if not lasciviousness, as a characteristic of this new golden age.

Under Milk Wood received its first broadcast in 1954, two months after Thomas had died, through the medium he had become adept at writing for.

The play was commissioned for the Third Programme, a new

national station that began transmission in 1946. The ethos of the Third Programme was one of cultural and intellectual betterment, a Reithian commitment to promoting a national appreciation of the arts. The activities of the inhabitants of Llareggub were first heard under this aegis; the eroticism of *Under Milk Wood* was presented as a public good.

There are sheep present in *Under Milk Wood* but no shepherds. The farmer Utah Watkins lies in bed in Salt Lake Farm and 'counts, all night, the wife-shaped sheep as they leap the fences on the hill', but Salt Lake Farm is primarily a dairy farm and Farmer Watkins 'hates his cattle on the hill'. This is despite the fact his livelihood would have significantly benefited from the transformation agriculture had experienced during the Second World War.

Unlike at the conclusion of the Great War, the protectionist measures the government had taken to ensure a food supply were not immediately removed in peacetime. Instead certain forms of farming – dairy farming, cereal and red meat – were assessed to be priorities and a decision was made that their production be guaranteed.

Towards the end of the 1930s, as war seemed increasingly inevitable, the National Trust and the Council for the Preservation of Rural England raised their concerns at the lack of any government planning for the fate of the countryside. Unless decisions were taken at the highest level, another conflict would ensure the return of the rural desolation of the early 1920s. Their concerns were supported by other single-issue pressure groups such as the Smoke Abatement Society and the Council for Clean Rivers, who together put forward the case for agriculture to be considered a national resource. Although wary of directly intervening with farming, the government recognised that during a decade of mass unemployment, agriculture remained a significant if parsimonious employer. In order to support the industry the decision was taken to create a series of marketing boards whose purpose was to extol the benefits of British produce. The most dynamic of these, the Milk Marketing Board, survived until the 1990s.

At the outbreak of war in 1939 the CPRE used its members' military experience and Establishment links to position itself as the voice of wartime rural Britain. The government spent much of the war without an official agricultural policy and relied on the Council's influence in policy decisions for countryside during wartime. An Emergency Powers Act that offered farmers £2 per acre to plough up pasture and turn it over to cultivation was passed immediately. The distribution of these funds and co-ordination of activities such as crop plantation was undertaken by a War Agricultural Committee appointed for every county. These institutions acted as a civilian chain of command for the countryside Home Front and had first been established during the Great War. Their powers included the rarely used authority to appropriate agricultural land; instead the 'War Ags' concentrated on working with farmers to ensure an increase in food production. The government carried out its own programme of acquisition and by the conclusion of the war had temporary ownership of over fourteen million acres.

In 1942, as part of a propaganda campaign, the Army produced a poster by the artist Frank Newbould titled 'The South Downs'. It shows a farmer replete with crook and sheepdogs guiding his flock towards a large set of farm buildings, as shadows are cast over the rolling Sussex landscape. The scene is accompanied by the strapline 'Your Britain – fight for it now'. Such imagery was considered a stimulating means for promoting patriotism and was circulated within the ranks, even if the poster depicted a way of life far beyond the reach of the ordinary citizen, who visited this notional representation of 'the countryside' rarely. The army he had joined was overwhelmingly urban and working class. There is a further significance to the Newbould poster: for the majority of the war the government deliberately avoided producing works of such emotive force. From 1940 onwards a decision was taken to stop printing overt propaganda and to concentrate instead on posters that appealed to actions not feelings. Some public bodies, such as the GPO and London Transport, printed material in short runs that included propaganda, other working groups such as The War Savings Committee concentrated their resources instead on promoting prosaic activities such as investing in national savings and the recycling of materials for munitions; their publicity urged Britains to 'Lend to Defend' and was accompanied by a campaign instigated by the Board of Trade to 'Make Do And Mend'. The Newbould poster was an anomaly in the war effort but has since been widely reproduced. People in far greater numbers than originally intended have now seen and interpreted its message. That a poster portraying such forceful nostalgia, which was considered overbearing at the time, should subsequently prove so popular illustrates how ahistorical our relationship to the landscape has grown.

The British landscape also featured in recruitment campaign posters for the Women's Land Army, another institution that had been resurrected from the previous war, whose contribution to the success of the government's wartime agricultural measures was of the greatest significance. At the outbreak of war Britain had been producing a little over a third of its own food, but by 1945, due greatly to the efforts of the Land Army, the country could produce nearly half of the food it required.

The triumph of farming in the Second World War had justified the role of state intervention and centralised planning. In contrast with its predecessor, the Attlee Labour government that came to power in 1945 had distinct policies on land use and ownership. During the 1930s the Labour party had regularly considered the nationalisation of land as the most appropriate means of securing the livelihoods of agricultural workers. The party had also met the formulation of marketing boards with a degree of scepticism, sensing conflicts of interest and the creation of cartels within each sector.

As late as 1943 Labour continued with its policy of outright governmental land ownership, but soon accepted there was little justification for nationalising an industry that had flourished during the war, even with the aid of state intervention. Farmers found themselves in a strong position of soft power; having fed the nation and helped avert economic collapse they could now expect its continued support. Nevertheless, the Labour government still remained committed to producing a change in the country's relationship with its landscape. Attlee's Chancellor, Hugh Dalton, who was also chair of the Ramblers' Association during the period, proposed that land requisitioned during the war be used for the creation of model farms and smallholdings, which were to be offered to returning servicemen and their families. Such plans proved too ambitious, and in 1946 Dalton instead created a National Land Fund with the aim of purchasing property of historical or cultural value to be made accessible to the public as a memorial to the war dead. The fund was rarely utilised and never administered in the way Dalton intended.

Three years later the momentum of public opinion regarding increased access to rural areas was realised in The National Parks and Access to the Countryside Act. Although it denied those who had fought for their country the opportunity to live and work in rural Britain, the population would now be able to visit ten designated sites of upland Britain and a handful of smaller areas of 'natural beauty'. Such a degree of access to rural Britain would have been unthinkable at the beginning of the century. The land chosen for the National Parks was of mixed use and where applicable would continue to be farmed. In certain areas the poor quality moorland and dense forestry would struggle to be described as 'beautiful'. Nevertheless, the Act secured for the population a fellowship with the landscape that was without precedent – a decision as radical as the government's creation of a National Health Service and its commitment to building social housing.

The organisations that had maintained a custodial role for rural Britain returned to peacetime with their reputations and land portfolios increased. The National Trust almost doubled its acreage holdings during the war, and by the end of the conflict the Council for the Preservation of Rural England could declare, in terms that suited its image as custodians of the landscape, that it saw 'no conflict between use and beauty in the English countryside'.

Despite Utah Watkins spending his days at Salt Lake Farm hating his cows, farming had also done well out of the war. By embarking on a policy of nutrition for all, the government had created an assured market for farmers such as Watkins, who between 1939 and 1945 had seen a fivefold increase in their profits. For landowners the fear that a Labour government would nationalise the countryside passed, although the subsequent voting pattern of rural Britain suggests a suspicion of such a policy and belief in the imminent threat of land ownership by the hands of the state became entrenched.

The Ministry of Agriculture and Fisheries was renamed the Ministry of Agriculture, Fisheries and Food in 1955, the new responsibility added in order to continue the impetus agriculture had achieved in the war. Although it sought greater capacity in farming, MAFF encouraged agricultural workers to find employment in other enterprises. The government's vision for agriculture was increasingly technological, and through the use of model farms, which trialled new techniques and machinery, it intended to oversee a mechanised British farming industry whose priorities were efficiency and productivity and which would quickly transform the character, profitability and appearance of the landscape.

The journey Dylan Thomas took to New York in May 1953 for the premiere of *Under Milk Wood* would be one of two visits to the city that year. The second trip Thomas made was for a further series of performances of the play at the Poetry Center where it had debuted. It would be his last – he died in the city six months later. In all Dylan Thomas completed four tours of the United States within three years; he had found an audience eager to treat him as a literary celebrity and his frenetic itineraries were arranged to consolidate this popularity. For his first visit in 1950 Thomas had made the return journey aboard the transatlantic liner *Queen Elizabeth*; for his second, which he undertook with his wife Caitlin, the couple sailed on a different ship, the *Queen Mary*.

Both oceangoing vessels were owned by the Cunard Line, whose motto 'Getting there is half the fun' was manifested in the performances given by the dance bands the cruise ships employed. Although the music they were forced to play for the seafaring clientele was rarely to the musicians' tastes, dance bands were a popular source of employment for British jazz musicians in the 1950s; a position in 'Geraldo's Navy', named after the impresario and bandleader who recruited band members for Cunard, guaranteed a passage and a few days' stay in New York City.

A Musicians Union regulation prohibited American musicians from performing in Britain for much of the decade, ensuring the only means dedicated British jazz players had of witnessing the music's innovators in person was to travel to the source. It was by such an arrangement, as a member of the dance bands aboard the ships *Queen Mary* and *Caronia*, that the young pianist Stan Tracey was able to see the musicians he venerated: Charlie Parker, Dizzy Gillespie, Duke

Ellington and Thelonious Monk in particular, play in their natural environs of Birdland and other clubs on Broadway.

Over a career that would span half a century Stan Tracey would duly be recognised for his role in the development of British jazz and accorded the same degree of influence he himself credited to Ellington and Monk. The recording that secured his legacy was *Jazz Suite Inspired by Dylan Thomas's 'Under Milk Wood'*, an eight-song instrumental adaptation of the radio play, the first album released in the idiom of British modern jazz, and possibly its apotheosis.

No record exists of whether Tracey was performing in the dance band aboard the *Queen Mary* during the Thomases' voyage out to America; if Tracey had recognised the usually exuberant couple, his natural reticence, which regularly extended to diffidence, meant it unlikely the pianist would have approached them. Tracey was born an only child in Denmark Hill in South London in 1926. He stopped attending school by the age of twelve and refused to be evacuated during the Blitz. Tracey instead grew transfixed by the music he heard while eavesdropping on the wireless broadcasts coming from neighbours' doorways. His father, who worked in nightclubs, gave Tracey his first instrument, a piano accordion that the boy taught himself. At the age of sixteen he was working professionally, playing in an ENSA group before joining the RAF Gang Show where his contemporaries included Tony Hancock and Peter Sellers. After a spell aboard the *Queen Mary* and *Caronia* he became a member of Ted Heath's dance band and was finally able to devote himself to playing jazz full time as the house pianist of Ronnie Scott's club in Soho, which, with a symbolism that celebrated the area as the epicentre of a soon to be flourishing jazz community, opened its doors during the final months of the fifties. For the next seven years Tracey would accompany the visiting American musicians now legally entitled to play in Britain and attracted to the Soho club for its growing reputation. At Scott's Tracey played a minimum of three sets a night, six nights a week. It was in the club that he met, then befriended the Glaswegian saxophonist Bobby Wellins, with whom he played in the house band when Wellins deputised for the proprietor, who sometimes found his priorities lay in the nearby bookmakers rather than on stage.

Wellins had served a similar apprenticeship to Tracey and many of the musicians of their generation: study at the RAF School of Music in Uxbridge during National Service, followed by a period in show bands and a stint playing on transatlantic liners. Wellins and Tracey also shared a wry sense of humour and, after years of the gruelling regimen at Ronnie Scott's had taken their toll, an addiction to heroin that, despite the drug's prevalence and low cost in early sixties Soho, they would each eventually escape.

In 1961 the duo's interests and musical empathy were formalised when the pianist formed the Stan Tracey Quartet featuring Wellins, Tracey, the drummer Jackie Dougan and bassist Jeff Clyne.

The nights of supporting visiting Americans at the club led Wellins and Tracey to consider the possibilities of a distinct British jazz sensibility, one steeped in the country's history and musical heritage of folk song. After reading *Culloden*, John Prebble's haunting account of the last pitched battle on British soil, published that year, Wellins was inspired to write *The Culloden Moor Suite*, a five-part evocation of the defeat of the clans and the landscape over which they fought. No tapes exist of the 1961 recording session Wellins had arranged to commit his composition to vinyl. Tracey and Wellins were also members of the New Departures Quartet, a group formed to accompany and improvise poetry readings organised by Pete Brown and Michael Horovitz, the editor of the periodical from which the quartet took their name. The single piece 'Culloden Moor' features on the quartet's eponymous album, a fragment from Wellins's initial period of inspiration. Several decades later Wellins would revisit *The Culloden Moor Suite* with the National Jazz Orchestra of Scotland; the depth of his compositions and the ethereal tone he employed during his performance, which drew on folk melodies to convey a sense of loss, were met with reverence and great acclaim.

Between his commitments at Ronnie Scott's, an increasingly busy recording schedule and his experiments with Horovitz and other poets, Tracey found the time to write the suite that would become *Under Milk Wood*. He later admitted he had composed much of the music for the eight pieces on the early morning workman's bus on which he travelled from Soho to his home in Streatham. Although Tracey was frustrated that his request to use the lyrics to Polly Garter's song in order to set them to music was declined by the Thomas estate, the eight pieces he wrote capture the irascible but melancholy tone of the play.

Jazz Suite Inspired by Dylan Thomas's 'Under Milk Wood' was recorded in a single day during 1965, perhaps in tribute to the time span of the play, or more likely due to the era's meagre recording budgets. Certainly, the brevity of studio time has helped create a folklore around the album, enhanced by the fact the record has never been out of print.

The album opens with 'Cockle Row', which in the play is the site of the town's awakening: 'Spring whips green down Cockle Row, and the shells ring out. Llareggub this snip of a morning is wildfruit and warm, the streets, fields, sands and waters springing in the young sun.' The phrase 'wildfruit and warm' captures the interplay between the quartet throughout the record and on the lead track in particular. Wellins plays fewer notes than Tracey; his saxophone, rich in tone and occasionally ruminative, summons the atmosphere of Llareggub. In contrast Tracey's piano is unpredictable to the point of volatility; the runs he plays are deliberately hurried, if magical, and complement the neurotic reverie of the town's characters.

On 'I Lost My Step in Nantucket', the quartet is reduced to a trio. The rhythm section creates a pattern for Tracey to wander up and down the scales locating unexpected melodic turns in the spirit of Thelonious Monk, before playing a series of pairs of dissonant notes that leap between octaves, from low to high and back again. Throughout the record Tracey uses his instrument to express the polarity between the interior and exterior spaces of the play, between the character's monologues and the day's occupations with which they busy themselves. The unsteadiness between these two worlds provides the momentum that drives both Thomas's original version and the uninhibited performances of the Tracey quartet on record.

The closing number, 'AM Mayhem', commences with an energetic burst of Wellins's sax before he and Tracey trade phrases as the quartet builds on their sense of shared exuberance. On this final piece Tracey sounds almost euphoric as his piano tumbles through the music with an insistence and barely controlled impetus that is equivalent to Thomas's characters rolling down Llareggub hill together in the dusk.

The title of the most widely known number on *Jazz Suite Inspired by*

Dylan Thomas's 'Under Milk Wood' is taken from a phrase that appears within the opening two lines of the play: 'Starless and Bible Black'.

Few pieces of music have been so perfectly named. In contrast to much of the record the ballad is an ensemble tone poem, a tribute to the darkness of the 'spring, moonless night', or, to use the title of another of Thomas's celebrated poems, 'owl-light', the hours before dawn breaks, when the horizon and sky are indistinguishable. Tracey's piano clusters, played with great use of the sustain pedal, create a chamber in which Wellins's notes echo as if being cast adrift on the tide, pulled on its current towards the seas inhabited by the fish, ghosts and dream figures of the play's opening scenes.

During his celebrated solo Wellins plays an improvisation around three semitones, in which there is sufficient space in his phrasing for the listener to imagine hearing the first birdsong of a spring morning. 'Starless and Bible Black' concludes with Tracey playing a short descending run, and as the play's First Voice narrator informs us: 'You can hear the dew falling.'

Jazz Suite Inspired by Dylan Thomas's 'Under Milk Wood' captured the distinctiveness of the radio play, as well as the changing face of the national character at the arrival of the 1960s; a perfect document of the modernism of jazz and Thomas's pastoral. Within months of its release Tracey made his departure from Scott's in deteriorating health, and for him a lean decade followed during which tastes in the musical form he had done so much to establish altered so dramatically that he was forced to give serious consideration to abandoning playing music entirely.

Mystery seems essential to the biography of all jazz musicians. It is unknown whether Stan Tracey visited either Laugharne or New Quay, the two small coastal towns Thomas drew on as the location for Llareggub. I was lucky enough to see Tracey play 'Starless and Bible Black' in the small parish hall of Hay-on-Wye, a town near my home in Mid Wales. Tracey was performing with Michael Horovitz at an evening organised by the town's poetry bookshop. Both men were in their seventies but retained the air of bohemianism that had defined their lives. Though more frail, Horovitz had the same boyish frame and sense of incredulity with which he had performed, in a striped Breton sweater, at The International Poetry Incarnation at the Royal Albert Hall in 1965, and filmed as *Wholly Communion* by the director Peter Whitehead. Horowitz had helped organise that event, which marked the point in the middle of the decade when the era of poetry and jazz he and Tracey had helped initiate would be superseded by pop music. For the evening on which I saw him, Horowitz had arranged for the hall to accommodate around fifty seated audience members. A printed newsletter was placed on every chair. It listed some of Horowitz's recent publications, but was mostly concerned with his ongoing campaign against the newly introduced parking charges that had come into force on his street in Notting Hill. He accompanied himself on a kazoo-trumpet as he read some recent poems before Tracey joined him for a long improvisation. Horowitz's voice and demeanour slowed a little during this section of the per-formance. The poet informed us that after the set had concluded, we were to consider the moon and nothing else as we left the parish hall on this cold and cloudless evening in late May. During their improvisation these two rather frail-looking men barely exchanged glances, but the energy and intuition between them was palpable.

Tracey, who wore an overcoat for the duration, had played a short solo set before his performance with Horovitz. He had opened with 'Cockle Row' from *Under Milk Wood*, and in so intimate a venue the percussive manner and intensity with which he attacked the keys was breathtaking. The drama of his playing was in contrast to his reserved demeanour. As he struck the keyboard, illuminated by a solitary soft white spotlight, his head and body remained perfectly still apart from his mercurial hands.

After acknowledging the applause with which the first piece was met, he commenced a busy improvisation based around some discordant clusters that gradually slowed and led to the opening, sustained notes of 'Starless and Bible Black'. He moved through the piece with a detached authority which suggested that although he was surely aware of the beauty of this composition, he was reluctant to register the effect his performance was having on the small audience, many of whom, myself included, were reduced to tears. As he concluded the number the last rippling notes were played in counterpoint to the heavily sustained modal chords and left to drift around the hall in rapt silence. There was a flicker of acknowledgement, a nod of the head at the reaction he had caused, and for one brief moment the face of this giant figure of British jazz, who in the 1970s had contemplated becoming a postman when he found work difficult to come by, broke into a smile.

The camp circle at the fourth Kibbo Kift Althing, Ballinger Grange, Great Missenden, 1923. 'White Fox' stands within the circle to the left, awaiting the arrival of the Kist and its bearers. (The Kibbo Kift Foundation/Museum of London)

4 : Sun Awareness

'Rise up, rise up, brother Diverus
And come you along with me.
There is a place prepared in hell
For to sit upon a serpent's knee.'
'Dives and Lazarus', Trad.

At the end of the 1930s, as Britain prepared again for conflict, many
of those who considered themselves champions of rural life regarded
elements of German National Socialism favourably. In certain cases
they identified closely with fascism and the views of Sir Oswald
Mosley's British Union of Fascists in particular.

Throughout the decade a persistent strain of fascism was prevalent
among custodial arguments over the landscape, made by men who presented their interpretation of environmentalism as a birthright or a priv-
ilege, one only truly understood by adepts such as themselves. Mosley,
formerly a Labour MP and government minister, was aware of the
growing sense of betrayal among rural communities, still seething at the
manner in which farming had been cast to the fate of the international
market once the armistice had been declared in 1918 and the support
systems temporarily put in place for agriculture were withdrawn.

The British Union of Fascists adopted an explicitly pro-agrar-
ian position. Jorian Jenks, an academic and gentleman farmer

who experienced the plight of agriculture during the 1920s and 30s at first hand, acted as the party's spokesman on rural matters and drafted its policies on farming. Jenks was influenced by the 'blood and soil' ideology expounded by Richard Walther Darré, a leading Nazi intellectual who eventually graduated to the higher echelons of the SS. Darré's theories made a direct link between race and land, claiming that the purity of both led to a dynamic relationship between a nation's health and therefore its supremacy. Darré served as the Nazi agriculture minister from 1933 to 1942, a position he used to disseminate his belief in the ground as a spiritual entity. The earth, Darré was convinced, should be garlanded with traditional songs and dances. In 1937 Germany's Ministry of Agriculture partially funded the Ancestral Heritage Research and Teaching Society, or *Ahnenerbe Forschungs- und Lehrgemeinschaft*. This research institute was founded by Heinrich Himmler as a means of justifying the ideology of the Nazi Party with pseudo-historical theories that included the role of folk music in German identity. Music, according to Darré, provided an immediate and profound means with which to restore the communion between the soil and its people.

Among the members of the British Union of Fascists who found Darré's ideas persuasive was the former army officer and ruralist Henry Williamson, the author of *Tarka the Otter*, who, like many countrymen returning from the Western Front, found solace and temporary respite from post-traumatic stress disorder by immersing themselves in the landscape. In a similar manner to Jorian Jenks, Williamson's attempts at farming had ended in failure; he visited

Germany in 1935 and attended that year's Nuremberg rally. There the vitality and discipline of the Hitler Youth struck him as an embodiment of the healthy outdoors he found absent in Britain. Within two years Williamson had joined Mosley's party; such was his attachment to their ideology he decorated his farm at Stiffkey in Norfolk with British Union of Fascists insignia. Williamson wrote that in the Hitler Youth he observed 'the former pallid leer of hopeless slum youth transformed into the suntan, the clear eye, the broad and easy rhythm of the poised young human being' and was so impressed by their display he considered whether an associate body could be started in Britain.

The rise of the Hitler Youth had its antecedents in two earlier German youth movements. At the turn of the century the Wandervogel (wandering bird) were founded with a mixture of romantic escapism, idealisation of the country's Teutonic era and an emphasis on testing the individual's endurance on long hikes through the countryside. These walks were undertaken in medieval dress and accompanied by folk songs sung on guitar, or lute, and performed with the innocence of pastoral shepherds. The Wandervogel considered singing ancient tunes accompanied by antiquated instruments an invocation of the past. Every step they took on their walks in the wild was purified by song.

Initially the Wandervogel were a brotherhood of some several thousand males aged between sixteen and twenty-five, self-organised into small groups. Within a decade young women were accepted as members, a decision which only amplified the Wandervogel's reputation for arcane eccentricity and the image of unabated youth setting base camps in remote rural locations, before wandering off together into the mountain mists.

Neither the Wandervogel nor their idealism survived the Great War. Prior to its outbreak a new, more radical alliance, Jungdeutschland (Young Germany), had been formed, which proposed a 'revolution of the soul' in dramatically nationalistic terms. In place of the mysticism of the Wandervogel, Jungdeutschland provided its members with military training, discipline and a prurient set of ethics. This was an ideology that proved sufficiently attractive to subsume the German Boy Scouts and much of the Wandervogel under its wing. On returning from the trenches to their defeated country, the depleted Jungdeutschland and remnants of the Wandervogel splintered into new formations, from which a substantial number of youth associations grew throughout the 1920s. These various associations were known by the term, Bündische Jugend – the Youth Movement – or by the shortened Bunde, and were united in their contempt for the libertarianism of the Weimar Republic, and scathing of its artificiality, insincerity and materialist obsessions.

Although each grouping had distinct identities and interests, they were united by a belief in self-reliance, fitness and the significance of the land to national identity. Several proclaimed themselves as *völkische*, steadfast in their rootedness to the soil, in comparison to nomadic or uprooted peoples, such as the Jews. At this highly uncertain political moment during the 1920s and 1930s the energy and idealism of youth found similar expression in Britain, in two esoteric groups led by charismatic individuals, one of whom considered music as sacrosanct in the marriage of blood and soil.

Rolf Gardiner was a 1920s pioneer of organic farming, a forester, rural revivalist and folk dancer who by the end of the thirties was an associate of Jorian Jenks and Henry Williamson. All three men shared a desire to reassert agrarian values of toil and belonging within the British countryside, but Gardiner, who was significantly younger than his acquaintances, felt this impulse with a singularity learned from an immersion in the activities of the Bunde groups of Germany and northern Europe.

Rolf Gardiner was born in 1902, the son of a distinguished Egyptologist and an Austro-Hungarian mother of Jewish descent. His interests in ruralism extended further than the reassertion of traditional farming methods and employment for the rural labour force that Jenks and the British Union of Fascists proposed. Gardiner shared with Richard Darré the belief in the ritual power of folk dancing and the holistic, proto-Gaian relationship between the ploughman and the sod. He would practise and advocate for these beliefs in a series of innovative experiments throughout the 1920s and 1930s and often do so under the patronage of the era's most disturbing political currents. Photographs of Gardiner performing in a Morris troupe from the time show a determined young man with a powerfully straight back. A look of fierce concentration born of his belief in the mystical nature of dancing is etched across his handsome features.

While an undergraduate at Cambridge in 1921 Gardiner edited *Youth*, a journal inspired by the Wandervogel and the Bunde, which he had witnessed at first hand when travelling with his father. The influence of his exposure to both is evident in the first editorial Gardiner wrote for *Youth*. He intended the publication to be 'the most significant journal of our time' and announced his intention to live 'in the physical, live, tangible world of sense, to be part of the sensual rhythm of life, with its birth, marriage, parenthood and death, with spring, summer, autumn and winter'. Music was the means by which Gardiner would realise these ambitions; his dedication to folk dancing had grown to be an obsession. According to the folk music historian C. J. Bearman, it had 'taken the place that love affairs or ambition occupy in the minds of other young men'.

Gardiner was also enamoured of D. H. Lawrence and took inspiration from the author's belief that 'What the blood feels, and believes, and says, is always true.' Gardiner made plain his devotion to Lawrence in the pages of *Youth*, writing: 'You may laugh, you may sneer, you may snivel, you *may* say or do any darned thing you like, but I tell you and foretell you, that the words of D. H. Lawrence will burn and tingle on the lips of men, in days when the dingy carpings of minds like James Joyce and Marcel Proust, of Lytton Strachey and Sigmund Freud, of Sidney Webb and Maynard Keynes will have long, long been consumed beneath the vanished debris of potty civilisation.' In particular, Gardiner was an advocate of what Lawrence termed 'sun awareness'; the author wrote to Gardiner about the need 'to have a silent, central flame of *consciousness* and of warmth which radiates out bit by bit'.

Through *Youth* Gardiner established several connections throughout the Bunde groups during the 1920s, including the Artaman League in Germany, a group with profound commitment to the 'blood and soil' philosophy and the revitalising of the Aryan race. He also had close ties to the Deutsche Freischar, who considered themselves more aesthetically driven and whose interest lay in re-enacting arcane ceremonies and dances from the nineteenth century. As someone so consumed by folk dancing Gardiner was enthralled by the commitment of the Freischar. 'It was the Germans who taught us the secrets of a true, nourishing discipline in music,' he later wrote. Gardiner was also determined that the occult properties of the dance should be experienced by young men as a means of restoring their virility. An immersion in the ritual of the Morris led them back to 'the soils from which they sprang' and gave them the strength needed to renew them. To facilitate this revival Gardiner instigated the Travelling Morrice troupe with a Cambridge friend Arthur Heffer, in 1924. This was a decision met with great concern by the English Folk Dance Society, then regarded as the custodians of the form's revival.

The archivist, teacher and revivalist Cecil Sharp founded the English Folk Dance Society in 1911. Ralph Vaughan Williams credited Sharp, who led the revival of folk music at the start of the century, with discovering and sharing 'something entirely new to us and yet not new'. Composer-archivists such as the flamboyant, Australian-born Percy

Grainger and Vaughan Williams's close friend George Butterworth, who was killed at the battle of the Somme, shared Sharp's enthusiasm and energy for collecting. Vaughan Williams wrote that he himself was drawn to folk music as it represented 'an art which is indigenous and owes nothing to anything outside itself'.

During Christmas 1899, Cecil Sharp had witnessed a Morris troupe by chance at Headington Quarry, near Oxford. The concertina player William Kimber, whose knowledge of folk tunes was thorough, accompanied them. Sharp was seduced by the liveliness and expertise with which they performed a musical tradition he assumed to be extinct, as the depletion of the countryside's population, the effects of industrialisation and the ageing of those for whom the singing of folk songs was part of daily life had threatened its survival. Sharp realised the common stem of folk music was withering and determined to preserve what remained of the tradition. In his opinion there was little worth in collecting a folk song from anyone under the age of fifty, as only singers of the older generation could provide a song's provenance.

Sharp and his colleagues subsequently travelled the country accumulating a library of rural folk songs. In 1920, with the revival now underway, Vaughan Williams published *Twelve Traditional Carols from Herefordshire* with Ella Mary Leather, a pioneering collector with an expertise in the gipsy tradition of her native county. Leather was the wife of a solicitor and ignored her social standing to participate in the seasonal hop picking in order to gain the trust of the traveller community and learn their songs. In 1911 Leather, Vaughan Williams and his first wife Adeline visited a camp near Weobley in rural Herefordshire to listen to their camp-fire singing. There they received a warm reception and Leather used a phonograph to record the songs, which were then added to the small canon she had compiled while writing a history of the county's folklore, from which she and the composer selected the twelve carols for their collection. Twelve Traditional Carols from Herefordshire included little-known carols such as 'The Angel Gabriel' and 'God Rest Ye Merry Gentlemen' that were rarely sung in church as their tunes, sung unaccompanied in the fields, were considered overpowering.

In Weobley Vaughan Williams encountered another version of the ballad 'Dives & Lazarus'; its story of the dispossessed beggar Lazarus achieving salvation, in contrast to the wealthy Dives, was a popular rural song. The accompanying tune struck a deep chord within the composer, for whom the song already held great signif-icance. Recalling how he first heard the tune in 1893 at the age of twenty-one in the presence of his friend Gustav Holst, he wrote 'that it was just what we were looking for. Well we were dazzled, we wanted to preach a new gospel, we wanted to rhapsodize on these tunes just as Liszt and Grieg had done on theirs; we did not suppose that by so doing we were inventing a national music ready-made, we simply were fascinated by the tunes and wanted other people to be fascinated too.' He added that the two young composers 'felt that this is what we expected our national melody to be'. Vaughan Williams included a setting of 'Dives & Lazarus' in his *Folk Songs Suite* of 1923, and in 1939 he composed *Five Variants on Dives and Lazarus* for harp and string orchestra, a commission he received from the British Council as part of the 1939 World's Fair in New York, where it was conducted by Sir Adrian Bolt.

Over three decades earlier Vaughan Williams had used the melody of 'Dives & Lazarus' for the tune 'Kingsfold', to accompany 'O Sing a Song of Bethlehem' in *The English Hymnal*.

The idea for a new collection of indigenous hymns originated from the clergyman and charismatic liturgist Percy Dearmer, a lifelong socialist and vicar of St Mary-the-Virgin, Primrose Hill. Dearmer had previously written *The Parson's Handbook*, a work that sought to revive an especially English form of singing. *The English Hymnal* was to be an accompaniment to this principle in musical form. Dearmer arrived unannounced at the door of Vaughan Williams from a hansom cab in 1904 and requested that the young composer help him realise his ambition, which Dearmer anticipated would take two months.

After reflecting on the offer for twenty-four hours Vaughan Williams accepted Dearmer's invitation and spent the following two years compiling music for the *Hymnal*. Among the most notable contributions the composer made were to include tunes from medieval music previously used in church services and folk songs he had recently collected, to accompany the texts of the hymns. By doing so he reintroduced forms that had been lost or ignored in popular worship. The hymn 'He Who Would Valiant Be' was set to a tune which Vaughan Williams heard sung to him by a Mrs Harriet Verrall of Monk's Gate, Horsham, and was derived from the traditional song 'Our Captain Calls'. He also adapted 'The Ploughboy's Dream', a tune he had heard 'sung by a labourer' in Forest Green, Surrey in 1903 to accompany 'O Little Town of Bethlehem'.

The composer also wrote new accompaniments of his own, which to our ears are now so familiar as to seem traditional. Out of what Vaughan Williams termed 'common modesty' he credited these tunes to 'my old friend Mister Anon'. These include 'Sine Nomine' (without a name), his setting of 'For All the Saints', 'All People That On Earth Do Dwell' and 'Down Ampney', the tune he composed for 'Come Down, O Love Divine' which he named after the Gloucestershire village of his birth. Liturgical in emphasis and ordered according to the church's calendar, the *Hymnal* also included supplementary material such as texts and plainsong for feast-days including Palm Sunday and Good Friday. These inclusions may appear established and commonplace to us today, but upon its publication in 1906 *The English Hymnal* was met with resistance. The Archbishop of Canterbury Dr Randall Davidson was firm in his disapproval and suggested that the church's clergy should refrain from using it.

The English Hymnal was published in the light green colour emblematic of High Church; its preface stated the *Hymnal* was 'a collection of the best hymns in the English language'. In the preface Vaughan Williams emphasised: '. . . it ought no longer to be true anywhere that the most exalted moments of a church-goer's week are associated with music that would not be tolerated in any place of secular entertainment.' And later continued: 'It is a great mistake to suppose that the result will be inartistic. A large body of voices singing together makes a distinctly artistic effect, though that of each individual voice might be the opposite. And it may be added that a desire to parade a trained choir often accompanies a debased musical taste.' Above all else, the composer selected tunes that might help facilitate the rediscovery of the joys of singing together.

Vaughan Williams ensured a 'large body of voices' might sing from the *Hymnal* together by setting the tunes it contained at as low a pitch as possible. His belief in song as a birthright and in 'music as the art of the common man and the art of the humble' was expressed in this decision to allow as many voices as possible to join together as one, regardless of ability or background. The priority for the young composer was that every voice in the large body should be heard. The act of singing should be allowed to run in the blood of everyone, otherwise a nation had no means with which to reveal its soul. A performance of the *Five Variants of Dives & Lazarus*, once more under the baton of Sir Adrian Boult, would be heard in 1958 at Vaughan Williams' funeral at the composer's request, at Westminster Abbey, where the ashes of Pearcy Dearmer had previously been interred.

Vaughan Williams' friend and biographer Michael Kennedy described the moment when the folk tune that the composer had first encountered as a young man, and had thereafter inhabited his consciousness, was played at the service:

> Into the silent of the Abbey came the first notes
> of the *Five Variants of Dives & Lazarus*. It was as if
> Vaughan Williams himself had spoken. The tune which
> he had loved all his life, which came from the soil of
> England, ageless and anonymous was the perfect device
> to create a mood of remembrance which will haunt those
> who experienced it to the end of their days.

In this place of coronations and royal weddings, a folk tune from the fields played as a requiem for the composer who had bequeathed the country the gift of its own national music.

Almost two decades after the publication of *The English Hymnal*, Rolf Gardiner had grown impatient with both the English Folk Dance Society and Vaughan Williams's opinion of folk music.

In 1922 a tour of the Cotswolds was arranged for the Travelling Morrice. Gardiner envisaged the trip would be made in the similar spirit of open-air mysticism of the Wandervogel, a monastic pilgrimage by a group of young men who sought a unification of earth and dance. The method in which the dancers travelled, however, would be more influenced by the rigour and discipline of the Bunde. In his diary Gardiner wrote of strenuous bike rides, the pitching of ascetic camps on stony ground, dances held by the roadsides, on village greens and market squares, and frugal meals: 'Bread and cheese were our ambrosia, ale our nectar; in fact we assert that never in England has that sterling fluid been pressed into more fitting occasion than on Travelling Morrice tours.' According to Gardiner the dancers received a generous welcome throughout the Cotswolds and he was encouraged, despite protestations from Cecil Sharp, who considered the Gardiner troupe's technique to be insufficient for demonstration, to take a version of the Travelling Morrice on a tour to Germany. There, Gardiner gained further attention and familiarity with the Bunde through his dancing style.

The esoteric nature of his interpretation of the Morris and contempt for Sharp's opinions led to a final confrontation with the English Folk Dance Society. 'The EFDS don't like my dancing,' he lamented to his diary in May 1923, 'bad cess to them. To hell with their fiddly-fuddly blundery bourgeois technique. Of course I'm eccentric in this point, and glad to be . . .'

In the ensuing years Gardiner organised hikes through the area he called the Wessex Downland of Wiltshire and Hampshire. A 'dozen or so men' Gardiner had met through outdoor or camping fraternities would meet on Boxing Day to take to the fields and hills. 'In that time of systole, of withdrawal to the roots of the sap, in those days of suspense, of hovering darkness illumined by Christmas stars . . . in such dark days we marched.' Music was a significant element in these expeditions, and a 'dedicated choirmaster' led the men in singing. Gardiner's description of a hike undertaken in 1926 evokes the stillness and darkness of midwinter in the Downland:

> A radiant winter's afternoon spread its sheen upon the
> Ogbourne downs. A threshing-machine hummed among
> yellow stacks, a tractor-plough crawled over a distant
> firle; rooks cawed as they travelled from beech clump to
> beech clump. In this world of self-absorbed activity our
> company made its way across the downs.

Gardiner and his men gathered twigs for fires, then slept in blankets, enraptured beneath the stars, to be awoken by their choirmaster or 'chantyman', who was 'sustained with a blanket round his shoulders facing an evening star' as he 'very slowly' began singing a fifteenth-century carol to greet the new day. As they rested one evening in a pub at Woolstone, below the White Horse Hill at Uffington, Gardiner and his associates 'exchanged songs with the village men', one of whom sang the ancient folk song 'The Jolly Ploughboy', before they left in good spirits to journey along the Ridgeway in good voice.

The disagreements between Gardiner and Cecil Sharp were ones the young firebrand shared with the social reformer and suffragette Mary Neal. The history of Neal and Sharp's long-standing arguments is convoluted and remains disputed. Neal's interest in folk dancing preceded Sharp's and she was concerned that the founding of the English Folk Dance Society proved he was more concerned with preserving traditions than celebrating the rituals of the Morris dance.

Neal's interest in the Morris revival had been kindled by witnessing a dance by the same Headington troupe led by William Kimber that Sharp had encountered during his epiphany of Christmas 1899. Neal had invited the dancers to perform at the Espérance Club, an institution she founded with her friend and colleague Emmeline Pethick-Lawrence. The club was established as a secure working environment for girls in the rag trade who had previously been subjected to poor and exploitative conditions. Within two years Neal had published a book of Morris tunes, and an all-female Esperance Morris, drawn from members of the club, performed dances regularly throughout the South of England.

Mary Neal's interest in the form grew in parallel with her strong reputation for social activism – Vaughan Williams once attended a fancy dress party as her – that ensured the Espérance Club performed dances at suffragette rallies. Cecil Sharp, whose sister Evelyn participated in the suffrage movement and had been arrested, is said to have disapproved of what he considered Neal's politicisation of the Morris. Their relationship deteriorated into a bitter dispute and was played out through a series of inflammatory letters written to national newspapers.

Neal's belief in the ritual aspect of folk dancing unsurprisingly brought her into contact with Rolf Gardiner, whom she met and corresponded with. Neal was clearly struck by the strength of Gardiner's convictions.

In a letter to him, she expressed her curiosity and fascination with the magical powers of dancing:

> What I want to know from anyone who can tell me
> is: – The inner history of the morris when it was (if
> ever) white magic if there is a lost tradition of what
> the feminine side was as a discipline and a gesture and
> [word erased] how that is related to the male dance. If
> there is a mutual dance expressing the highest religious
> side of sex as a symbol of cosmic union. When (if ever)
> the dance degenerated into black magic and why and
> what causes underlay this change. If I had any part
> in either the black or white side what had Sharp and
> MacIlwaine to do with its past history and with me.

Where any records are to be found which would help
us to use the old tradition as a foundation for the new
and revived dance?

For all the strong impression Gardiner made on such authorities
as Mary Neal, he was driven by the belief that the cosmic union
between blood and soil was only understood by those who shared in
his ideology, which in the 1930s manifested itself with a dangerous
malevolence.

Poster advertising *The Nomad*, the monthly newsletter of the Kindred of the Kibbo Kift, 1923. The poster was designed, drawn and painted by the newsletter's editor and founder of the Kindred, 'White Fox' (John Hargrave). (The Estate of John Hargrave/Museum of London)

5 : The Wide World's Drift

'All Hael! All Hael! We wield the lashing flail,
That beats the golden life out of all things stale
We come, we come, we come, the Kibbo Kift,
Children of the Fire and the wide world's drift.
Whoso wrong our fiery throng stuns.
We are the strong ones, we the Kibbo Kift,
We come, we come, the Kibbo Kift
Children of the Fire and the wide world's drift.'

Rolf Gardiner, 'All Hael'

The interest in mysticism Mary Neal had confided to Rolf Gardiner ensured she would also cross paths with 'White Fox', or John Gordon Hargrave, the founder of the Kindred of the Kibbo Kift. An intense and charismatic man who in later years would practise as a psychic, Hargrave was brought up in the Quaker tradition and continued to place an emphasis on the light within.

Hargrave, an author, book illustrator and designer, had been an active member of the Boy Scouts Association, before growing dis-illusioned with what he perceived to be an increasing emphasis on prosaic militarism over scouting's earlier interest in woodcraft and outdoor skills. This disenchantment led to Hargraves being accused of disloyalty and he was subsequently asked to leave the organisation.

The Kindred of the Kibbo Kift was founded in 1920 as a separatist movement to the Boy Scouts Association. The Kindred was constituted at a meeting held at the home of Emmeline Pethick-Lawrence, the suffragette and colleague of Mary Neal in the Espérance Club. Neal herself was a member of the Kindred's Advisory Council and frequently received Hargrave as a house guest.

The name Kibbo Kift came from what Hargraves insisted was an archaic piece of Cheshire dialect meaning 'proof of great strength'. Its members would be illuminated through tribal training, remain resolute during hardship and experience the best physical health. These were the attributes, Hargraves was certain, that would help the Kibbo Kift realise their ambition for world peace. To demonstrate the seriousness with which they approached their task and to display a universality of commitment, the Kindred wore a hand-sewn uniform of cowls, hoods and jerkins. Hargrave declared this costume 'an outward, visible indication of the spirit of the age'. The Kindred of the Kibbo Kift appeared in the green hills of Buckinghamshire as pilgrims carrying wooden staffs, driven by their own divine purpose.

Each Kinsperson was assigned a name either derived from, or suggestive of, Native American custom. Hargraves himself was 'White Fox'. The Lodges into which the Kindred were divided each created a totem pole to stand beside the richly decorated banners and ritualistic artefacts that rendered the Kindred spirit in material form.

At their official camps, known as Althings, Kin members wore ceremonial robes made from rich fabric. A carved oak chest, known as the Kist, would be presented to the Head Man, carried on poles by four Kistbearers wearing distinctive tabards. White Fox himself was resplendent in a brilliant white robe, lined with regal purple. During sessions of physical exercise the Kindred wore slips and zephyrs modelled on the Ancient Greeks. It was in these garments Kindred members practised a bespoke martial art known as 'thewstrang', a form of all-in wrestling in which contestants proved their strength by attempting to grapple one another to the ground.

The Kibbo Kift was co-educational and recruited adults and children, which was an egalitarian, almost revolutionary policy among outdoor associations in the 1920s.

Despite these displays of non-conformity Hargrave was keen to assert the Kindred were not a secret fellowship but an 'open conspiracy': the Kibbo Kift was a living example of health, ritual and hardiness. In a similar manner to Rolf Gardiner, Hargrave had found inspiration in the Wandervogel and imagined the Kibbo Kift would create a self-reliant 'New Race of Scout Men'. This was a phrase redolent of the acceptance of social Darwinism in the 1920s and the increasing consideration of eugenics as a means of rectifying societal ills such as poverty, disease and unemployment. The Kin's Covenant, which every member had to sign, promulgated an ambitious blend of radical measures to 'counter-act the ill effects of industrialism and overcrowding in towns and cities'. These ideals were disseminated in *The Nomad*, the house journal of the Kibbo Kift, which featured Hargrave's beautifully drawn and coloured designs. His use of free-hand and bright inks was as distinctive and eye-catching as the Kindred costume.

Hargrave proved a charismatic, if intense, leader and received encouraging correspondence for his ideas and the activities of the Kindred from five Nobel Prize winners and from H. G. Wells, whose ideas Hargrave admired and, in private, considered to be a great influence.

The more fantastical elements of his controlling nature, which his perceived brilliance hid, are evident in the declaration younger initiates were required to make: 'I wish to be Kibbo Kift, and to (1) camp out and keep fit; (2) help others; (3) learn how to make things; and (4) work for world peace and brotherhood.'

New Kindred recruits over the age of eighteen were asked to undergo nine initiation tests devised by White Fox: the Tests of the Supple Limb, Keen Eye, Sharp Nose, Fleet Foot, Listening Ear, Silent Paw, the Wander Camp Test, the Test of Silence and the Test of the Sunburnt Skin.

Anyone undertaking the Test of the Silent Paw was required to walk barefoot through woodland without making their presence known. Higher-ranking Kindred members were given more onerous tests, which according to one member were seldom completed. These included the Test of the Hindu *Bhagat*, during which the appellant, having taken a cold bath, rubbed themselves down with dock leaves. Now rid of the scent of a human they were directed to walk naked into a forest and return with six drawings of wild animals.

Mary Neal, who was never a full member herself, assumed Rolf Gardiner would find common ground with the esotericism and faith in the spiritual properties of the outdoors of the Kindred and introduced her young friend to White Fox.

Hargrave's sense of performance and ritual and his propensity for discipline attracted Gardiner, who shared the Kibbo Kift's enjoyment of hiking and camping. In turn, Gardiner's links and friendship with the Bunde groups in Germany were an attractive asset for Hargrave. White Fox suggested that the newly named 'Rolf the Ranger', accompanied by four Kindred, represent the Kibbo Kift at the North European Youth Assembly staged near Dresden. Within a year of joining, Gardiner rose to the rank of 'Gleemaster'. His principal contribution had been to enhance the role and influence of music within the Kindred. As he had on his Downland marches, Gardiner encouraged the singing of old English folk songs, as well as compositions of his own, written specifically for Kindred hiking expeditions and Althings. An issue of *The Nomad* gives a report of the Easter Hike of 1925, during which Gardiner introduced the song 'All Hael':

All Hael! All Hael! We wield the lashing flail,
That beats the golden life out of all things stale
We come, we come, we come, the Kibbo Kift,
Children of the Fire and the wide world's drift.
Whoso wrong our fiery throng stuns.
We are the strong ones, we the Kibbo Kift,
We come, we come, the Kibbo Kift
Children of the Fire and the wide world's drift.

This was sung to the tune of 'The Monk's March', a traditional Morris tune. At another Althing, Gardiner led a sunrise tattoo.

This consisted of six men carrying tree branches processing through the camp at daybreak singing a 'stirring song' he had written for the occasion. By the mid-1920s, a *Kibbo Kift Song Book* had been published. The collection included compositions by Rolf the Ranger but, notably, White Fox had written the majority of entries.

Gardiner's involvement with the Kibbo Kift was as dynamic as it was short-lived. The source of the fissure between Rolf the Ranger and White Fox was their differing views on folk dancing. For Hargrave the type of Morris dancing Gardiner enjoyed and proselyted symbolised regression. In turn Gardiner thought such an opinion proved White Fox was in denial of the ancient rhythms of the soil.

Gardiner wrote of how 'the old mystery, the fire and the blood of the Morris must be infused into the dances of the Kibbo Kift; the dances of every new and genuine brotherhood must be inspired with the magic breath of *ancient* rituals.'

White Fox was bemused by the earnestness of Rolf the Ranger's beliefs and dismissive of his ideas, and made clear his opinion in an issue of *The Nomad*: '. . . bands of Young Flaxen-Haired Giants Morris Dancing in the Sun – what can it possibly signify beyond giving a pleasant harmless outlet for young fellows who can afford the pastime and who find it easier to revolt against the intellect than to set their minds and "rhythms" to any constructive analysis of human needs.'

Gardiner had also grown weary of this increasing despotism on Hargrave's part and also found White Fox to be manipulative. In his diary Gardiner questioned Hargrave's motives and considered the Kibbo Kift to be over-concerned with what he described as 'sect-theatricality' and airy notions of divination that placed too little emphasis on the land and the business of its cultivation. He wrote of his concern that the Kibbo Kift displayed '. . . no living roots in the earth of England, no blood-contact with the living part of English earth'.

White Fox, who had left school at twelve, was anti-intellectual, almost anti-educational and discouraged the Kindred from keeping pens or notebooks about their person. Instead, Gardiner decided, Hargrave was preoccupied with ephemera such as copses, fairy rings, fossils and standing stones, and neglected to acknowledge the primal vitality and opportunity represented by an abandoned field ripe for ploughing. The fact Hargrave had settled in a bungalow at Kings Langley, Hertfordshire, confirmed to Gardiner that the Kindred of the Kibbo Kift, whose adult members included Metroland teachers, civil servants and librarians, were little more than a costumed and over-theatrical, if intellectually curious, equivalent of the weekend picnickers motoring through the countryside with *Shell Guides*. To Gardiner these Sunday drivers in search of authentic rustic locals, megalithic monuments and the comforting sight of lychgated parish churches represented a failure of imagination. Such a suburban, romantic perception of rural Britain, with its nostalgic emphasis on the rustic or overgrown, was anathema to someone with his vision of the countryside as a thriving agriculture in which the toil and expertise were clearly visible in orderly furrows.

D. H. Lawrence encouraged Gardiner's dismissive attitude. In a letter the novelist urged Gardiner to strike out on his own from the fanciful tyranny of Hargraves and the Kibbo Kift and to rid himself of '. . . wandervogling and piping imitation nature tunes to the taste of a cake of milk chocolate . . . all this blasted snivelling of hopelessness and self-pity and stars and wind among the trees and campfires and witanagemotry – shit!'.

Gardiner marked his resignation from the Kindred of the Kibbo Kift in equally forthright terms. He published an article in *Youth*, which he continued to edit, titled 'Suburbia Delenda Est' that asserted, in similar terms to his repudiation of the English Folk Dance Society: 'The Kibbo Kift is the supreme instance of suburban idealism trying to create order out of the chaos of its own excreta. Behind its whole creation there is a ghastly vacuum and absence of belief, belief of the blood and the soul.'

Although his departure was rife with animosity, Gardiner had left his mark on the Kibbo Kift. Vera Chapman, a member of the Kin known as 'Lavengri' who would go on to found the Tolkien Society, become a member of the Ancient Order of Druids and write on the Arthurian legends, wrote in her diary:

> Rolf Gardiner was a very gorgeous and magnificent young man. He brought to us something of what the Wandervogel were doing and that, at the time, was entirely idealistic. It was peace, better education and the breaking of various taboos; the taboo against discussing sex, the taboo against throwing off your clothes in camp and the taboo against discussing anyone else's religion. We broke the seals and brought them into daylight.

After his departure from the Kindred, Gardiner determined to create his own cadre of young, single-minded and invigorated English countrymen. In 1927 his uncle, the composer Henry Balfour Gardiner, gave him use of a dilapidated estate, Gore Farm, in north Dorset. The land was in the typically poor condition of a farm left to ruin during the decade's agricultural depression but provided Gardiner, then aged twenty-five, with further inspiration to build a centre for the rural renaissance he was determined to bring about. 'The task of making a balanced and economic estate out of the farm lands and woods acquired piecemeal from the wreckage of the old hereditary units, broken up in the nineteen twenties, fell on myself as owner of Springhead,' Gardiner wrote.

This economy that would rise from the wreckage would see England once more growing its own, nutritious produce. Farmers would no longer be mere agricultural labourers but fit, healthy conduits of uncontaminated yeomen stock, who understood the doctrine between man and soil and become guardians of its continuity. Their endeavours would be celebrated in the dances and songs of the seasons and recorded in simple paintings and drawings evoking lives lived entirely to the growth rhythms of the land.

Gardiner named his centre the 'Gore Kinship' and invited sympathetic groups from the Bunde and other northern European groups to assist in the restoration of the farm and to work and study together to restore life to the ground. Within five years Gardiner's opportunity of realising his vision had increased dramatically. With no little encouragement from Gardiner himself, his uncle acquired the neighbouring Springhead mill and farm, a more substantial estate including a working mill and courtyard around which Gardiner's new group of enthusiasts would muster throughout the 1930s under their own flag bearing a George Cross and Dragon. Gardiner formally described the site as a 'centre for the gathering and training of men and women for the weal of Wessex', which he christened the Wessex Centre Group, or the Springhead Ring. Gardiner was also keen that the Ring be open and generous in its dealings with its Dorset neighbours. Rather than gain a reputation for being a 'sect', Gardiner saw the activities of the Ring as a means for the community to meet and hold celebrations together; these festivities would recognise the rebirth of the land as a source of the area's energy and celebrate the journey back to prosperity from the era of rural decrepitude.

During his trips to Europe Gardiner had become familiar with several communal camps from which he drew inspiration for the Springhead Ring. In Jutland he had stayed at the Danish Folk High School, an institution where he had witnessed folk history, nationalism and productivity taught under the principle of a school for life.

The institution that had the most profound effect on his ideas was the Musikheim at *Frankfurt on Oder*, in Brandenburg, founded in 1929 by the former Wandervogel and friend of Gardiner, Georg Götsch. The Musikheim attempted to restore the arts to the 'common calendar' of the local community in order to revitalise its primal foundations. Gardiner described these centres as 'islands of spirit' which shone like a beacon in the midwinter of the 'new dark ages' of the twentieth century.

The Springhead Ring held regular annual camps with a similar emphasis of national renewal and taught attendees agrarian skills and customs, which Gardiner believed provided a more holistic alternative to the increasing prevalence of the tractor as a means of earning a living from the land during the Great Depression.

There are accounts of unemployed miners Gardiner had encountered on his Morris tours attending the Ring courses. In a report he wrote for the Minister of Labour he enthused that the Springhead camps attracted members 'from different walks of life' who gained 'a direct experience of community by thinking, playing and working on the land'.

The activities of the Ring were publicised in a biannual journal, the *North Sea and Baltic*, which appeared at Whitsuntide and midwinter. The Whitsuntide edition of 1933 gives great insight into the momentum Gardiner had created in Dorset. There are essays on 'The German Revolution', a profile of the Orientalist and educator Carl Heinrich Becker, in whom Gardiner recognised 'Sun-Awareness', and a report on the Third Cleveland Work Camp, which Gardiner had organised near Whitby and included activities such as allotment digging, folk dancing and a lecture on smallholdings.

In his later years Gardiner wrote that 'music was the soul of our camps and it was a musical sort of discipline at which we aimed in everything'. The day would conclude in song:

The Earth has turned us from the sun,
And let us close our circle now to light,
But open it to darkness, and each one

Warm with this circle's warming,
Go in good darkness to good sleep
Good night.

Then torches would be extinguished and the camp, after a day of intense singing, dancing, digging and learning, fell silent.

As well as evocative descriptions of camp life, the *North Sea and Baltic* also contains several instances of anti-Semitism, including the line: 'How sick Europe is of the Jewish monotheistic string!' Gardiner would later deplore the manner in which Nazism had ruined the 'German Revolution' instigated by the Bunde, but many of the activities at Springhead were informed by a doctrine associated with the rise of Hitler.

The culmination of the Springhead Ring year was the Harvest Home festival. After a communal feast 'all would go out into the starlit courtyard and sing': 'Spin smoothly earth, / Lie quietly man / Sleep in good darkness / While you can.' 'Smoothly round the earth is turning, / Turning always on to morning / And from morning round to night.'

Gardiner described these songs as 'simple words sung with a listening intentedness and quietude'. This description and the vocabulary of the verses sung at Springhead are familiar to anyone with a passing knowledge of the canon of late 1960s and early 1970s songwriters inspired by the rhythm of the seasons. It is hard to think of a better description of the music of Nick Drake than 'simple words sung with a listening intentedness and quietude'. Drake's subject matter bears a strong similarity to the natural world Gardiner celebrates, and songs such as 'Fruit Tree', 'Harvest Breed', 'Saturday Sun' and 'Pink Moon' share a responsiveness to the earth, or Sun Awareness, with which the Springhead Ring might have found affinity.

The musical policy at the Ring, Gardiner stated, was 'new texts and new tunes, adaptations of old folk songs, rounds and chorals'. Three decades after the pinnacle of the Springhead Harvest Home festivals, Ashley Hutchings of Fairport Convention would visit the library of Cecil Sharp House to study English folk songs. He would include them with the group's own compositions on *Liege and Leif,* the album justifiably regarded as the definitive coupling of new texts and new tunes with traditional English music. 'To Every Thing There Is a Season' was a song popular at Springhead that would later be recorded by The Byrds as 'Turn! Turn! Turn!'. In the second half of the twentieth century, folk music and the styles it inspired was associated first with the protest movement and later the counterculture of the mid to late 1960s. The era's affinity with environmentalism suggested the resources of the natural world were in the custody of those who cared for it most, people of a liberal or left-leaning outlook who sang of its wonder. At Springhead, Gardiner and his acolytes took an equal degree of inspiration from the environment and the time of the seasons. Much of the philosophy he espoused was the converse of the ideals that the landscape later inspired, during the Aquarian Age. The earth provided inspiration to both, but no judgement.

While cultivating the Springhead Estate, Gardiner utilised the theories Rudolf Steiner, the Austrian educator, philosopher and esotericist, had developed under the term biodynamic agriculture, which Steiner expounded as a manifestation of his philosophy of Anthroposophy. Although he had little direct experience of agriculture himself, Steiner believed farmers should allow their crop cycles to be governed by the moon, and the regular activities of ploughing and harvesting should be undertaken in consultation with the lunar calendar. Steiner also advocated the use of rituals, such as filling cow horns with manure, before burying them in the soil for the duration of winter. The horns were then exhumed, the manure added to water and the mixture sprayed on the ground as a fertility rite in preparation for sowing. Such eco-mysticism and deification of the soil proved seductive for Gardiner, who followed Steiner's principles closely.

Springhead would be farmed using his biodynamic methods and the handicraft and rural skills, lost for a generation, would once more be taught and circulated among the Ring's initiates. Those present would also be instructed in recreation and in the feast-days of each season, to ensure the bonds of village life would be reasserted, and to convey that 'behind all husbandry and craftsmanship and using such things as drama and festival, stood sacramental ideas of worship and offering, as opposed to the etiolation of modern life by the decay of reverence and mystery'.

The esoteric nature of Gardiner's methods, his enthusiasm for an agrarian form of nationalism and his stirring correspondence with officials concerning rural economic revival ensured he became a figure of note for those in positions of authority who shared his interests. The Conservative MP for Basingstoke, Viscount Lymington, had a passion for farming and was drawn to Gardiner through their mutual interest in manure; dung was something of an obsession for Lymington, who urged the government to consider appointing a 'Minister for Manure'. Lymington held equally trenchant views on the use of imported bamboo canes in horticulture in place of native hazel sticks and, like many during the decade, including John Betjeman, considered tinned foods to be a symbol and symptom of national decline.

Like Springhead, the considerable Lymington estate at Farleigh Wallop was a centre for innovative organic farming practices. Lymington deplored the government's abandonment of agriculture after the Great War and considered the establishment of the Milk Marketing Board, on which he had been invited to sit, to be an act of 'state socialism' that would undermine the livelihoods of small farmers, going so far in 1934 as to resign his seat in Parliament in protest. Four years later he published *Famine in England*, a short book that warned of the consequences of the country's continual vulnerability as a net importer of food, a position that would become grave should there be another war. Lymington's message was duly noted and proved influential within government, while he and Rolf Gardiner found they had much in common. There are reports that in 1939, on the eve of conflict, both men travelled to Germany and met with Richard Darré, the Nazi agriculture minister and creator of the 'blood and soil' movement, and Rudolf Hess, a homeopath, naturist, and fellow enthusiast of Rudolf Steiner's biodynamic farming methods.

Despite having clear fascist sympathies – he had previously met with Hitler and Mussolini – Lymington declined an invitation to join the British Union of Fascists as he disagreed with the party's position on monarchy, which he considered insufficiently deferential. Gardiner too resisted both an invitation to become a member of the party and the suggestion, from its spokesman Jorian Jenks, that Oswald Mosley be asked to visit the Springhead Estate.

Lymington and Gardiner were instead both members of the clandestine English Mistery. Founded by William Sanderson in 1930, the organisation was male-only and small in number. Its members included Lymington, Gardiner, J. F. C. Fuller of the British Union of Fascists and A. K. Chesterton, who would later be a co-founder of the National Front and, along with Lymington and others, edit the *New Pioneer*, a journal of organic farming techniques and vehement anti-Semitism. The Minister of Agriculture in Chamberlain's government at the outbreak of the Second World War, Sir Reginald Dorman-Smith, the man who instigated the 'Dig for Victory' campaign, was one of a handful of members of the Mistery who were serving MPs.

The creed of the English Mistery was stated in the conclave's first publication, *English Mistery, Order of 1933, No. 1*: 'The English Mistery is a stronghold for all who are activated by motives of English patriotism. Our race can be saved and its vigour increased by the revival of instinct and tradition, and by the protection and development of national breeds, on which the existence and continuation of culture depend.'

Its founder William Sanderson was a freemason and had been active in the Imperial Fascist League, but by the 1930s was a disenchanted writer of tracts and opinions including *That Which Was Lost: A Treatise on Freemasonry and the English Mistery*, the book from which his society took its name. He had also produced a pamphlet entitled *Statecraft* that set out the need for an 'Anglo Saxon Revival' and bemoaned the 'lost secret of race' in British government. Sanderson founded the Mistery to promote a return to the feudal system, to do away with capitalism, to agitate for the recognition of the rural way of life over the urban and to promote the reinstatement of the peasantry and the subjugation of women. These views were broadcast in obscure pamphlets written and edited by the Nietzschean philosopher, author and lifelong opponent of miscegenation Anthony Ludovici.

The Mistery met in a clandestine atmosphere at headquarters Sanderson had secured in Lincoln's Inn Fields to discuss how to disseminate its principles of royalism, anti-Semitism, the purifying of the English race and the reinvigoration of the soil; activities overseen by its 'Council of Strength'. The Council may have had Sanderson as its sole member, as the Mistery's founder was vehemently anti-democracy.

At one meeting Gardiner gave a reading from a paper he had written for the Mistery titled 'Reflections on Music and Statecraft'. It began: 'Music is the supreme political exercise. Yet today the statesman as such has little use for music, the musicians as such still less use for the State.' He went on to lament that although music was 'the essential magic of the vital State', a rupture had occurred between music and action. 'The common people has for the most part lost all traditions of musical recreation, all traditions of ritual and festival.'

In his conclusion Gardiner's animosity towards the English Folk Dance Society resurfaced: 'The middle class which at present dominates England with political leaders is musically inarticulate and barbarous; it regards song and dance as objects of sentimental indulgence . . . as an opportunity for a letting go, not as a disciplined restoration of community order and vitality.' Such lassitude was a form of decadence, and Gardiner singled-out the composer of *The Lark Ascending* as an accomplice in the weakening of English song: 'Musical forms today are pieces of lyric utterance, or they are, as in the Vaughan Williams setting of the Wassail song, attitudinations. They are not part of a living epic context. They are either purely compartmental recreations on a par with cricket, tennis, bridge or other amusement or they are formalities. A nation which takes refuge in such compartmental amusements on the one hand and formalities on the other has ceased to make history.' The fact Gardiner believed in the ritual power of folk as a means of abnegating middle-class pursuits is one of the most dramatic instances of the dogma he followed. The only revival folk music required was one that reconnected its songs and dances to the soil and thereby venerated its sacred authority.

Viscount Lymington tired of Sanderson's insularity and in 1936 reconstituted the Mistery as the English Array, effectively the same society, with the same members, but without Sanderson. The Array was named after the massed rows of English archers at Agincourt and promoted, via the *Quarterly Gazette of The English Array*, an agrarian ideology that drew greatly on Gardiner's beliefs and the activities of the Springhead Ring: biodynamic farming, rigorous exercise and self-reliance, the communion of body and earth and the primacy of a self-governing agriculture. The Array was also absolute in its belief in the divine authority of the monarchy and of the necessity to reverse the gains in equality made by the suffragettes.

In keeping with its forbear the Array too had a written creed. Its members swore: 'to strive to restore the King to his rightful position as the mirror of his people's virtues, as their protector from private interests, and as their supreme executor of Government. For he alone can guarantee permanence.' They also declared: 'I have faith in the surviving stock of my own people. I have love for them and for the English soil from which they have sprung.'

Rolf Gardiner is said to have provided wholemeal flour for the Array's Dorset division, King Alfred's Muster, from the mill at Springhead. This was not the only quasi-military rustic cadre in Dorset at the time; the aristocratic George Lane-Fox Pitt-Rivers had similarly founded the Wessex Agricultural Defence Association, with further branches in each of the other districts of the Anglo-Saxon kingdom: Hampshire, Somerset and Wiltshire.

Although it numbered a handful of MPs, influential journalists and some genuine 1930s rural yeomen and ploughmen from East Anglia and Dorset, the activities of the Array were short-lived. At the outbreak of war a number of far-right ruralists, including Henry Williamson, Jorian Jenks, George Pitt-Rivers and Anthony Ludovici, were either arrested or interned. Rolf Gardiner served on the Dorset War Agricultural Committee, and concentrated on developing his techniques for forestry; he had volunteered immediately for the Home Guard but, owing to his exceptional interest in Germany, his request to join was declined.

The beliefs these men shared in the preservation of the soil did not diminish during wartime. In 1941 Gardiner, Jenks and Lymington would reconvene with a dozen or other associates as

Kinship in Husbandry. They would be joined in this new society by H. J. Massingham, one of the era's greatest chroniclers of rural life who, unlike several of the Kinship's other members, had remained immune to the distillation of ruralism into fascism.

The Kinship was a more informal association than the quasi-Masonic and secretive Mistery and Array. In essence it was a group of acquaintances with a common belief in self-sufficiency and the need to protect the countryside, and a particular belief in the benefits of organic farming. Through its Establishment connections the group had the ability to influence policy decisions explored in the symposia it held on subjects such as 'The Return to Husbandry' and 'The Natural Order'. At the conclusion of the war, Kinship in Husbandry was disbanded and in 1946 a new society was created from its ashes: the Soil Association, which went on to promote organic farming methods for over seventy years, considerably longer than the esoteric, eco-mystical societies it succeeded.

The two principal founders of the Soil Association were Lady Eve Balfour and Oswald Mosley's former agricultural adviser Jorian Jenks. Balfour had served on War Agricultural Committees and in 1943 published *The Living Soil*, an account of the trials she had carried out for three years comparing organic and artificial fertiliser methods at two adjoining smallholdings in Haughley Green, Suffolk. *The Living Soil* is still considered one of the definitive guides to organic farming and for decades to come the results of her conscientious research would greatly influence the organic movement in Britain, which by the 1950s had finally rid itself of its *völkisch* sympathies. It had taken a woman to separate the blood from the soil.

Many of the decisions the government made at the end of the war – to continue to subsidise agriculture; to increase the country's capacity to feed itself; to promote a nutritious natural diet; to consider the welfare of rural workers and communities and to preserve rural landscapes and heritage by the creation of ten National Parks – would have met with the approval of members of the Kindred of the Kibbo Kift, the Springhead Ring, the English Mistery and the English Array. The fascist element in these societies would doubtless have taken umbrage at state intervention and the government's increasing belief in the benefits of the technological advancements in farming.

Throughout the war and for much of his later life Rolf Gardiner's association with National Socialist Germany during the 1930s over-shadowed his brilliance as an agricultural pioneer. In the surrounding villages of Springhead there was gossip that he had planted a forest in the shape of a swastika to prevent bombs falling on north Dorset. Although such rumours were unfounded he remained tainted by his politics. The estate continued to develop agricultural methods, with-out, as Gardiner pointed out in a letter in 1951 'the lavish facilities, amenities and comforts of a Dartington Hall'. Gardiner had studied forestry at the nearby Dartington after the war and was considered to be an expert in plantation for the rest of his life, until his death in 1971. The Springhead Ring continued in the years that followed the war. Its final News Sheet, which had replaced the *North Sea and Baltic*, was dated Winter Solstice 1962. It was during these last years that Gardiner was reconciled with John Hargrave of the Kibbo Kift, who is said to have stayed at Springhead.

In contrast to many assets, land is exchanged rarely in Britain.

The same fields may be owned for generations and the sense of timelessness this produces can lead to the idea that the land itself is a sacred constant during times of dramatic change. Gardiner, Lymington, Williamson, Jenks and their confederates projected just such a sense of the eternal onto the land. They convinced themselves the directions back to a nobler age, one of peasantry, hierarchy and – for those not landowners themselves – misery, lay in the abandoned fields of Wessex. Instead of finding richness or humus in the soil, these men discovered only aridity.

Rolf Gardiner's love of folk music and dancing was as intense as that of Mary Neal, Cecil Sharp or Ralph Vaughan Williams. Where others find contemplation and a sense of identity in the landscape Vaughan Williams evoked in *The Lark Ascending*, Gardiner saw a resource for authority and the demonstration of strength. The green fields and hills have no say in either interpretation. They remain mute in the presence of anyone who regards their existence as a means to an end, whether for good or evil.

In the late 1950s Ewan MacColl, the author of 'The Manchester Rambler', would introduce many traditional songs into folk music's Second Revival. His politics were decidedly of the left, as were those of many of his contemporaries with whom he trespassed on Kinder Scout. Twenty years before MacColl played 'The Jolly Ploughboy' and other tales of working life for a new generation in folk clubs, these songs had been held in similar admiration by Rolf Gardiner, a man whose beliefs were of an entirely different ideology, but whose love of the tradition was entirely, pathologically, unwavering.

NORTH SEA and BALTIC

WHITSUNTIDE 1933.

Contents.

*Issued for the Wessex Centre Group by Rolf Gardiner
at Springhead, Fontmell Magna, Dorset.*

Cover of *North Sea and Baltic*, Whitsuntide, 1933, written and published by Rolf Gardiner, Springhead, Dorset. The 'Books To Read' section includes *Apocalypse* by D. H. Lawrence and *Statecraft* by William Sanderson, founder of the English Mistery.

ISLE OF ISLAY

How high the gulls fly o'er ISLAY
How sad the farm lad deep in play
Felt like a grain on your sand

How well the sheeps bell music makes
Rovin' the cliff when fancy takes
Felt like a tide left me here

How blest the forest with birds song
How neat the cut peat laid so long
Felt like a seed on your land

© DONOVAN (MUSIC) LTD.

One of twelve inserts housed in a portfolio that accompanied *Phonograph Record/ The Second*, the second half of the original edition of *A Gift From a Flower To A Garden*, 1967. Each insert was individually coloured and featured the lyric to a song and an illustration by Sheena McCall and Mick Taylor.

6 : Pebbles on a Hebridean Shore

A solo instrument played in a high register that evokes a solitary bird in flight and captures a sense of unfettered freedom in a few short trills. The short piece 'Kes Flies Higher', taken from the original soundtrack for the film *Kes*, has an antecedent in the birdsong of *The Lark Ascending*; the flute on which it is played is the archetypal pastoral instrument. In the film about a boy and his kestrel – a bird of prey known to hunt and feed on a fledgling lark – this music accompanies images of the airborne bird as it climbs with regal authority before diving towards the lure held by the film's protagonist Billy Casper.

The contemplative score written by the composer and arranger John Cameron is only an occasional presence in *Kes*. The official soundtrack album, eventually released some thirty years after the film, lasts less than half an hour. The instruments employed, clarinet, penny whistle, flute and harp, create an ethereal atmosphere that is rarely present in the film's narrative, an atmosphere suggestive of a serenity unobtainable to the characters. When it is heard, the score alleviates the earthbound reality of waterlogged football pitches, shifts at the pithead and the austere social conditions in which Billy and his family live, and complements the contrast provided by the film's occasional moments of peace, such as when sunlight falls through the trees in the woodlands close to the film's central location, the pit village of Hoyland, South Yorkshire.

The use of natural lighting and a cast drawn from members of the public who speak in broad Yorkshire dialect are signatures of the English form of *cinéma vérité* developed by the director Ken Loach. They temper the bleakness of the story of a disadvantaged boy who finds solace and temporary redemption in his relationship with a kestrel.

I walked through the landscape of *Kes*, Hoyland and its surrounding countryside, on a day in early winter when the fall in temperature the night before had produced clear skies. My guide was Richard Hines, whose brother Barry wrote *A Kestrel for a Knave*, the book from which the film's screenplay, also by Barry, was adapted. The deep affinity Richard felt with falconry during his childhood was the basis for Billy's relationship with Kes; although Richard was quick to inform me that other than this ardent obsession with birds of prey he and Billy shared little in common.

In the pale sunshine we wandered towards the ruined tower of Tankersley Old Hall from where Billy steals Kes, an incident based on Richard's own experience. 'All the farms here were tenant farms,' he told me, 'and this place, where you see Billy climb the Old Hall, I did that in real life.' Richard explained to me he had crept there, just as Billy does, at the dead of night, his path illuminated by the moon. 'We walked past a building site nearby where they were putting up council homes. This was in 1965. A few years later they used one of them for Billy's house in the film. We borrowed a ladder that we carried through the woods and it was really bright. We placed it against the wall and reached in for the kestrels.'

On his route through the woods, from the village towards the Old Hall Tower, Richard felt as though he was travelling between two moments in time. He was leaving the present, where new houses were being constructed at the edge of a mining village, and returning to the seventeenth century, when the building had belonged to a royalist diplomat.

> We went when the farmer was asleep at about eleven o'clock at night. As I went across the common, my heart was racing, because I knew all the history. Sir Richard Fanshawe had lived there, he was Charles II's right-hand man. I was thinking of hawks from 'The treatise of hawkes and hawking' by Edmund Bert, a book which Fanshawe would have read, including the quote 'There is no way but gentlenesse to redeeme a Hawke'. I was going to take this bird, and I had this vision that he wouldn't drive us off; he'd hold us to find out why we were there and then give us advice on our kestrel. In later years, I realised he would probably have set the dogs on me, because we were trespassing and we hadn't got a licence for a bird so it was illegal as well.

Bert's falconry advice that there was 'no way but gentlenesse' made a vivid impression on Richard at a young age, and much later in life he would use part of the phrase as the title of a memoir. Richard broke off our conversation and stared at the trees. He noted the extent of change in the woodland species, how dense it had become and pointed at the path through which he had quietly crept by the light of the moon a lifetime ago.

In the film Billy makes the same journey Richard had taken but in the daylight of morning. The music that accompanies his stroll is the most wistful on the soundtrack, conveying his moment of solitude with the weightlessness of a daydream. 'Somehow, the countryside and everything around here didn't feel like that to me,' said Richard. 'It didn't feel like flute and woodwind, it was the sound of the birds. There was nowhere in the pit village more than a couple of hundred yards away from the countryside; on summer mornings I could hear a skylark singing and the call of a nightjar at the end of the day.'

One of the many strengths of *Kes* is its depiction of the relationship Billy and his neighbours in the village have with the natural world; the surrounding fields and hills are as familiar to the inhabitants of the coalfield village as they are to those who live in Llareggub. During a school break time he and his classmates suggest going on a nesting expedition, a regular occurrence with which they are all familiar. As Billy's half-brother Jud begins his shift at the mine, the cage lift he enters is emblazoned by sunshine as luminous as the accompanying music. The characters interact with a similar instinct and immediacy to their landscape as that of the inhabitants of Milk Wood. As we strolled around the fields where the powerful scenes of communion between Billy and Kes were filmed, Richard indicated a ridge in the distance that had once been the site of the Hoyland mine.

'Round the pithead, there were fields of gold wheat and crops,' he said. 'There was a bluebell wood a stone's throw away from us at that pit tip; we could see the spoil heap from our window.' And in these few phrases Richard had defined the pastoral character of *Kes*.

'All of us, everybody, we were always in the fields, bird-nesting and exploring. Every time we went out of the house we used to walk through the fields,' he continued. 'But it was about the mine round here as well, and I was upset about the hawks being wiped out. I kept magpies and jackdaws, and in the 1960s they were on the verge of being wiped out by pesticides, almost blasted out of existence by shotguns.'

As we concluded our visit, the passion for falconry was evident in Richard's profile and bearing. The lightly worn learning accumulated over a lifetime made him a powerful presence as a guide and walking companion. His agility and natural kinship with birds had allowed Richard to cross social divides with an ease that the ending of *Kes* suggests is unavailable to Billy Casper. As we sat in the car ready for departure he offered me an explanation for the source of empathy and kindness he exuded.

When I pulled my glove on, I felt as though I was reaching into this animal world. I've never felt such a vivid awareness of living in nature. We've all evolved from the same origins, and we live these fragile, transient lives where chance advances and a wrong decision means the difference between life and death, and as a result of that, I learned that living in nature, we've got to look after each other, we've got to look after the world.

Ken Loach filmed the fields and woods that neighbour Hoyland in a manner that is neither bleak nor bucolic and is familiar to many, as walking through fields near villages or small towns is an everyday experience of the countryside. A sense of the effortless shift in the film's backdrop between the built-up streets of the village and its rural location was one that registered with John Cameron, the composer of *Kes*'s soundtrack.

'I was always struck by the way the industrial side of things was very much part of the landscape,' Cameron told me over the phone. 'You never needed to walk far before you were right in the middle of nowhere, but you never needed to walk far in the other direction before there was a mill, or a mine.' The hardships of the rural mining community are current throughout *Kes*, as is people's capacity to enjoy life. The rural scenery is filmed with a similarly neutral eye. This non-judgemental, semi-documentary style would grow to be a signature of Loach's direction. 'There's no extra emotion in the way Ken shoots *Kes*,' Cameron continued. 'You don't beg the audience to feel, they just do.'

Loach and Cameron had first collaborated on the director's debut feature *Poor Cow*, featuring Carol White and Terence Stamp. That film included three songs by Donovan, for whom Cameron acted as arranger, but for *Kes* it was agreed that the compositions would be entirely instrumental and that the ambience of the film would lead the soundtrack. 'We'd start to talk about thematic ideas. But I was very much sort of given free rein on it,' Cameron said. 'Something I really love about it is the penny whistle at the start. That piece is actually in 3 plus 2 plus 3/8, so it's both very simple and not simple. It's sort of slightly restless. The penny whistle to me was Billy Casper, and the alto flute is the hawk.'

The technology of the time meant that the soundtrack was recorded in a manner that matched the realism that Loach favoured for the filming. The penny whistle that accompanied Billy's wandering and the flute's evocation of Kes in flight were both recorded in real time directly on to the optical mono print of the film, in a single mix. The unavailability of overdubs or editing ensured a feeling of spontaneity in the music and the sense that the musicians, like the cast, were happy to hold their performances in check.

> The way Ken had shot it put its own parameters on it; the nearest we got to emotion is the piece where the young boy walks through the woods very early in the morning. There's a sense of slight, quiet expectation, which is not necessarily there in the rest of it. It was Harold's alto flute, which he'd bought the week before. I asked him if he had an alto and he said, 'No, I'll go and buy one'! – he was always a phenomenal jazz flautist.

Harold McNair was born in Kingston, Jamaica, and attended the Alpha Boys School, an institution for wayward youths that was run by Roman Catholic nuns and specialised in providing musical education. Many of the school's alumni went on to define the sounds which Jamaica would become identified. Rico Rodriguez, Cedric 'Im' Brooks, Leroy Smart, Yellowman and four founding members of The Skatalites all received their education at Alpha Boys, whose staff had a reputation as disciplinarians. In 1960 McNair moved to London, where his reputation as a flautist and saxophonist spread through the clubs of Soho and led to an invitation to join Ronnie Scott's house band, in which he played alongside Stan Tracey. McNair, who was softly spoken but exuded the quiet confidence of a highly respected professional musician, was used to playing in several different contexts throughout the working week: a soundtrack recording, an evening set at Scott's, or as a session musician for pop or folk artists. In photographs he is impeccably dressed in the Italian-tailored suits of the period and projects an enigmatic self-assurance.

> Harold was happy to play jazz, film, funk, blues, I don't
> think I ever heard him not be musical whatever he
> did. He was quite reserved and private, almost a magic
> figure, who kept himself to himself. Once we'd been
> in Stockholm, working with Donovan, and on the last
> date we ended up at an all-night party somewhere and
> didn't manage to get back to the hotel. We all trooped
> in just about in time to get the plane, a real sixties gig.
> And for some reason they upgraded us all to first class,
> where Donovan already was. About half-way through
> the flight, Harold got his alto saxophone out – we were
> the only people in first class – and he just started play-
> ing, and it was like something out of a movie. I'll never

forget it. It was beautiful: quiet, lyrical phrases at thirty thousand feet. He was totally unpredictable.

On the handful of solo albums he made McNair collaborated regularly with Cameron. 'The Hipster', a freewheeling, flute-driven composition that evokes late-night London streets is his most celebrated piece. The buttoned-up energy of the music ensured its popularity among DJs who played for the small but well-informed crowds that danced to jazz in the ensuing decades. Perhaps this was the material – lyrical, modern, slightly restless – on which he wished to concentrate, but shortly before his early death from cancer at the age of thirty-nine, McNair was in demand for the pastoral tones heard on the soundtrack to *Kes*.

Shortly after completing work on the film, McNair and Cameron were recording the album *Barabajagal* with Donovan. The flautist and arranger had first worked together with the singer-songwriter on his 1967 record *Mellow Yellow*, but it is on the acoustic half of the double album *A Gift from a Flower to a Garden*, recorded in the same year, on which McNair's presence is most notable.

A Gift from a Flower to a Garden was released in a box that contained two albums and twelve individual lyric sheets that accompanied songs on the second record. These were printed in separate colours and illustrated in the style of a psychedelic treasury. Liner notes written by Donovan were glued to the box's interior, and the singer began his message to the listener with the declaration 'Oh, what a Dawn Youth is Rising to'. This introduced the theme of the first record, 'music for my age group, an age group which is gently entering marriage'. Its companion piece – 'Phonograph Record / The Second', as it was described in the box

– was dedicated to the 'dawning generation' that Donovan, at the time a father-to-be, suggested would spend the early stage of their life in wonder: 'We shall fill their days with fairies and elves and pussys and paints, with laughter and song and the gentle influence of Mother nature.' On 'Phonograph Record / The Second' along with field recordings of the sea, spring birdsong and occasional percussion, Harold McNair's flute is the principal instrument accompanying Donovan's voice and guitar, as he sings a collection of sparse lullabies with titles such as 'Song of the Naturalist's Wife', 'The Lullaby of Spring' and 'The Magpie'. The lyrics to these songs resonate with the bliss of the first warm breeze of the year. Although its tone is fractionally less ethereal than the one he employed when recording *Kes*, McNair's flute fits perfectly in the space left between Donovan's voice and the guitar. Its presence there gives flight to the daydream quality of many of the lyrics.

The records Donovan Leitch released in the late 1960s are elaborate documents of his generation's newfound commitment to a rustic ideal. They represent a British equivalent to the gilded innocence of California popularised by the singer's contemporaries in America, where his commercial success had made Donovan their equal. Leitch was in the vanguard of the music world's reimagining and revitalisation of rural Britain. In 1969 he acquired three uninhabited isles off the northwest coast of Skye: Isay, Clett and the twenty-five-acre Isle of Mingay, known as 'the Blue Isle' due to its carpet of bluebells in summer when the surrounding seas are populated by dolphins.

On 'Isle of Islay', the song on which Donovan hymns the nearby Islay, the Queen of the Hebrides, the singer is alone, accompanying himself on guitar and making great use of his voice's vibrato. The song is neither happy nor melancholy, but racked with lysergic fragility. Its lyrics suggest that Donovan's time on the Inner Hebrides was spent sitting on its barren beaches embarking on psychedelic journeys, which left him feeling 'like a grain on your sand' and 'like a tide left me here'. In the liner notes Donovan twice implored his listeners to eschew drug use. 'Yes I call upon every youth to stop the use of **all** Drugs and head the Quest to seek the Sun.'

The singer similarly disowned drugs on the *In Concert* album that followed *A Gift from a Flower to a Garden*, but the penetrating sense of the infinite experienced while on LSD, which allows the user to condense the size of the universe into a single pebble, washes through many of these songs.

In addition to the three dreamlike Hebrides isles Donovan owned a cluster of dilapidated stone buildings near the town of Stein on Skye itself. They included a schoolhouse on which basic work had begun to convert the property into a recording studio; a group of trailers and caravans were assembled around the buildings and formed the basis of the commune Donovan hoped to establish on the island.

This was the destination of Donovan's friend Vashti Bunyan when she left London by horse and cart for a new life away from the Soho recording studios that constituted the working environment of session musicians and arrangers such as Harold McNair and John Cameron. Over the decades the two-year journey she made has grown in myth, as captivating as it is now almost inconceivable, and provided the inspiration for her debut album *Just Another Diamond Day*, a record initially heard by very few until it was rediscovered, like the music of *Kes*, at the turn of this century.

The supporting cast of musicians on *Just a Diamond Day* were drawn from the Witchseason production and management company run by the record producer Joe Boyd and included members of Fairport Convention and The Incredible String Band. Both groups had latterly relocated to secluded areas of rural Britain, Fairport Convention to Hampshire and The Incredible String Band to Pembrokeshire, Wales.

A photograph used on several versions of the 1968 Incredible String Band album *The Hangman's Beautiful Daughter* features a raggle-taggle group of adults and children, who share a taste in clothes of natural fibres, bright colours, tunics and felt hats, and a dog, assembled around the bare branches of a winter tree. The picture is suggestive of a family portrait, although in this instance it is not clear how the family might be related. Their outfits, together with the healthy glow they exude, suggest the vigorous hand-to-mouth outdoor life of a commune. The romantic tale of Vashti Bunyan's pilgrimage to Skye and the feral grace of The Incredible String Band, their entourage and children, gazing from the sleeve of *The Hangman's Beautiful Daughter* are among the most vivid examples of 'getting it together in the country': a phrase increasingly heard in the recording studios of late sixties London, the period when pop stars of the stature of Donovan owned Hebridean sanctuaries and his friend John Lennon purchased Dorinish, an uninhabited island off the west coast of Ireland. In 1966 Paul McCartney, so often one step ahead of his contemporaries in the mid-sixties, had bought High Park Farm, a dilapidated farmhouse and its accompanying two hundred acres of land overlooking Machrihanish Bay on the west coast of Kintyre in Scotland. The acquisition of rural boltholes was not limited to household names. John Cameron found himself 'a little thatched cottage outside Harpenden'; such purchases were, he told me, with great amiability, 'the thing'.

On the records on which he played for Donovan and on the soundtrack to *Kes* McNair's flute was used to evoke an airy pastoralism. There are few shared experiences of the countryside in the film or *A Gift from a Flower to a Garden*?

The psychological landscape of *Kes* is often arduous, even as the physical landscape is occasionally beautiful. The songs that Skye and its neighbouring islands inspired Donovan to write are homages to the carefree, seashore life of children's stories, one replicated by him and his contemporaries. A pastoral idyll is a familiar setting in children's literature: the riverbank of *The Wind in the Willows*, the '100 Aker Wood' of *The House at Pooh Corner* and *The Secret Garden*. For Donovan and those musicians who had experimented with LSD, the rabbit hole of *Alice's Adventures in Wonderland* proved an especially significant location, as its transformative powers represented a perfect point of departure to a psychedelic other place. *A Gift from A Flower to a Garden* contains an adaptation of the Shakespeare poem 'Under the Greenwood Tree', to which Donovan added the refrain 'Will you, won't you . . . join the dance?' a quotation of the chorus of 'The Lobster Quadrille', from the book's tenth chapter. The trip back through one's early years, which the drug often precipitates, ensured that LSD users would refamiliarise themselves with these charmed landscapes.

The Wind in the Willows is an overt presence on one of the first

British psychedelic albums. Pink Floyd founder member Syd Barrett chose the title of the seventh chapter of the book, 'The Piper at the Gates of Dawn', as the name for the group's debut album, released in the same year as Donovan's *A Gift from a Flower to a Garden*.

The imagery of Edwardian children's stories is rendered as hallucination in several of the album's songs. On 'Flaming' Barrett describes himself 'watching buttercups come to light / sleeping on a dandelion'. He has shrunk to the size of Alice in the *Adventures in Wonderland* and is experiencing the Garden of Live Flowers of *Through the Looking Glass*. The conflation in Barrett's memories of the two books on which he drew to describe a psychedelic now, is a perfect illustration of LSD's state of benign bewilderment.

A scarecrow who 'stood in a field where barley grows' is the titular character of a later song. Barrett uses the language of nursery rhyme to describe 'The black and green scarecrow as everyone knows / Stood with a bird on his hat and straw everywhere / He didn't care.' This is a heedlessness with which Barrett, whose relationship with acid proved perilous, was familiar. During the final chorus the band change gear, and the simple melodic lines they have been playing grow more expansive, evoking an open sky above the head of the scarecrow and the rural kaleidoscope landscape he occupies.

The canon of psychedelic and psychedelic-inflected folk music of the era suggests Ratty, Mole, Christopher Robin, the Cheshire Cat et al were often encountered by the user as a friendly chaperone on their lysergic journey through the past and inspired them to record these meetings in song; the records on which these characters from childhood feature also view the countryside through a similar lens. The

Beatles' 'White Album' is partly considered an attempt to achieve clarity after the long period of LSD experimentation that culminated in 'I Am the Walrus', a song inspired by a character in Lewis Carroll's *Through the Looking Glass*. Two of the more introspective songs on the 'White Album', whose working title was 'A Doll's House', are largely acoustic. 'Julia' by John Lennon is a song that laments the childhood he never experienced with his late mother or her 'sea shell eyes'. The subject of 'Mother Nature's Son', principally written by Paul McCartney, is a 'Poor young country boy … swaying daisies … sing(ing) … a lazy song beneath the sun.' As well as sparse instrumentation both songs share an understanding that childhood and the countryside are largely uncorrupted places, where life is simpler and lived to older rhythms.

It was out of a similar desire for a return to innocence and the past, even the fictional past of bedtime stories, that many people moved to the countryside at the end of the 1960s to 'get it together' away from modernity, towards an ideal that was rarely attainable.

The phrase 'getting it together in the country' is most often attributed to a press release issued by Island Records in 1967 to announce *Mr. Fantasy*, the debut album by Traffic. The record had been written and rehearsed in a secluded former gatekeeper's cottage near the hamlet of Aston Tirrold in Berkshire, where the band had relocated from London at the suggestion of Steve Winwood, the vocalist and multi-instrumentalist in a group predicated on the idea of a band as a democracy; the interior and exterior of the cottage feature heavily in the elaborate artwork included in the album's gatefold sleeve. The band's rural isolation was much discussed in reviews and by their peers as the source of their debut's free-flowing music: the sound of psychedelic pop gone to seed.

In the late sixties Berkshire was evidently sufficient distance from London to achieve a change of pace and separation, and several of their contemporaries followed their lead. It was perhaps inevitable that folk-rock groups such as Fairport Convention and The Incredible String Band would retreat to the rural source of many of the songs in their repertoire. More surprising was that musically divergent contemporaries such as the Small Faces shared in the impetus and followed Traffic to the Home Counties for seclusion and recuperation. Three of the band, Steve Marriott, Ian McLagan and Ronnie Lane, rented Monk's Corner, a large cottage near the riverbank at Marlow in Buckinghamshire, the location of Kenneth Grahame's childhood summers, the source of the memories on which he drew to create the sleepy habitat of *The Wind in the Willows*. Monk's Corner had once belonged to Jerome K. Jerome, who had written *Three Men in a Boat* at a desk in a room now occupied by the band's equipment.

The relaxed atmosphere the Small Faces sought was enacted on stoned boating trips and can be heard in one of the first songs they wrote at Marlow, 'The Universal'. Birdsong and the barking of a dog are clearly audible on the recording, which is as loose and ramshackle as the song itself; its antecedents lie more in knockabout music hall and bluesy chord progressions than in the dropped D harmonics of folk tunings customarily associated with pastoral songs.

This joyous, informal approach to songwriting is one 'The Universal' shares with much of *Ram*, the record Linda and Paul McCartney began recording in 1970, inspired by time spent on their farm in Machrihanish Bay. In a promotional film made to accompany the song 'Heart of the Country' the McCartneys and their infant children have the authentic air of post-psychedelic crofters. Paul and Linda wear thick Shetland jumpers and ride horses through wildflower pasture, or drift barefoot along a deserted shore. A fully bearded McCartney is also seen gamely attempting to corral a flock of sheep; he would reprise the role of shepherd on the album's cover, while the dereliction of the farm's outbuildings suggests they had yet to consider any renovations. This homespun mood is present throughout the record, in the freshness and earthiness of the performances and in the carefree nature of McCartney's songwriting; the sound of people who have been reinvigorated by the sea air rather than seduced by the sea's mythology.

The retreat by musicians to the living, natural world at the end of the decade was an international phenomenon led by the pop aristocracy. Visitors to Traffic's Berkshire retreat included Bob Dylan, who had, along with his manager Albert Grossman, relocated to the dappled town of Woodstock in New York State. Grossman invested heavily in the surrounding area's real estate and established another of his charges, The Band, in a rented house in nearby West Saugerties which they christened Big Pink. Woodstock had much to recommend it to musicians whose resolve had withered and who sought inspiration and rehabilitation in a restorative environment. The town was enclosed in a verdant landscape and the deep winters brought snow and a sense of isolation. Its proximity to New York, barely a two-hour drive away, also meant that business could be attended to – an idea that was impractical and soon forgotten by those spending any time on the Isles of Islay, Clett and Mingay. For Donovan, Vashti Bunyan and their friends the immersion in the landscape was all engrossing, a psychological as well as physical retreat into nature.

Drawing of life at The Broom by Sally Seymour, from the first edition
of *The Fat of The Land*, 1961.

7 : The Julian Calendar

'Iechyd da i chi foneddigion, dewch i weld os yw'r
gwin yn dda.
Dewch i weld, O, la, la, dewch i weld, O, la, la,
Dewch i weld os yw'r gwin yn dda,
Peidiwch dweud with y diaconiaid rhag i ni gael ein
torri mâs
Dewch i weld, O, la, la, dewch i weld, O, la, la,
Dewch i weld os yw'r gwin yn dda'

Traditional West Walian folk song

In 1969, the year in which *Kes* was released, the rural population of
the United Kingdom increased for the first time that century. Many
of those who participated in this migration to remote parts of the
country were inspired by the photographs on records such as *The
Hangman's Beautiful Daughter*. It was a journey made by the generation who shared with Vashti Bunyan the urge to leave urban Britain
behind, for the promise of a new life in the hills.

This desire to go back to the land had been formalised by the
author and broadcaster John Seymour, whose work and character
cast a long shadow across the 1960s and 1970s. It was during these
decades when living simply in harmony with nature developed
from a marginal, radical set of concerns that rejected the increased

mechanisation and technological change in society, to its position in national light entertainment as the subject of the sitcom *The Good Life*.

1969 was also the year in which Seymour produced a short, twenty-minute black and white film for BBC Wales. Its title *I, a Stranger – John Seymour Among His Neighbours* would be adapted by Seymour a decade later for *I'm a Stranger Here Myself: The Story of a Welsh Farm*, one of the author's many books on the subject of self-sufficiency and the utopian association of soil and manual labour which Seymour popularised, even mythologised, throughout his long, eventful life.

As he addresses the camera in *I, a Stranger*, Seymour's charisma and force of personality are obvious. The film opens with him playing the accordion, sitting at the fireside as he and his companions ring in the New Year with songs sung in *Cymraeg*, the language of Wales spoken in the 1960s throughout the Preseli Hills in Pembrokeshire where the film is set. In the only moment where his arresting on-screen presence deserts him, Seymour explains with a slightly mannered casualness that the date is 12 January, where in this mysterious, timeless place, life is lived by the Julian rather than Gregorian calendar. In the north of Pembrokeshire the New Year falls a fortnight later than is customary.

A few minutes later Willy Jenkins, a neighbour of Seymour's 'who lives all alone', is seen sitting on a milking school, working the udders of a cow as he unselfconsciously describes some of the supernatural phenomena he regularly encounters nearby:

'There are many queer things happening on that road over there.

I could see a light in the distance about a yard from the road. The light passed me quite quiet, and three of four days later there was a funeral.'

'And what do you call that?' asks Seymour.

'Well, it's a spiritual thing, and it does happen now, but there is so much speed about today no one notices it. It's the spirit of the person being buried. *Canwyll corff* they used to call it in the old days. But it's a spiritual thing.'

'What's that in English?'

'Well, the light of the dead person, about two or three o'clock in the morning is the usual time; if it's a young person going to be buried it's earlier, but the later the thing is seen at night, the older the person is.' A literal translation of the phrase *canwyll corff* is 'body candle'.

In another scene a fellow farmer, George Hughes, described by Seymour as 'seventy-one but can race me up the mountain and is the most contented man I have ever met', explains why he has rarely left the hillside: 'I'm not rich but I have never been in need of money all my life, never needed a bun, I want to spend the last of my days in the same old fireplace as where I was born. If something might happen to me and they take me to hospital they will have to carry me back here across these fields.'

Although it is often a harsh subsistence, if enlivened by mysterious phenomena of the type witnessed by Willy Jenkins, Seymour clearly considers his situation to be one of rural bliss. His days are spent scrimping the natural resources of the Preseli Hills, where the farming community ride horseback, share their time, equipment, folklore and homemade beer in a manner that appears ageless and determinedly at ease with itself. Standing outside Fachongle Isaf, his smallholding, wearing a bobble hat and dressed in well-made clothes that have begun to show their age, Seymour makes a convincing case to the camera for this charmed life on the far west coast of Wales.

In the next scene his neighbours are shown at worship in their local chapel in the nearby town of Trefdraeth. The congregation incants passages from the bible written in *Cymraeg*. This is done in a collective, singsong voice, without musical accompaniment, that suits the austere interior of the chapel and the sonorous, guttural character of the language. Their chanting fades and is mixed with the more familiar sound of children singing in school. Seymour's narration indicates one of the pupils in the scene is his daughter Anne; her presence there, singing a traditional Welsh song with her classmates, is further evidence of how embedded and accepted the Seymour family have become in the valley, since moving there four years earlier in 1964.

From that year when he made his base in West Wales, Seymour would dedicate his life to environmental causes that were then of little public interest beyond the Council for the Preservation of (later the Campaign to Protect) Rural England.

This is a part of Wales with which I am very familiar. The first summer I spent here was as a child during the heat wave of 1976, when my parents began restoring a small cottage nearby they had acquired for a meagre sum as my mother had conducted the negotiations in *Cymraeg*, her first language. This had ensured a favourable price and the assurance that we were not perceived as incomers in the usual sense. I became familiar with the neolithic and megalithic sites that abound in north Pembrokeshire, the dolmen at Pentre Ifan and how any mention of it was usually qualified with the fact that the blue-stones for Stonehenge, which Pentre Ifan predates, had miraculously been transported from these hills.

The summit of the Preseli Hills which looms over Pentre Ifan and the Seymours' former smallholding is Carningli, the angel's rock, a name that perfectly evokes its gentle features and the calm, almost celestial atmosphere of these hills which gaze out over the coastline towards the Irish Sea.

As a child I was unaware of the free festivals that were taking place less than a few miles away from Pentre Ifan that dense, sticky summer. Other than the two hippies who had been paid cash by my parents to rewire the cottage, there was also little visible evidence of the gradual colonisation of the area by a new generation of incomers. These were young people often interested in building new forms of communities, many of whom had previously visited or arrived at the Seymours' door asking for advice, or a blessing of approval from John, whom many considered to be some form of guru, living off the land at the foot of Carningli, occupying himself in the beguiling, ancient atmosphere of the area carried on its breeze.

'John was born into a wealthy, almost aristocratic environment in Frinton-on-Sea but he just went out every day and worked with the fishermen in the village,' his daughter Anne told me on the day I made my own pilgrimage to the Preselis. 'He absolutely loved it and felt he had discovered a more honest society than the one that he lived in.'

This rejection of the conventions of his upbringing inspired Seymour to lead a peripatetic life, and at the age of twenty he duly left England for Africa to undertake a series of menial jobs either on the land, as an agricultural labourer, or at sea on boats as a fisherman or skipper. At the outbreak of war in 1939 Seymour was living in Kenya, where he enlisted with the King's African Rifles.

'My father came back after fighting in Burma,' Anne continued. 'He'd been away for twelve years, living in Africa mainly, but India as well. He'd seen primitive societies, he had loved living with the Kalahari Bushmen. When he came back here and saw that there were people who would like to have land but couldn't have it, he just thought that was so wrong. And also, he just hated this headlong rush to an industrialised society and industrialised farming in particular. He came back and thought, "What the hell is going on?" There was obviously a surplus of nitrates left over from the war, and away they went spraying it over everything.'

The government's desire to industrialise agriculture had led to highly visible changes in the landscape, including the large-scale removal of hedges and the conversion of chalk grassland, heathland and meadows to the wide, easily managed fields necessary for arable production. A substantial amount of moorland had similarly been lost to the continuing policy of forestation and the creation of monotonous rectangles of dark spruce conifers over the country's hillsides.

The findings of the first *Atlas of the British Flora* produced in 1962 were a dramatic illustration of the effect the post-war rationalisation of farming had had on the environment. It recorded a significant loss of biodiversity, including the extinction of numerous localised plant and flower varieties, and revealed that a dramatic overall decline in the number of species had coincided with the construction of Britain's first motorways. Seymour was among the first people in Britain to sense this change in the natural world was underway. 'My father worked for the War Ag in Suffolk,' said Anne. 'He was so horrified with the way farming was turning out that he just wanted to escape, and that's really what he did.' Many of the changes in agriculture had been facilitated by Seymour's employers at the Ministry of Agriculture through their grant aid programmes to farmers as part of the government's drive towards efficiency, yet no formal consideration or assessment had been included for the environmental impact of their schemes, which promoted the use of nitrates and other fertilisers.

The 'escape' of which Anne spoke was recorded in *The Fat of the Land*, Seymour's pithy and at times visceral account of his family's experience as smallholders living frugally, from the spoils of four or five acres included in their lease of The Broom, a pair of derelict Suffolk cottages they renovated and revitalised on their own terms. The property became a homestead, where Seymour's wife Sally had a studio for her work as a ceramicist and artist and where their three daughters experienced an animated outdoor childhood in rural isolation. *The Fat of the Land* often reads as an exercise in determination and bloody-mindedness. 'If the rest of the world blew itself up tomorrow,' the book's second paragraph begins, 'we could go on living quite happily here and hardly notice the difference.'

The trenchant quality of Seymour's writing acts as a balance to the romantic aura that takes hold as the family rehabilitate the smallholding and become adept at living by their wits. Seymour implies their successes are a matter of trial and error and above all, common sense. He also emphasises that this experiment in the peasant economy is subsidised by regular stipends from publishers for his freelance work and from Sally's pottery. This fact is easy to forget and was doubtless easily forgotten by many reading such an arresting account of healthy labour, survival and communion in the Suffolk countryside. Despite his intention to be realistic, if not blunt, about their life at The Broom, Seymour undoubtedly accentuated its high points. A reader might also be seduced by the illustrations by Sally that are included in every chapter. They suggest an idyllic existence: wicker baskets full of produce sitting on kitchen flagstones; gumboots leaning against a wall under barrels of homemade beer; geese grazing under fruit trees; pumpkins curing in the vegetable garden; more produce and preserving jars side by side atop a sturdy kitchen table; children and animals, reeds and flowers, all rendered in elegant, simple lines that complete the image of harmony.

Seymour is also swift to dispel any notion that their undertaking is particularly ideological. 'Thoreau lived at Walden,' he writes, 'with very little apparatus indeed, and grew all his own food. He gives a very complete list of his belongings, and a complete balance sheet of his financial transactions. But he only lived there for two years. And he had no family. He was prepared to live almost exclusively on beans.'

The Fat of the Land was published in 1961 (the Seymours had moved to The Broom in the mid-1950s), but it would be another decade before the way of life Seymour evoked became formally categorised as self-sufficiency. A decade during which copies of *The Fat of the Land* were widely shared and its contents proved seductive for many of its readers.

Seymour would subsequently embrace the term self-sufficiency in his books and television and radio programmes and profit greatly from its usage, but the richness in his description of the family's life in *The Fat of the Land* is deceptive. 'He was never advocating "do everything in this book yourself". It was self-reliance as opposed to self-sufficiency and that would have been a much better term,' Anne told me. 'It was a philosophy of independence: you can change your life if you want to, even if you change it in a tiny way. Even if you live in a city, you can put vegetables in your back garden.'

Three years after the publication of *The Fat of the Land* the Seymours made their home at Fachongle Isaf, where the skills that Seymour suggested were necessary to adapt in a new community were brought to bear. Upon their arrival on the west coast the family found a marked contrast with Suffolk.

'I came to this place from East Anglia, a country where farms are huge, productive and farmers are very rich,' Seymour states during his narration of *I, a Stranger*. 'There everybody minded his own business, nobody seemed to know or care whether his neighbour sank or swam; it's very different here.' Seymour was able to use his affability, empathy and considerable knowledge and openness to farming methods to ensure the family was accepted.

'When we first moved here, we were one of a very few English families and the Welsh people were so welcoming,' Anne said. 'We were part of the community instantly but they saw us as total eccentrics, but this was our whole life here: social life, farming life, work life, everything centred around this little valley for us. We hardly had to go anywhere or did go anywhere, except my father, who had to go away to write and make programmes.'

The Preselis held a further appeal of which Seymour may have originally been unaware. The land is of only reasonable quality and its topography ensured scratchy hill farming was the only viable form of agriculture. Although significant areas of Britain were witnessing the spread of motorways across rural areas, the transport and infrastructure in and around West Wales remained basic. The 'soil mining' of East Anglia with its use of pesticides and fertiliser that Seymour so detested was untenable in the foothills of Carningli. Seymour had made their home among a community that farmed in the prelapsarian manner that matched his beliefs.

The sense of inaccessibility and distance from what Seymour and his neighbours regarded as the outside world was acute. Seymour was naturally attuned to the unceasing rhythms of hill farming, and if its returns were sparse, they suited his conception of what the landscape was for and how best it should be maintained: a hedge should be cut and laid by hand using a billhook; ploughing could be efficiently carried out by horse, and the horses could be left to graze by themselves on the hillside when not in use; hops for beer should be allowed to grow along the sides of a sheltered outbuilding and harvested communally and drunk in the same manner. Seymour had found one of the few remaining parts of the deep countryside in Britain, where the second agricultural revolution of the post-war area had been forestalled. The Preseli Hills had yet to be included in the new era of industrialised farming, and their topography and character would continue to resist definition from outside agencies.

The strength of the community bound together in penury on the mountainside of Carningli, the rock of the angel, compensated for the poor nutrition of the soil. 'This area, post-war, was so poverty-stricken. It was really hard to scratch a living, farming at its barest,' Anne said. 'Everything was shared. There was one baler in the valley, there was one bit of machinery somewhere, somebody would have the yeast for the beer.'

At the end of the 1960s Britain had yet to join the Common Market and the meagre subsidies for which hill farmers qualified were administered as a form of social security. In more successful, arable areas the 'technological' farming Seymour had known in East Anglia was thriving under the new methods utilised. Through the widespread removal of hedgerows and trees (occasionally by the use of dynamite) the landscape was adapted to the industry's needs. The result was an English equivalent to American prairies and the new, incongruous sight of infinite acres of wheat extending to the horizon, before their stubble was burned, to add to the soil's nutrients, once the harvest was complete. The intensification in agriculture was similarly evident in the straight lines and sharp boundaries in lowland crops and a further increase in the blanket squares and rectangles of forest plantations on hillsides.

Concern about the consequences of these developing monocultures led to a burgeoning ecological movement. A new organisation, Friends of the Earth, was founded in 1971. It proved finely attuned to the new social energies of the era and adept at developing sophisticated media campaigns to raise environmental awareness. One of its first published reports estimated that if farming continued with such intensity, within a generation 'a quarter of our hedgerows, twenty-four million hedgerow trees, thousands of acres of down and heathland, a third of our woods and hundreds upon hundreds of ponds, streams, marshes and flower rich meadows will have disappeared, systematically eliminated by farmers profiting from a complex web of economic and technological change'. The report went on to note the deleterious effect the widespread use of fertiliser and stubble burning was having on the country's bird and wildlife population.

A decade earlier the American author Rachel Carson had researched and written the book that achieved the greatest impact on public thinking about the devastation occurring in the natural world, including the formation of bodies such as Friends of the Earth. *Silent Spring* was published in 1962, serialised in the *New Yorker* magazine, and its revelations about the consequences of modern agricultural use on the environment were stark. Carson's conclusions were immediately debated, then refuted, by the chemical industry and their lobbyists, before being eventually accepted and acted upon by government.

Her investigation and analysis queried the acceptance that scientific progress was inherently beneficial to society. This was a radical departure from received opinion, at a time when the nuclear age families of the United States placed great faith in large corporations and the avuncular image and sense of reliability they projected to the public in advertising campaigns. Carson's scrupulous research into the extent to which the wildlife population was being annihilated by the manifold use of chemicals, DDT in particular, established this new threat in the mind of a generation. In *Silent Spring* Carson introduced environmentalism to, if not mainstream America, then to a readership that would be spurred into action by her research.

The large bio-technological fertiliser companies immediately rejected Carson's findings and organised publicity stunts to discredit her. Monsanto printed five thousand copies of *The Desolate Year*, a leaflet that parodied *Silent Spring* and dismissed its message as a liberal conspiracy. Other manufacturers of DDT were quick to indicate that Paul Hermann Müller, the scientist who first synthesised the chemical as an insecticide, had been awarded the Nobel Prize and issued warnings of a 'return to the Dark Ages' of disease and pestilence.

A former US Secretary of Agriculture wrote of his concerns that Carson was unmarried and 'probably a communist'. The attacks on Carson, a well respected and bestselling author prior to *Silent Spring*, concentrated on her gender and the assumption that as a woman she was prone to 'hysteria'. However, her experience and discipline as a researcher ensured that the arguments she presented could not be countered merely by smears and insinuation. The evidence in *Silent Spring* was supported by many of Carson's peers working in biotech and its related fields and eventually prompted the White House to order a review into the usage of DDT. Carson, who was suffering at the time from cancer, testified before Congress herself.

Though in great pain and losing her hair, she kept her illness from the watching world. On the strength of Carson's evidence an Environmental Protection Agency was established which in 1972, a decade after the publication of *Silent Spring*, issued an aggregate ban on the use of DDT.

The author Margaret Atwood, who regularly cites *Silent Spring* as an influence, once wrote that Carson 'knew how to explain science to ordinary readers in a way that they could understand; she knew that if you don't love a thing you won't save it'. One of the principal arguments of *Silent Spring* was that DDT was indiscriminate, that it not only eradicated one species of pest, it simultaneously eradicated many others with which it came into contact. Carson was able to illustrate how terrible the effects of such an unforgiving approach were to the biosphere and how a likely consequence would be the destruction of the natural world if its usage continued. In combining vigorous accumulation of evidence, personal testimonials and an overriding argument for greater understanding of a developing crisis, Carson wrote about the environment with a voice that had not previously been heard. The counter argument against such a voice seeks to discredit whoever is speaking. It consists of little more than insinuation and denial and continues in our lifetime, particularly if the voice belongs to a woman.

Silent Spring would eventually sell over two million copies, was widely translated and gave international recognition to concerns that had been fermenting amongst Seymour and his associates in Britain, who had previously regarded their opinions to be of only minority interest, but now realised environmentalism was developing into a participatory cause.

During 1970, the song 'Big Yellow Taxi' by Joni Mitchell was being heard daily by millions of Americans on FM Radio. The inclusion of the lyric 'Tell the Farmer to put away the DDT now' was due to Carson's popularisation of the awareness of the chemical's malignant presence in our ecosystem. For all the failures of the utopian dreams of the 1960s it is easy to forget that environmentalism counts as a success of the era's idealism. It would be the generation inspired by Seymour and his friends who had settled in Pembrokeshire that further established ecological concerns in the public mind, to the point where national and local government accepted the need for action. Although dismissed as hopeless idealists or hippie dreamers, their cause was successful; Carson, who campaigned, almost single-handedly against the destruction of the natural world died in 1964.

Original silk screen poster for the Meigan Fayre, 1974, by Bill Hamblett. The image is based on an ink drawing by David Collier, which was inspired by the floor labyrinth at Chartres Cathedral.

8 : The Fourth World

The war in Vietnam, the Unilateral Declaration of Independence in Rhodesia and the activities of a Peace Action Centre at Frodsham in Cheshire were all interests close to the heart of the editor of *Resurgence* magazine, the iconoclastic clergyman John Papworth, a veteran peace campaigner who had been imprisoned with Bertrand Russell for protesting against nuclear arms. First published in 1966, *Resurgence* commissioned contributions from many of the era's notable thinkers, such as R. D. Laing, and representatives of an older generation, such as E. P. Thompson and Herbert Read, who wrote on 'The Limits of Permissiveness'. Within a few years *Resurgence* and some of its contributors had followed John Seymour to Pembrokeshire, where the author of *The Fat of the Land* was joined by several of his contemporaries. They sensed a transformation in the area. In their minds West Wales was now blossoming into a centre of an ecological consciousness with several interrelated disciplines.

'Once we'd moved here an ecological movement started happening. My father was one,' Anne Seymour told me. 'There was Satish Kumar and Schumacher, Leopold Kohr, all these people were involved in *Resurgence* at the beginning.'

In the late sixties the philosopher Leopold Kohr taught at the University of Wales in Aberystwyth, and one of Kohr's former pupils at a previous institution, E. F. Schumacher, was a regular contributor to *Resurgence*. In 1973 Schumacher would publish the landmark text on countercultural economics *Small Is Beautiful*, a phrase he attributed to Kohr and one regularly introduced to explain the evolving idea of sustainability. The timing of Schumacher's book was propitious: within a year Britain was undergoing a series of crises including the Three Day Week and the OPEC oil dispute, while inflation was running at 16 per cent. The subtitle of *Small Is Beautiful* was *A Study of Economics As Though Humans Mattered*. Schumacher's arguments for an end to corporate 'gigantism' were being played out in daily life. His theory that business had dehumanising effects was also evident in the sense of societal breakdown in the country. The intensity of the IRA mainland bombing campaign increased in 1974, a year in which Britain held two elections, emigration from the country was at a record high and the stock market lost over two hundred points. The latter collapse in financing was indicative of one of *Small Is Beautiful*'s key tenets, that growth for growth's sake was unsustainable.

In the same year, the editorship of *Resurgence* was passed to Satish Kumar, a pacifist, activist and former Jain monk who was a neighbour of the Seymours. Kumar, who would go on to edit *Resurgence* for the next forty years, made his home in the Preselis at Pentre Ifan Farm, which overlooked the megalithic site and doubtless inspired the synthesis of New Age mysticism, environmentalism and small-scale localised economics that its adherents gathered in the hills now practised. This philosophy was made overt in *Resurgence,* which by the early 1970s was subtitled 'Journal of the Fourth World'. Its stated editorial policy was to publish 'articles on alternative life styles, human technology, eco-logical-organic living and small, simple decentralised power struc-tures'. *Resurgence* was a rather meek analogue to the stylishly pro-duced *Whole Earth Catalog,* the periodical published and edited by Stewart Brand, one of Ken Kesey's original Merry Pranksters and an associate of Buckminster Fuller. In contrast to *Resurgence,* the *Catalog* was large format, nearer A3 than A4 in size, and by its final edition, published in 1971, ran to almost 450 pages. Its cover featured a picture of the earth in shadow taken, according to notes on the front inside page, from space:

> Taken November 9, 1967, from NASA's Apollo 4 at
> a distance of 9850 nautical miles. This is probably the
> first American photograph of the 'whole Earth'. You're
> looking west over the Atlantic Ocean, with the Antarctic
> Continent just visible at the bottom of the crescent. The
> picture was released in 1967 but no one seemed to care
> about noticing it or publishing it. I think it was the
> shadow, which frightened people. There are no shadows
> on our maps.

In the pages of the *Whole Earth Catalog* it is easy to detect the energies that would coalesce into the self-improvement tropes of the New Age, whose concentration was directed toward the individual not the communal, but the energy contained in the *Catalog*'s pages is one of collective endeavour. The *Catalog* lasted for the five years when people attempting to build their new utopia continuously occupied the country's wilderness and turned to Stewart Brand's publication for guidance and inspiration and placed their faith in his strange handbook that described itself, in suitably millenarian terms, as 'an evaluation and access device'.

For a new set of incomers the deprivation and depopulation of the more inaccessible parts of rural Britain proved seductive. Many of them had read Seymour's books and come of age during the 1960s. Now they brought their experience of the emerging counterculture with them. Despite the poverty of the area appearing attractive to these romantic settlers, for local families the enduring hardships of subsistence farming were proving increasingly intolerable. Large parts of remote countryside were experiencing the transformative home comforts of central heating and indoor lavatories, and such comparative luxuries held an understandable appeal for many of the Preselis' inhabitants, even if such amenities were ones the newly arrived young people were happy to leave behind as they began their new lives in the comparative wilderness of West Wales. This was a generation for whom, as The Incredible String Band, now settled nearby, were discovering, the Preselis not only offered the possibility of self-sufficiency but the opportunity for ritual activity. The surrounding hillsides were rich with psilocybin and fly agaric mushrooms, oak trees whose trunks were carved with spells and ancient stone monuments. For those seeking a complete retreat from modernity in exchange for a more pagan existence of rites and magic, West Wales represented a psychic playground.

The Preseli natives met this influx of visitors and settlers with a mixed response. Although the Seymours had seemed arcane, not to say eccentric, in their desire to live the penurious life of an upland farmer, Seymour's social skills in particular had ensured their position within the community; a community that valued its language, in which it conversed at all times, and despite its hardships wished to maintain the way of life it represented.

'In the seventies, the land was really cheap and there were houses everywhere ready to collapse, and there was a huge influx of young, golden-haired hippies, and then the trouble started,' Anne said, 'because I think people around here just – there was too much of a gulf, you know, whereas my father was trying to understand the old ways and to go back, the local people were actually trying to get away from it, and they were just, "We don't want to live like this any more, we want to modernise." And I think once more people began moving in there was separation.'

Although idealistic, many of those making their home in the hills of West Wales lacked Seymour's work ethic, which, accompanied by an Epicurean enjoyment of fine wines, homemade beer and good food, placed conviviality and neighbourliness at the heart of his activities. The Dionysian tastes and nocturnal habits of the newly arrived hippies were at odds with the reserved stoicism of the local population.

Until the United Kingdom joined the Common Market in 1973, and the Common Agricultural Policy four years later, land values suffered from fluctuation and were sensitive to outside forces such as the oil crisis. The further away from urban areas land was located, the less it was worth. It was not uncommon in remoter parts of the country such as West Wales for dwellings to be thrown in for free in the sale of any acreage that they stood upon. For those seeking to flee the modern world the dilapidated farmsteads of Pembrokeshire represented a rare opportunity of free housing. Along with a return to nature in the hidden British countryside, the hills offered the advantage of buildings ripe for appropriation by communities ready to expend their energies on new experimental methods of living.

'There were lots of small communities. Somebody would rent a farmhouse, and then somebody would go and do up an outbuilding, and then two or three families would get together and not necessarily do much on the land, but aim to,' Anne continued. 'But then a lot of them went again, because it was harsh – if you didn't get up in the morning and work bloody hard and go to bed tired, you weren't going to make it.'

John Seymour's commitment to the antiquated methods of farming allowed little for the rejection of work symbolised by dropping out. The more solipsistic politics of the self, as they had come to be defined by the late 1960s, left Seymour bemused at best.

'Somebody tried to grow some marijuana in the woods there, and John came across them and he came back and he said, "They're never going to grow there, it's far too shady! Use some common sense!"'

Seymour, who continued to inspire his guests, would show visitors around the farm and indicate what plans he had for developing certain fields into thriving single variety plantations, but as one former visitor once told me, using a turn of phrase redolent of the era, 'It was a case of "You only see it because you believe it" – people would be walked around these muddy fields thinking it was Narnia.'

This new generation of incomers brought a particular form of hedonism to accompany the marijuana seeds they planted in the Preseli Hills and the mushrooms they collected there. For three years in succession in the mid-1970s the young golden-haired hippies Anne described held Meigan Fayre, a free festival. A short amateur-made film exists of the third Fayre, and the faded earth tones of the colour film suit the richness of the summer landscape. There is a great deal of nudity among the gathering of people who are visibly, at times energetically, tripping on LSD. The music played by some of the lesser-known lights of the free festival circuit, including Zorch and Mazariba, is at times rather challenging. Under the right circumstances their performance may have produced feelings of transcendence, but to the sober ear these bands sound tuneless and clumsy.

The most jarring aspect of the presence of these musicians in the Preseli Hills is how little of what they play has any connection to their surroundings. The stoned jam sessions heard on the film are the very opposite of *genius loci*. One of the strengths of the late sixties records made by musicians who had retreated to rural Britain was the extent to which the atmosphere of the natural world was an audible presence. In the case of Donovan's *A Gift from a Flower to a Garden* this included the recorded sound of waves and birdsong, as well as the effect the landscape had had on his songwriting. The records made by The Incredible String Band offer a musical equivalent to the life depicted on the front and back covers of their albums. When the ISB's Robin Williamson or Vashti Bunyan sang of the coming of winter, they did so with the authority of people who had chosen to experience the season at its rawest and the ability to filter the music of the past with their new surroundings.

The tunes of Zorch and other bands playing at Meigan Fayre are manifestly second rate in comparison. They presumably sounded better when listened to under the influence of drugs, but any sense of kinship with the landscape is entirely absent.

The ancient spirit of the Preselis remained instead in the songs heard in the houses and pubs of the mountains, where they had been sung from generation to generation and survived without the need of a revival or archivist such as Cecil Sharp.

The film of the third Fayre opens with panoramic views of the Preselis and Pentre Ifan, as a well-educated male English voice begins a narration: 'In the beginning God was in heaven, then he descended and was visible to man in certain places of power. This is the teaching of the ancient Celts whose stone monuments still stand today. Here in West Wales young people have come to live by these sites and to honour this teaching.' The film then shows long-haired young people gamely chop wood as a group of wide-eyed friends strum guitars and tap out rhythms with enthusiasm.

'Everywhere we find a longing to strip away the artificial and unnecessary. In response to this desire many have come to the country,' the narrator continues, 'to live in small communities. Where they grow their own food, learn the forgotten crafts, build their own houses, deliver their own babies.'

Over the course of the next hour footage of the free festival is intercut with testimonials from its organisers and from those attending who recognise the Meigan Fayre as part of a return to a forgotten form of being. One contributor, who is dressed in white robes, insists that the indigenous population of the hills have 'lost knowledge of themselves' and are unaware of the spiritual connections abroad in the hills of West Wales. He is later seen clambering up Pentre Ifan (presumably his own spiritual connection takes precedence over protecting the condition of a neolithic site).

At times it is difficult to watch these visitors to the area making such pronouncements without wondering what John Seymour's aged neighbours, George Hughes and Willy Jenkins, men who had witnessed little but the mysteries of these hills throughout their life, would make of the self-righteousness of these incomers. These quiet, venerable farmers would doubtless have been grateful for being born with the forbearance that had allowed them to endure in this landscape for generations. Perhaps of even greater value was their equally strong sense of humour.

The specific location of the Fayre was a large field borrowed from a farmer who appears in the film wearing a countryman's white shirt and tweed tie. His only grievance, he explains, is that the festival-goers he knows draw social security and he wishes 'they could find a way to earn a living'. In all other respects, he says, with some warmth, he finds them agreeable. The success of the arrangement is confirmed by an announcement printed on the festival's poster, which states: 'Special Thanks to Mr. Jones, Pantyderi, for the use of his land and much more besides. We need the names of people willing to pay for the field by helping on the corn harvest in August.'

The farmer of Pantyderi had recognised an opportunity to exploit free agricultural labour when it had presented itself. As the film concludes, the credits run: 'This was a documentary of "A free Festival filmed in the Prescelli Mountain, Wales".'

The location of the Fayre was one the film's participants considered unique, yet this misspelling of its name reveals, as much as the music of Zorch, that the empathy they express for their new surroundings is limited. However well-intentioned, it is brokered by a confidence in their own naive rectitude. A few local people bristled at the new incomers' attitude. For a short period a self-appointed vigilante group, 'The Friends of the Preselis', embarked on a spree of overturning hippy vehicles. In recognition of the tension their presence caused in the community, some festival-goers who stayed on from Meigan Fayre, to settle in the area, started a 'Meigan Workforce', a service that offered skills and labour to the agricultural community, including to Mr Jones, Pantyderi during the corn harvest. The majority of their contemporaries departed the hills; a handful, following the trajectory of their generation, returned to West Wales in their later years to scour property investment opportunities.

'There was a wave of people who went away after the Meigan Fayres,' Anne told me. 'After a while they just got completely fed up with the poverty and the damp, and they came back recently, having made a lot of money.' The idealism of the old ways had been replaced with the rent-seeking pragmatism of holiday lets and Airbnb.

The combination of John Seymour's frequent absences and his habit of extending the invitation to visit Fachongle Isaf to anyone he met on his travels placed a further strain on to an already over-burdened household. Self-sufficiency, environmentalism and a new impetus in the anti-nuclear movement coalesced at the moment the Seymours' attempt at living in the hills began to founder. The most obvious signifier of the anti-nuclear movement was the sticker created by two Danish activists in their early twenties of a smiling sun framed with the phrase 'Nuclear Power, No Thanks'. By the mid-1970s the phrase had been translated into over forty languages, including *Cymraeg*. The Welsh version could regularly be seen on the back of many of the vehicles using the West Wales lanes, occasionally including ones driven by people unable to speak the language, who had placed the anti-nuclear sign on their rear bumper or back window as a signal of intent; the driver understood the unique and attenuated conditions of the area and wished to demonstrate that they had come in peace. The gesture was sensible, as the number of arson attacks on second homes in the area carried out by Welsh Nationalists had increased.

During the heat wave summer of 1976 John Seymour published

a large-format picture book, *The Complete Book of Self-Sufficiency*. It proved to be a phenomenon.

The generously illustrated and simply laid-out pages were designed to elicit the feeling of can-do enthusiasm in the general reader. The new book offered an accessible version of the *Zeitgeist* created by the works of E. F. Schumacher (who provided an introduction) and Leopold Kohr and presented them as a How To book for the high street market of W. H. Smiths, where its popularity was considerable. *The Complete Book of Self-Sufficiency* eventually sold over a million copies, was translated into almost two dozen languages and provided Seymour with a considerable income, which he squandered with enthusiasm.

'He was absolutely appalling with money,' Anne continued. 'He would just splash it about on whomever. He was like a Bushman. If you found the pot of honey, you ate it all, there and then, and then he moved on. The big self-sufficiency book brought in a lot of money. I remember him saying, "I've earned as much as the Prime Minister this year," and I was thinking, "Where is it? Why haven't I got any shoes, Dad?" He liked to live well, and he liked pretty women and to wine and dine them.'

The desire for the footslog life of open country which Seymour had captured in his early works was absent from the large format self-sufficiency manual. Trial and error in the name of rosy cheeks and a good night's sleep had been substituted with a more methodical, prosaic form of home economics. Where he had once written lyrically of 'the cries of the marsh birds coming to us at night as we lie in bed, and the song of the nightingales in the summer time' and in so doing beguiled a generation, Seymour's tone was now more didactic. In an early chapter he attests that 'A further preoccupation of the self-sufficient person should be the correct attitude to the land.'

There are apocryphal stories of early editions of the book being printed either with errors, such as a diagram of a one-acre holding that appears to be of a scale significantly larger than one acre, or with crucial pieces of information missing.

The popularity of self-sufficiency had certainly entered the mainstream, to the point of its satirisation in *The Good Life*, the Surbiton-set sitcom starring Felicity Kendal and Richard Briers, which began broadcasting in 1975.

It is unlikely Seymour ever watched an episode. His belief in congeniality was matched by his belief in his ruralist forebear William Cobbett's idea of 'The Thing': the encroachment of an overreaching Establishment 'other' into everyday life, of which Seymour considered the television to be a contemporary example. And, like Cobbett, the Reform Act radical who was also a committed monarchist, Seymour was a man of great contradiction. The John Seymour who regularly made television programmes throughout his working life distrusted and resented the medium. 'My father made a big point of never watching television,' Anne said, 'and he wouldn't have watched *The Good Life*. He hated television; he hated the whole sort of modern celebrity age. He hated his own success, actually.'

Seymour's disenchantment with his success was an emotion shared by the original generation of musicians who had fled the cities for inspiration and salvation in the countryside. On their final, listless album *When the Eagle Flies*, Traffic, the band once so associated with a new approach to rural life, had grown tired of its responsibilities. Their weariness is reflected in the song 'Memories of a Rock 'n' Rolla', in which Steve Winwood's lyrics inadvertently capture the naivety of his attitude to being a landowner and admit that the original impetus that brought him and his band-mates to rural Buckinghamshire has run its course.

By 1977 the location of Paul and Linda McCartney's remote Scottish farmstead was far from secret, as 'Mull of Kintyre' by Wings became the first British single to sell over two million copies. In the accompanying video McCartney is no longer the bearded smallholder of *Ram*. As the band of the Campbeltown pipers march along the shore, complete with bandleader and staff, their music summoning local families who assemble for a beach bonfire, he surveys them with the air of a highly affable laird.

The apotheosis of the British rock star as landed gentry occurred in the next decade when Roger Daltrey of The Who, dressed in Barbour jacket and peaked cap, appeared in an advert for the American Express credit card. Playing the part of the hobby squire, Daltrey introduces viewers to the purpose-built trout farm, Lakedown Fishery, in the grounds of Holmshurst, his East Sussex Jacobean manor. Presenting ad campaigns aimed at the spending habits of the newly upwardly mobile allowed Daltrey to finance the upkeep of his estate. By the time the adverts ran on national television Donovan's three islands in Skye were now uninhabited apart from the seals who made the waters and shoreline their breeding colonies. Few musicians in the 1980s produced work inspired by remote locations. Acoustic guitars were not heard on albums in the Top Forty to the extent they had been in the late sixties or early seventies. Outside the semi-cloistered environment of folk clubs, finger-picked intruments were rarely heard during the decade.

In 1981, following a mutually agreed separation from Sally, Seymour left Pembrokeshire for County Wexford in Ireland, where he established a smallholding and devoted himself to environmentalism. Age could not wither his determination, nor his wilfulness; in 1999 he was arrested for destroying a crop of genetically engineered sugar beet.

'John was really worried about what was happening and spent his whole time actively working towards environmental solutions for the last twenty, thirty years of his life,' Anne said. 'And he was able to express his opinions to wealthy landowners in a pleasant way, and also to go out in the dead of night with a Super Soaker and some Roundup and trash a GM crop, aged eighty-five! And when he went to court he claimed they were defending the country. It took a long time, but he won the case and they now no longer have GM crops in Ireland.'

The lack of Genetically Modified crops in Ireland can partially be attributed to Seymour's beliefs and his enjoyment of direct action. The legacy left by him and his colleagues, including those who believed in the idea that a Fourth World had been established in West Wales, is visible and palpable in the area, where the early incomers now have firmly established, generational roots.

'The roads were better,' Anne continued; 'by the eighties transport had improved and people had their own vehicles. Then there was the Steiner School, and that brought a lot of people down who were already well into the back-to-the-land movement: that's why they wanted their children to have alternative education. And now there are generations of them. And I'm just talking about this local area. I'm sure it happened all over the country. I mean, my father would never have believed that they would have got planning permission at Lammas to do what they're doing.'

The Lammas Ecovillage is a settlement of nine dwelling houses and a community barn. The buildings were constructed with natural materials such as straw bale insulation and local timber and situated on a site of nearly eighty acres, located approximately ten miles from the Seymour smallholding. The relative success of the Ecovillage encouraged the Welsh Assembly Government to introduce the 'One Planet Development Plan', a national low-impact policy to encourage the establishment of further smallholdings in the manner of Lammas. The willingness of policy makers to endorse the Lammas Ecovillage is recognition of the motives and success of the back-to-the-land movement that began forty years earlier. The values of the movement have not merely been formalised by the authorities, but become respected and understood as a necessary, viable set of principles with which to address the crisis of climate change.

To the casual onlooker Lammas is yet another idyllic and utopian

West Wales commune situated within sight of the mountains and the sea; the form of intentional community Donovan imagined founding in the Lower Hebrides now receives state approval. The name Lammas, the Anglo-Saxon name for the August festival of Harvest that thanks the earth for its blessing, would presumably meet with the approval of the generation who had held their own Fayre at Lammas time in the nearby hills.

In 1998 Wales was granted partial devolution from the Westminster government and was among the first nations in the world to include sustainable development in its constitution. This was a decision partly derived from the influence of the *Small Is Beautiful* eco-politics of the 1960s when Leopold Kohr, who coined the phrase, taught as a lecturer at the University of Aberystwyth. There Kohr shared in his students' belief in *cymdeithas*, the Welsh ideal of community, and was diligent in encouraging many of them in their goal of achieving, if not Welsh independence, then the degree of Welsh autonomy engendered by devolution. The idea of sustainability was similarly promoted throughout the 1970s and 1980s a short distance from Aberystwyth, in the nearby market town of Machynlleth, the location of the Centre for Alternative Technology, an institution where esoteric ideas of environmental science grew into academic and policy research.

The original, simple back-to-the-land impetus of the individual eking an existence from the soil and sharing in its rewards has also survived and, according to many long-term members of its communities, thrived. As concerns over the scarcity of our natural resources have become accepted mainstream thinking – although not without concerted efforts to challenge such assumptions – people who withdrew from society in order to live in communion with the environment have regularly lived contended, quiet lives.

'We have a friend now well into his seventies and he has lived in communities since he was eighteen,' Anne told me as we walked towards the brow of the hill where her father is buried. 'And he's just got on with it; he's a plumber, that's what brings in money when he needs it, and he plays chess for Wales.'

John Seymour returned to Pembrokeshire in his final years to live with Anne and her family at *Fachongle Isaf*, where he died in 2004. He was buried in an old blanket from the house in the top field, in an orchard that he had planted, within sight of the sea, Pentre Ifan and the mountain paths on which his neighbour, Willy Jenkins, saw *canwyll corff*, the body candle.

Within sight as well, of the junk shops, where a decade or more ago, if one's luck was in, one might find the remnants of record collections that once belonged to the original incomers of the late sixties and early seventies; records such as *A Gift from a Flower to a Garden* by Donovan, that in good condition are now a new kind of collectable antique. The few copies I have seen for sale in the past have all been loved but become somewhat dilapidated, an appropriate state for the music written by the songwriter who bought an island on Mull, where he intended to live in harmony with nature and his friends, one of whom, Vashti Bunyan, travelled by horse and cart to join him. The records now crackle and jump but the music remains audible, especially the flute of Harold McNair, whose instrument, like that of the Pied Piper, lured young people away from the town, across the hills, to get it together in the country.

Iceberg Illustration taken from an acrylic painting by Angela Bryars, used on the sleeve of the original pressing of *The Sinking of The Titanic*, 1975.

9 : Cold and Eternal Light

'God of Mercy and Compassion,
Look with pity on my pain,
Hear a mournful broken spirit,
Prostrate at thy feet complain,
Many are my foes and mighty,
Strength to conquer I have none,
Nothing can uphold my goings,
But thy blessed self alone.'

Episcopal Hymn 'Autumn'

Prior to the publication of *Silent Spring* Rachel Carson had for many years worked as a distinguished marine biologist. Among her many achievements was the discovery that the sea's temperature was gradually rising. Carson published her first notable essay, 'Undersea', in 1937 under the name R. L. Carson, as she assumed using her full name would put her at a disadvantage. 'Undersea' was a meditative account of the life of the seabed and drew on her experience in the US government's Fisheries Bureau, for whom she had originally written the piece. It begins:

Who has known the ocean? Neither you nor I, with our earth-bound senses, know the foam and surge of the tide that beats over the crab hiding under the seaweed of his tide pool home; or the lilt of the long, slow swells of mid-ocean, where shoals of wandering fish prey and are preyed upon . . .

Even less is it given to man to descend those six incomprehensible miles into the recesses of the abyss, where reign utter silence and unvarying cold and eternal night.

Carlson was twenty-eight before she ever saw, smelled or touched the sea. She spoke of being born with a fascination for the ocean and dreaming of it during her childhood in landlocked Pennsylvania.

Throughout the twentieth century our history was taught in terms of the country's relationship to the sea, from Drake to Trafalgar and, subsequently, the Battle of Britain. Our mastery of the waves, it is still habitually suggested, provided Britain both with an empire and national character that was physically and spiritually independent. We are an island nation but our island story is told by our earthbound senses. Even if some of the activity around our shoreline, such as fishing, takes place far underwater, we are prone to concentrate on the surface of the waves rather than the sea's depths; the recesses of the abyss remain largely unexamined in the more patriotic conceptions of the British Isles.

For the length of our coastline the twelve nautical sea miles that extend from the shore outwards towards the horizon belong to the United Kingdom. The figure, which is used by the majority of nations in the world, is the official definition of Territorial Waters. This strip of sea around a country's borders is usually owned by the nation. The majority of Territorial Waters and their seabed in Britain are owned by the Crown and managed by the Crown Estate. The patriotism evident in nautical music such as Sir Henry Wood's *Fantasia on British Sea Songs* is appropriate, as the Queen owns the sea that surrounds Britannia. The singing of 'Rule, Britannia!' and the other 'Sea Songs' occurs during the second section of the Last Night of The Proms, which many in the audience at the Royal Albert Hall regard as the evening's highlight. 'Land of Hope and Glory', 'Jerusalem' and 'Rule, Britannia!' are sung in sequence and the annual demonstration of the very English, ironic hysteria running through the crowd swells to a patriotic climax. For all the notion of tradition associated with this ritual demonstrated by the mass waving of Union Jacks, this final part of the evening's programme is a recent invention. The music of the second half of the Last Night was introduced in 1954, so is a tradition which began more recently than the reign of the current monarch.

In the United Kingdom, experience of the coast is formed early in life through its use as a regular location in children's literature and, for many, as a holiday destination. The sea is a constant presence, not only in our memory and imagination, but physically, in our country's geography. According to the Ordnance Survey, grid reference SK 257 144, a field at Church Flatts Farm, near the village of Coton in the Elms in Derbyshire, is the furthest point from sea in Britain. Even from this village, that has a claim to be the most inland point in Britain, the sea is only about seventy miles away, less than a two-hour drive. The twice-daily broadcast of what the poet Sean Street called 'the cold poetry of information' of the

Shipping Forecast on Radio 4 is a twice-daily reminder of how habitually the sea's rhythms lurk in the background of everyday life. Although mainly providing an essential service for mariners starting their working day, its familiarity and constancy can offer a source of comfort to anyone listening, awake in the dead of night.

Those who live within sight of the sea and spend their days in its company talk of its changing character as though the current were an expression of certain moods; the troughs and crests of a wave alter their constitution according to the temperament of the sea as well as the controlling pressure of spring or neap tides. The energy of the tide at our shoreline is a permanent process of arrival, confluence and departure, beyond which the visible currents of the sea recede towards a mass of water, past the offing, towards the depths and, for many of us, as Rachel Carson suggested, the unknown.

In Part VI of *The English Hymnal*, there is the heading 'To Be Sung in Rough Weather'. One of two suggested hymns is 'Eternal Father, Strong to Save', now recognised as The Navy Hymn and known from the final line in three of its verses, 'For those in peril on the sea'.

As a cathedral chorister in Newport in South Wales, a city that still maintained working, if not lively, docks, I regularly sang 'Eternal Father' during services when the city's dignitaries were present. I was always struck that the tune's major note resolution seemed forced, as though the very real peril of being at sea was, true to sailing super-stitions, a factor to be, if not ignored, then certainly to be given only the lightest recognition and seldom to be commented upon. This comforting note suggested the sea as a protective presence around our coast, the sea of the shoreline and Territorial Waters rather in contrast to the depths of the Mid-Atlantic.

Another piece of choral music whose subject was the sea had a very different effect on my senses. In its entry in the catalogue of the Royal School of Church Music, the anthem 'They That Go Down to the Sea in Ships', by the composer Hubert Sumsion, is described as 'One of the most popular anthems in the RSCM catalogue. Sumison's anthem is a dramatic setting of Psalm 107 that is a study in word-painting. It requires a good organist.'

This need for 'a good organist' is due to the series of long-held pedal-notes that require a degree of dexterity to play and create the foreboding undertone that captured my imagination.

When I sang 'They That Go Down to the Sea' in the 1980s it was a recent addition to the repertoire. Hubert Sumsion had premiered the anthem in 1979 at the age of eighty, following a distinguished career that included being simultaneously organist of Gloucester Cathedral and director of music at Cheltenham Ladies' College for over forty years. The composer was also richly decorated for his contribution to church music, his honours including the CBE and numerous awards from the Royal Academy of Music, the Royal College of Organists and the Royal School of Church Music. 'They That Go Down to the Sea in Ships' is just under seven minutes in length, and is based on a dramatic organ part over which the choir voices rise and fall in imitation of the great waves that are part of the anthem's subject. The verses of the anthem taken from Psalm107, which the RSCM described as 'word-painting', created a fearful picture in our young minds. Rather than the devil-may-care vigour heard in The Navy Hymn or in the tunes of reels and other working songs of the sea, 'They That Go Down to the Sea in Ships' evoked the sea's extraordinary power, its thousands of miles of unknowable depth and its drowning vastness:

> They that go down to the sea in ships, and occupy their
> business in great waters;
> These men see the works of the Lord, and his wonders,
> his wonders, his wonders, his wonders, in the deep.
> For at his word the stormy wind ariseth which lifteth up
> the waves thereof.
> They are carried up to the heav'n, and go down again to
> the deep; their soul melteth away because of the trouble.
> They reel to and fro, and stagger like a drunken man, and
> are at their wit's end.
> So when they cry unto the Lord in their trouble, he
> deliv'reth them out of their distress.
> For he maketh the storm to cease: so that the waves
> thereof are still.
> Then are they glad because they are at rest and so he
> bringeth them unto the haven where they would be

The Old Testament vocabulary that advocated for sinners to be thrown into the pit was familiar to us choristers. We regularly sang hymns marked with an asterix, which denoted a sensationalist subject matter not always suited to more sensitive congregations. The setting Sumsion had given this psalm, in which the souls of those at their wit's end melt in the great waters, was evocative of the depths and cold currents of the sea bed, a place of incomprehensible yet powerful darkness or, as Rachel Carson described it, 'unvarying cold and eternal night'.

In 1975, four years before Sumison's premiere of 'They That Go Down to the Sea in Ships', the young British composer Gavin Bryars had released his debut recordings: two sidelong pieces that bore the influence of contemporary American New Music and shared certain structural similarities with minimalism and the compositional methods of John Cage. Bryars had begun the first piece, *The Sinking of the Titanic*, in 1969 when working part time as a tutor at Portsmouth Art College. The work was inspired by the famous sea tragedy and has a sense of depth and awe at the limitlessness of the sea that is equal to the biblical fear of Sumison's adaptation of Psalm 107. The foreign topography of the sea bed is the location for Bryars's score, in which a mournful string part repeats, modifies and reflects itself in the manner in which sound travels underwater, by echo, or as notes drifting, carried along by a submerged, barely perceptible current.

'I had this idea of music existing underwater and being heard underwater,' Bryars told me in his studio in rural Leicestershire. 'It meant that the environment which it was in was the ocean, and sound will travel four times as fast underwater as it does in the air, therefore it will travel much greater distances, hence the use of sonar in the transmission of information between dolphins and whales and marine mammals in general, they use vocal sounds underwater, and they can carry for many miles. So the way in which the sound would travel great distances and bounce back and be deflected was part of the realisation of the piece.'

Bryars based his score on the chords of the Episcopalian hymn 'Autumn', which eyewitnesses stated was the final piece of music played by the ship's string orchestra on the *Titanic* as it gradually started to sink towards the ocean floor. Whether 'Autumn' was the ship's eulogy has subsequently been debated, but what is agreed with some certainty is that the orchestra continued to play as the ship submerged.

'The one reliable witness does say that they were still playing as they went down and he was Harold Bride, the only wireless operator to survive,' Bryars continued. 'So he was used to interpreting sonic information, and he was interviewed when the survivors arrived in New York.' Bryars had undertaken meticulous research before he began the composition of *The Sinking of the Titanic*. He had requested a copy of both the Board of Trade report and the ship's building plans, and through studying these documents he was able to establish the means by which a string orchestra might continue to play on a ship that had essentially been vertically upended, as he explained:

Someone described seeing a cellist running along the boat deck – his spike was dragging along the floor – outside the ship's gymnasium. There was lots of forensic evidence in the stuff I looked at, and I talked to survivors too; there were more of them alive in those days. This gymnasium was on the very top of the boat. So as the ship went from the horizontal to the vertical, like a duck that goes down for a dive, they were able to play, standing on the wall of the gymnasium. Two cellists and the bass player, who'd have obviously needed to alter their pegs and so on; the others were three violins.

This small ensemble played 'Autumn' as the boat sank. And in Bryars's imagination, their music fell with them to the deep, as the sound they produced reverberated on the undertow of the swell beneath the tides and was carried on its currents out towards the darkness. 'Autumn' provided Bryars with the basis for his composition, and its tune is repeated throughout as the primary musical motif. As well as a string ensemble similar in composition to the one that entertained passengers on the *Titanic*, Bryars used recordings of clock chimes, wood blocks that replicated the sound of dripping water, as well as fragments of Morse Code signals and interviews with survivors. The gradual introduction of these details has the effect of submerging the listener deeper into the composer's repetitive score, a process that resembles the fate of those aboard unable to survive; here the sinking of the title reflects the immersive properties of the music and the moment when, at the conclusion of the piece, anyone who has found themselves lost in Bryars's chord progressions might sense they have yielded to an experience with a powerful undertow.

Few pieces concerning the sea that surrounds us have such a sense of the scale of the ocean. One of the lasting effects of listening to *The Sinking of the Titanic* is to feel as though one has witnessed a passage to another world. Bryars also reflected that the disaster signified the passing of an era. 'It's a kind of threnody, in a way, it's a sort of requiem', he told me.

> There's a sense in which Victorian England ended in
> 1912, when Victoria died, and the nineteenth century
> ended then, rather than 1900. It was a moment when
> people had thought that science, technology, industry
> could conquer everything, and suddenly, at a stroke, a
> ship which had been foolishly billed as unsinkable was
> struck down on its maiden voyage, with all the most
> privileged people in the world on board. It was just one
> of those things, God saying, 'Hang on, you've got it
> wrong.' And it was almost as if a new century started
> from then, which involved uncertainty, involved hesi-
> tation. The First World War was just as if some people
> hadn't realised that was the moment, and it dragged on
> for a bit longer. And there were other kinds of disas-
> ter, like Scott of the Antarctic, which suddenly struck
> regarding imperial power and control, like ownership of
> the world was gone. In a way, the *Titanic* is almost like
> an emblem of that.

The end of the seafaring empire Bryars described would have an effect on the population of the towns and cities that had grown dependent on its economy, in the form of ports, shipyards, docks, ferries, trawling and fishing fleets. Almost half a dozen locations can claim a relationship or sense of ownership with the *Titanic*, either through its construction or its maiden and final voyage. 'Southampton, Belfast, Liverpool; Cork makes a claim, because Cobh was its last point of call, where it dropped off the pilot, and the last photograph of the *Titanic* was taken by an Irish priest from Cobh, of it going out to sea; all major shipbuilding ports that have become marinas, or a Tate Gallery in the case of Liverpool.' The heritage industry being more important than any other.

Bryars had begun composing while living in a port himself as a part-time lecturer at Portsmouth School of Art, in a spirit that reflected the institutional bohemianism of art colleges in the late sixties and early seventies; where comparative, often experimental ideas were taught and explored in parallel with the core syllabus, or what might have passed as a syllabus during the ferment of the era.

'I started teaching at Portsmouth when I came back from America, where I'd been working with John Cage. There was a course called Complementary Studies, which could be done alongside the main,' Bryars told me. 'But the difference with places like Portsmouth and a couple of others was that they employed musicians as art teachers. I used to work with the students on performing experimental music, and this meant doing things where their imagination was at a pre-mium, and it didn't demand specific musical abilities.'

It was while lecturing at Portsmouth and reflecting on the period he had recently spent with Cage, whose ideas of chance and inde-terminacy can be heard in *The Sinking of the Titanic*, that Bryars was inspired to begin a separate, very English project.

One day, we were just chatting, three students and me, and we had this idea of making an orchestra that played proper classical music. Their knowledge of classical music was not from being classical music lovers or knowledge-able about music history; it came from whatever they heard in popular culture. And so we did the *William Tell Overture* because that was the theme music to the *Lone Ranger* cowboy series. The things we knew were *Also Sprach Zarathustra*, because of *2001*, and similarly, the *Blue Danube*. We were like a rather low-grade Classic FM.

The orchestra was formally constituted in order to enter a talent show the art college had organised, and given the name the Portsmouth Sinfonia. The word 'sinfonia' is mostly used as a name for a chamber orchestra; having given themselves the challenge of performing as one, it was now necessary for Bryars and his colleagues to each choose a role and indeed an instrument.

One or two people already had instruments, which they played in a rudimentary way. I bought a euphonium from a bicycle shop. Some people could just about read music, others could see the shape of the notes and work out where they were, and then we also had to have a conductor, a guy called John Farley, who knew what he should look like and what the gestures were. He had a beautiful frock coat, long flowing black hair, a great profile, and this beautiful, dignified, haughty way of presenting himself.

In photographs the various members of the Sinfonia have the unmistakeable air of wry detachment that the enterprise necessitated. Their hair is long, regardless of gender; their clothes are scruffy and they more readily resemble a *University Challenge* team representing a plate glass institution than an orchestra. But they also have the stoical air of resignation seen in classical musicians the world over, clutching their instruments for comfort as they are corralled into posing for an album cover.

'We were English and mostly well brought up, and we also had a great sense of humour and a sense of the absurd. We also knew that to do things like that well you have to do it with a straight face,' Bryars said. 'And the thing was, the Portsmouth Sinfonia was hilarious, but the hilarity came from the huge gap between what people knew we were trying to do and what we actually achieved. That was the funny thing about it.'

As the Sinfonia's confidence grew, the orchestra was invited to play at other art colleges, the progressive venues on London's South Bank and more esoteric locations such as Wormwood Scrubs. The members also felt sufficiently emboldened to attempt a studio recording.

'We cut a mono version of the *William Tell Overture* and put it on one of those flexi discs you used to get with *Private Eye*. We mailed them to various people around the world who we knew or admired. We sent one to Mao Tse Tung – whether he got it, I don't know; we sent one to Rodney Marsh at QPR; we sent one to Leonard Bernstein, to Pierre Boulez, and lots of other people.'

The various activities of the Sinfonia, which might reasonably be described as 'actions' or happenings if the warmth and humour at the heart of the enterprise were not so evident, soon came to the attention of Brian Eno, then a student at Winchester Art College, who had previously taken an interest in Bryars's activities and attended performances he had given in the Purcell Room at the Royal Festival Hall. Bryars and Eno struck up a friendship that resulted in Eno both becoming Bryars's lodger and joining the Sinfonia as a clarinettist.

'After he'd been at Winchester Brian moved into this one-room flat I had in Kilburn, and I think he joined the Sinfonia when he was in Roxy Music. That then gave us the inroad to a proper recording studio, which we didn't have before, and by then we did have more repertoire.'

Eno is credited as the producer on the resulting album *Portsmouth Sinfonia Plays the Popular Classics* which was released in 1974. He can be seen on the record's cover in significantly less make-up than he wore as a member of Roxy Music. The record is a seductive combination of hesitancy, incompetence and the peculiar rigour associated with British amateurism. It can also be heard as the culmination of various strains that had developed over the previous decade: the academic inquiry of experimental music, the flourishing open-minded approach in education represented by art schools, and the idea that a record label saw fit to release a record of ad hoc student tomfoolery.

The album contains attempts at or, if one were being generous, interpretations of the Sinfonia's repertoire: 'In the Hall of the Mountain King', 'Dance of the Sugar Plum Fairy', 'Jupiter' from *The Planets* and 'The Blue Danube'. There is a pleasure, almost catharsis, in listening to this music decades after its recording. In the hands of the Portsmouth Sinfonia *Also Sprach Zarathustra*, familiar to contemporary audiences as the portentous soundtrack to the moment when an ape discovers violence in Stanley Kubrick's film *2001: A Space Odyssey*, achieves a semi-controlled hysteria. The listener, already familiar with the drama of the score and its culmination in an ecstasy of high notes, can only listen in trepidation as the moment nears when the musicians are required to play at the upper end of their register. The joy in hearing the Sinfonia's unsuccessful but valiant attempt to stay loyal to the score is immeasurable.

Although *Portsmouth Sinfonia Plays the Popular Classics* sold modestly, to say the least, the reputation of the Sinfonia had grown sufficiently for the ensemble to perform at the Royal Albert Hall, the home of the Last Night of the Proms and the bedrock of the more conservative classical music establishment.

'The Sinfonia was at its largest when we played at the Albert Hall; there must have been fifty of us. We did the "Hallelujah Chorus" there. Our solution was for everyone to bring three friends, which meant immediately we had a 150-strong chorus ready to join in.'

Bryars's career as a composer continued in tandem with the activities of the Sinfonia, and had seen the completion of a new work, *Jesus' Blood Never Failed Me Yet*. Eno, who can be seen singing heartily during the Sinfonia's Albert Hall performance of the 'Hallelujah Chorus' in the scant few minutes of footage that exist, had left Roxy Music at the time of the *Classics*. His interest in New Music had developed, as had his ideas about recording and what he termed 'generative music', compositions created by effects and machines that played themselves, and he suggested to Bryars that a record company might be founded in order to release their experiments.

'Brian and I had a meeting in 1973 at Island Records,' said Bryars, 'to discuss putting this stuff out on a new label, which Brian would supervise. Then, there was the 1973 Arab-Israeli War, the three-day week, 55-mile-an-hour motorway speed limits, all that, and the whole oil shortage, and because vinyl was a by-product of the petroleum industry, any experimental vinyl work was stopped. So it didn't happen.'

The plan was revisited two years later. Eno was convinced that the reputation contemporary experimental music had for inaccessibility was undeserved, and there was a significant number of composers working in the field whose methods could produce recordings that were attractive and approachable. With a mixture of wilfulness and playfulness the new label was to be called Obscure Records. 'Brian asked Michael Nyman and myself to help him as advisers. The two of us worked with Brian, because we were friends and Nyman and I were next-door neighbours.

Jesus' Blood Never Failed Me Yet, the companion piece to *The Sinking of the Titanic*, is a composition of equivalent emotional weight, and at around twenty-five minutes, of equal length. It is based on a tape recording of a homeless man singing the phrase 'Jesus' blood never failed me yet / This one thing I know for he loves me so' under the arches at Waterloo, made by a documentary maker friend of Bryars, which the composer then looped to form a thirteen-bar rhythm track from his voice.

Bryars's use of this tragic, almost pitiful recording is unflinching.

For the first three minutes of the piece the voice is heard alone on a loop as the listener becomes familiar with the background sound of seagulls and the occasional snatch of voices in the distance. A string arrangement is gradually introduced, and over the course of the ensuing twenty minutes Bryars's ensemble, which includes Michael Nyman on organ and Derek Bailey on guitar, accompany a loop of the man's fragile voice in a gentle and, due to the imperfection of the loop's time signature, a literally staggering waltz.

Although the homeless man's circumstances are tragic, Bryars's score reserves judgement and instead offers empathy in its accompaniment as it supports his singing and, therefore, his situation. *Jesus' Blood* resists the mawkish or sentimental, although listeners who were feeling life's woes themselves might easily find the piece overwhelming.

'People are affected by it,' Bryars told me. 'There are people who hate it violently, but almost as many people who like it.'

Bryars first became aware of the reaction that the recording elicited by chance. One day while lecturing in the Fine Art department of Leicester Polytechnic he had run the loop through a recorder in the faculty's small studio while he took a break to drink a cup of coffee. The studio shared a door, which Bryars had left open, with one of the college's large open-plan painting studios. Bryars returned to find that the mood there had become subdued, and in one corner of the room he noticed a student weeping. During the time it had taken Bryars to drink his coffee the tape had continued playing on a loop and reduced some of the students to tears and created an atmosphere of poignancy throughout the studio.

There is an unassuming but overpowering spirituality contained in both *The Sinking of the Titanic* and *Jesus' Blood Never Failed Me Yet*, one set in the past during a moment of national tragedy, the other recognising the condition of a man incapable of making ends meet as he nears the end of his life.

'Both pieces do involve ideas about mortality, about the passing of time, but for me, the man singing "Jesus' Blood" is clearly religious,' Bryars said. 'He was the only one out of all the people who was interviewed by this friend of mine when he was making his film who didn't drink, so he was entirely someone who was living rough, and what I heard in his voice was this great kind of simple faith, but a great humanity, a rather curious optimism, it was a kind of a whole human-ness of the man . . . and yet the words – if anybody had been let down by Jesus, he had. He was close to death; he had nothing. But he didn't think so.'

At the time of its initial release Chris Blackwell, the MD of Island Records, was among those who was mystified, if not horrified by the recording. The mogul had a system of listening to forthcoming releases while simultaneously holding a conversation on the telephone. Few records he heard distracted him from concentrating on his call, but in the case of the Bryars recording he was unable to sustain his equilibrium and snapped.

> As *Jesus' Blood* was playing, he was getting more and
> more annoyed and actually put the phone down: 'What
> the fuck's Brian doing? This has gone too far this time!'
> because it really annoyed him. Brian had to persuade him,

'Well, look, jump a bit further in, in the first three minutes, nothing much happens, this guy's just going round, and then three or four minutes in, something starts to happen.'

Eno felt confident that despite the low profile New Music experienced as an abstruse or academic genre, he knew of enough people working in the field whose output was engaging and melodic and capable of reaching an audience, albeit a small one that would respond with interest to experimentation. It was also an approach Eno himself was taking to his own release on Obscure Records and the label's third, *Discreet Music*: his earliest attempt at producing a record of generative music. The liner notes to *Discreet Music* contain a diagram of how the title piece was created, accompanied by detailed descriptions of the equipment Eno utilised and an explanation of the process of repetition, echo and delay by which he was able to produce the melodic, contemplative sound forms on the record.

Once Eno had established his methodology he allowed the music to create itself by a theoretically endless pattern of repeating itself, with each repetition producing a subtle change in character and tone. The track 'Discreet Music' lasts for 45 minutes, as that is the maximum length of audio that can be contained of one side of vinyl played at 33 rpm. The system Eno had established in his studio would have allowed the music to continue for as long as he was prepared to keep the machines running. On subsequent recordings he would develop and modify these methods and, by coining the term 'ambient' to define them, pioneer an entire genre.

Side two of *Discreet Music* consists of another long piece, *Three Variations on the Canon in D Major by Johann Pachelbel*. For its recording Eno asked Bryars to act as the conductor. Members of the ensemble, which included many of the same musicians who had performed on *The Sinking of the Titanic / Jesus' Blood Has Never Failed Me Yet*, were each given brief excerpts from the score, which were repeated several times, along with instructions to gradually alter the tempo and other elements of the composition. 'Obscure itself was not a big label,' Bryars pointed out. 'At first it was only available on mail order, it was never promoted.'

Eno's burgeoning career as a record producer also hindered the label's momentum. 'As Obscure developed from 1975 to 78,' said Bryars, 'during that time Eno became increasingly involved in working with Bowie, and there was always a problem, because Brian had to supervise everything, he had to proof everything, he had to verify everything, so if Brian was away, nothing happened. "Can we do this?" – "Sorry, no, Brian's in Berlin for a few weeks with David." So that was what limited it. Over the four years, we got ten albums, which is not bad and it's actually an interesting document as a whole.'

To test his intuition that recordings of the modern instrumental music usually written about in specialist publications, and played in the side rooms of distinguished concert halls such as the Purcell Room on London's South Bank, could prove accessible, Eno had selected an album containing *The Sinking of the Titanic* and *Jesus' Blood Never Failed Me Yet* as the debut release for Obscure Records. Although a marginal concern for the management of Island Records who funded the label, there was little theoretical or detached about

Bryars's record. Both pieces are now considered to represent an apotheosis of British experimental music of the period; a compositional style that drew on similar influences as its American progenitors, John Cage in particular, but imbued them with a sense of memory and place. Bryars's works were written at a meditative pace, compared with the frantic tempos often used by the New York minimalists Philip Glass and Steve Reich. They ebb instead, with an English reserve, until the listener subsides, finally overwhelmed by the weight of their emotion and its accompanying release.

Cover to *Signs of Life* by Penguin Cafe Orchestra. Painting by Emily Young, 1987.

10 : The Holy Land

In 1978, the same year in which the Bryars recordings were released, Obscure Records issued an album that started the career of one of the most successful genre-less but popular British instrumental ensembles, the Penguin Cafe Orchestra.

The album's full title was *Music from the Penguin Cafe, Performed by Members of the Penguin Cafe Orchestra*. The recording and songwriting was credited to Simon Jeffes, the multi-instrumentalist composer and founder of the Orchestra. The music for the album was recorded in Jeffes's back garden in West London on a portable Revox recorder and a budget of £870.

At the time of his debut record Jeffes was in his late twenties, working as a freelance arranger and producer to supplement his compositions. Bespectacled and softly spoken and with the mild air of preoccupied diffidence that often seems to accompany originality, Jeffes created, in his tragically short life, a musical idiom as recognisable, idiosyncratic and innovative as any British composer in the twentieth century.

Like Bryars, Jeffes was an acolyte of John Cage and kept a framed telegram he had received from the American composer on the wall of his study. There was a further shared characteristic between the three composers: at various stages of their lives they had each practised Zen Buddhism.

'There's a word in Zen Buddhism, I forget what it is, but it means "direct pointing at the heart". It's an idea about pointing at the Moon, which encapsulates the difference between the finger that's pointing and the Moon itself. I remember my dad being very interested in this musically; that there's a difference, but both are part of the same world.'

This was how Jeffes' son Arthur explained some of the governing principles of his father's compositional methods to me when I visited his apartment-cum-studio in North London. The general air of bohemianism was given an additional atmospheric charge by the presence of the paintings of surreal Homo-Penguins familiar from the artwork of Penguin Cafe Orchestra album covers. The Penguin figures were the work of Arthur's mother Emily Young, who as a child had been the inspiration for the Pink Floyd song 'See Emily Play'. The paintings were larger than the records suggest. On the canvas the figures approach life size and their presence in the building was both cheering and mysterious, as though they inhabited the space on equal terms.

We lingered in front of the painting that had been used for the cover of the album *Signs of Life*. It shows a wooden interior room in which a male and a female penguin-person are in intimate embrace. Three other penguin-people serenade them on accordion, ukulele and what might be a djembe. A baby penguin rides a bike around the couple while waving a small football rattle, as his cycle makes circular marks on the room's wooden floor. Behind the couple a small boy places an arm around a penguin as they gaze out from the room's balcony, hung with coloured festoons, that overlooks a river or lake.

'The artwork and the music together create a world which is very familiar and somehow quite domestic – like the domestic face of Buddhist, avant-garde music,' Arthur said. 'I think it's part of the same conversation that strong, perhaps intimidating, personalities like Steve Reich and Moondog were having, but the Penguin Cafe, is much more friendly, a very English form of Zen Buddhism.'

Simon Jeffes once stated he was making music for a listener 'capable of enjoying Wilson Pickett, Beethoven, the Rolling Stones, choral music from West Africa, Bach, Stravinsky, Irish bagpipe music and even Abba on the odd occasion'. The Orchestra began to discover this audience with the release, in 1981, of the self-titled album that followed *Music from the Penguin Cafe*. The record includes 'Telephone and Rubber Band', which would become familiar through its use in advertising campaigns as the decade wore on. At the time of its debut the composition was an example of the synthesis of everyday objects, exotic instruments and melodic phrases with which Jeffes began to define and develop the Orchestra's sound and personality. Both would encapsulate some of the energy of the new decade.

On *Penguin Cafe Orchestra* Jeffes was joined by ten accomplished musicians to realise his compositions. One of the album's shorter pieces, 'Simon's Dream', refers to the much-repeated story of how Jeffes had decided upon the Orchestra's name almost a decade earlier. On a family holiday in the South of France, during a vivid dream that followed an acute bout of food poisoning, Jeffes encountered a figure that said, 'I am the proprietor of the Penguin Cafe. I will tell you things at random.' The visitation left an impression on Jeffes, who later stated he expected the Cafe was 'an imaginary and rather introverted place which didn't exist in the real world'. Four of the fifteen tracks on *Penguin Cafe Orchestra* are under two minutes long. These shorter pieces are as meticulously played as the longer compositions but have a concentrated intensity, as though the musical daydreams Jeffes had experienced in a 'rather introverted place' have been transcribed for the Orchestra.

Whichever way it might be described – idiosyncratic, wistful, lively – there is an equal sense of joyfulness and quiet reflection to the music of the Penguin Cafe Orchestra. Their compositions and recordings exist in their own singular genre, a world in which instruments such as the ukulele, kalimba and the Venezuelan cuatro, were paired together with household objects such as milk bottles and rubber bands. Jeffes created a world music for a world which doesn't exist.

Their style may be unthreatening, at times comforting, but the ensemble played with sufficient purpose and Jeffes's compositions were written with such integrity that they resist the accusation of being whimsical. Perhaps Simon Jeffes and the Penguin Cafe Orchestra's most singular achievement was to have such faith in the listener that their music became steadily more popular in the eighties and nineties as their audience and reputation grew, to the point where they were in a position to perform what were essentially avant-garde instrumental compositions on mainstream light entertainment television programmes.

We continued our short tour and Arthur pointed out a rather battered but clearly well-loved instrument. 'This is the found harmonium,' he said, pointing to the keyboard that became the title for one of the Orchestra's best-known pieces. In 1982 Simon Jeffes had found the instrument abandoned in a Kyoto side street while in Japan working on a collaboration with the composer Ryuichi Sakamoto.

Arthur told me the story of how, although immediately enamoured of the harmonium, his father wrote a note stating that he would return the following day to collect the instrument rather than removing it there and then. Jeffes placed his message on the instrument, and his assumption that the harmonium would remain overnight in the street proved correct. He took the keyboard back to his monastic Kyoto apartment, and from there home to London. The Penguin Cafe Orchestra took the harmonium across the world; and it can be seen in footage of their appearance on *Wogan*, the prime-time 1980s television chat show, on which they played the piece named after the instrument.

'The found harmonium was to do with *objets trouvés*,' Arthur told me. 'I think at a certain point, my dad found there were elements you could cast in quite a ridiculous light.'

Part of Jeffes's talent lay in tempering the ridiculous with a sense of purpose. Once Arthur returned from school to find his father recording a dripping tap with the intention of using the sound of water hitting the sink as a rhythm track. As Jeffes's arrangements for the recordings use percussion only sparingly, it is the stringed instruments that frequently generate the pulse of the Orchestra. The lack of drum kit, or dedicated rhythm section, also contributes to the records' air of intimacy and calm, which is enhanced by the inherent warmth of the Orchestra's acoustic instruments.

'There is an ebb and flow to so many of the compositions,' Arthur said, 'and they're essentially played on wood, and that kind of wood and the catgut of the strings and guitars produces a particular tone.'

The character of the music was further enlivened by the high calibre of the musicians who played alongside Jeffes. Their technical ability, which brought out the lustre of their acoustic instruments, greatly contributed to the Orchestra's appeal. In an era of synthesizers and dramatic studio effects, Penguin Cafe records offered a new form of reflective chamber music, a private space in an age of conspicuous consumption.

I mentioned to Arthur that I had vivid recollections from adolescence of seeing cassette tapes of the Penguin Cafe Orchestra albums strewn across the dashboards of cars belonging to parents of my friends, or lurking in fruit bowls in their houses. The domesticity he had mentioned was part of my first experience of Penguin Cafe; it provided a musical element in a world of Habitat stripped pine.

'When I play my father's music now, for a large part of the audience it's part of their childhood. When driving around as a family it was the music everyone could agree on. Holidays, as well, I've been told of so many family holiday drives soundtracked by Penguin Cafe. It's for a moving landscape, because there's no focal point in the music and no focal point in the landscape; the listener becomes immersed.'

I asked Arthur the destination of these journeys he had heard described. 'British holidays, to Cornwall, the coast and on the way to the ferry for Brittany,' he told me.

A pair of very impressive speakers that I assumed dated from the late 1980s were placed either side of the sofa on which Arthur and I were sitting. They were reminders of the era's obsession with perfecting sound technology, specifically the moment in the middle of the decade when sleek matte black hi-fi systems coalesced with a consumer demand for New Age music. Pleasant synthesizer washes, soothing solo piano pieces encased in reverb and atmospheric field recordings of the natural world, running water in particular, were the hallmarks of this genre. For over a decade New Age music had been released in small batches on cassette by a musical cottage industry whose audience was the self-improvement movement. By the middle of the 1980s New Age recordings were being bought in greater numbers in the new CD format, in record shops as well as health food stores, and was regarded by some of its aficionados as contemporary, high-end spiritual music. The Windham Hill record label of Palo Alto, California, was a market leader in sales of New Age releases and in the way its recordings were presented. The artwork on its albums combined minimal design with warm, earthy tones that suggested an ethos of gentle self-examination. The house sound of Windham Hill releases featured mellow instrumental compositions coloured with occasional folk inflections, contemplative and unchallenging but always recorded in pristine audio. Occasionally the music the label released was flattered by the sophistication of Windham Hill's design aesthetic and the size of its recording budgets.

I asked Arthur if he thought there had been an overlap between the Penguin Cafe Orchestra audience and the consumers of New Age music. 'These are my dad's speakers,' Arthur said, pointing to the impressive cabinets on either side of us. 'He was very much part of that side of music, he knew the people behind sophisticated hi-fi, and he used to listen to all sorts of stuff in the car, including some of that New Age material. For me there was a qualitative difference between Penguin music and New Age because it was all played live on real instruments by wonderful musicians.'

As the 1980s progressed, the Penguin Cafe that Simon Jeffes regarded as 'an imaginary and rather introverted place' became a seductive location for the increasingly assertive advertising industry. Several agencies licensed Jeffes's compositions for inclusion in campaigns promoting the Eurotunnel, IBM Computers and various phone companies. In an example of synergy between the Penguin Cafe Orchestra and many members of its audience 'Music for a Found Harmonium' was used in a television ad for the recently launched *Independent* newspaper in 1987. That same year Jeffes and the Orchestra were profiled for the *South Bank Show*. By then Penguin Cafe music had received a great deal of exposure but, aside from Radio 3, very little traditional airplay. Jeffes's music had become familiar to a large audience, one that enabled the Orchestra to tour the world's most prestigious concert halls, through innovative or atypical means, such as advertising, but most of all through word of mouth.

Brian Eno's instinct that the experimental recordings he had released on Obscure might prove accessible turned out to be correct. His own pieces were popular in advertising campaigns for mobile phone companies, in which the pace of Eno's music was a refined presence. The thoughtful lugubriousness associated with the ambient genre was a shrewd counterbalance to the rapid changes taking place in how people communicated. The Obscure alumnus Michael Nyman worked as a film composer, most notably for Peter Greenaway and Jane Campion, and also contributed music to television adverts. In a memorable promotional film for Milton Keynes in the mid-1980s, the rigid structure and process of his compositional style was paired with images of a child roller-skating through the town while clutching a red balloon.

The experiments of Jeffes, Nyman and Eno were now considered an appropriate score for the internalised world that advertising pioneered; where music functioned as shorthand for emotion. Faced with the eternal dilemma of commercial compromise, the British avant-garde of the late 1970s and early 1980s integrated into the corporate mainstream with comparative ease. The success of these campaigns, which ensured their compositions were in demand from the ad industry, is even more noteworthy.

For an act to appear on *Wogan*, *The Old Grey Whistle Test* and at Glastonbury, to be the subject of a *South Bank Show* documentary and find an audience among Radio 3 listeners as well as Balearic ravers suggests an across-the-board popularity. In the case of Penguin Cafe Orchestra it was perhaps the music's uniqueness to which so varied a constituency could relate: the cafe was a space, even a sanctuary, many felt they inhabited. Although a fusion of disparate global influences,

Jeffes's Englishness, a 'very English form of Zen Buddhism', registered with the listener through its grace, warmth and singularity.

The English landscape of the 1980s through which a car drove on a journey to Devon or Cornwall, or to a port to catch a ferry to the Continent with the Penguin Cafe Orchestra as a soundtrack, included new varieties of crops in the fields and a new sense of scale in the countryside. The value of land had increased significantly since the United Kingdom first joined the European Community in 1973, and was subsequently integrated into its Common Agricultural Policy four years later. Whatever its merits, by participating in this Pan-European agricultural funding scheme, British farmers were in a position to receive significantly higher subsidies than had previously been available. The Common Agricultural Policy, or CAP, had been established to guarantee a livelihood at the base level of European farming. Its main purpose was to supplement the impecunious life of a smallholder in the *pays profond* of south and southwestern Europe. The payments had also been conceived as a means of preserving the character of rural life. British agriculture, including smaller, upland farming, was of a higher material value than the subsistence levels of European smallholders. Once the United Kingdom was in receipt of CAP monies, its farmers benefited from such economies of scale.

The prices farmers might achieve for their produce and stock had been supported, in some cases guaranteed, by state provision at the end of the Second World War. The additional funding agriculture received from the EEC ensured the industry had prospered from the mid-1970s. The subsidising of the majority of agricultural production meant that the benefits of the CAP's market intervention were spread unevenly, with those least in need of financial assistance achieving a substantial return. Larger farms producing at high volume and scale were at the greatest advantage from this system. The majority of these in Britain were owned by the wealthy, as part of a wider portfolio of holdings, of which land represented only a component.

The Conservative government of the time also offered tax exemption schemes for land acquisition. The price of land increased dramatically and the sense of affluence in farming became palpable and concentrated in the areas of England whose topography suited grain and cereal production such as East Anglia, where the prairie farming John Seymour had fled was thriving.

This led to a marked increase in the levels of rural inequality within agriculture. Upland sheep farmers in areas such as Northumbria or Mid Wales experienced a much smaller financial advantage from being in the Common Agricultural Policy compared to their lowland equivalents, who were known, with envy along with camaraderie, as 'barley barons', or occasionally Piccadilly Farmers, after the St James's clubs of which landowner families had traditionally been members.

Arable farming was increasingly a sophisticated agribusiness that relied on state-of-the-art equipment such as self-propelled sprayers. The sector benefited greatly from the advances in agrichemicals that had minimised the risk of disease, weeds and wastage in crops. In 1940 the yield of wheat per hectare was 2.25 tonnes; by 1980 this had more than doubled to 5.9 tonnes. These gains further accelerated the industrialisation of farming that had begun with state intervention during the 1930s and 40s; capital investment was now concentrated on machinery rather than labour, with the result that far fewer people were employed in farming at a time when the returns in the sector were at their highest in a century. They would need to be, as the purchase cost of a new combine harvester was higher than the price of an average house in Britain. These riches were also a consequence of the continuing practices of hedge removal, stubble burning and a proliferation of chemical usage, along with the destruction of wildlife and habitat such methods ensured.

Nowhere were these changes more visible than in the lowlands of Southern England and the West Country. During the drive along the A40, M4 and M5 on the route to Cornwall, the journey would be enlivened by both the music of the Penguin Cafe Orchestra and the sight of acres and acres of a relatively new crop, oil seed rape, which transformed the colour of the green pasture and wheat brown fields of Albion into a luminous, practically Day-Glo yellow.

In the early 1970s such negligible quantities of the crop were sown that it had been impossible, indeed pointless, to quantify the percentage of oil seed rape grown in the United Kingdom. By 1982 it accounted for 5 per cent of total crop production, an increase of about 40 per cent in less than a decade. The governance that allowed farming to flourish, approved and resourced by the Common Agricultural Policy, eventually led to the overproduction that became a feature of European farming by the end of the decade: the butter mountains, milk and wine lakes emblamatic of a continent-wide surplus of goods.

As farmers utilised technology and subsidy to increase productivity, the government encouraged the appropriation of previously marginal or unsuitable land. A programme of ploughing up moorland, reclaiming land from the sea and the draining of marshes was advocated and supported by the Ministry of Agriculture, Fisheries and Food. The now established ecological movement continuously challenged the increasing and often malign impact on the environment of such measures. Two incidents at the beginning of the 1980s became emblematic of the argument between conservationists and agriculture over how the British landscape should be managed. The first was the proposal that the moorland of Exmoor be ploughed, which resulted in a series of disputes between government agencies at the highest level and the plan being eventually abandoned. The other source of conflict was the marshland of the Norfolk Broads.

The Halvergate Marshes in the Broads is an area of 4,500 hectares of wetlands and is recorded in the Domesday Book as a site for sheep grazing. In the early 1980s the Marshes were home to a number of rare and threatened indigenous plant and bird species, but had nevertheless been assessed as a suitable site for drainage. Environmentalists indicated any erosion of endangered wildlife that followed would be as a result of public monies and governmental policy. They argued that the funds should instead be spent on maintaining the Marshes as a conservation area. Aware that they faced accusations of hypocrisy the Ministry of Agriculture, Fisheries and Food was persuaded by the environmental lobby, which resulted in a change in strategy. Instead of funding 'improvements' such as drainage, the government now made payments to the farmers of Norfolk to conserve the landscape. The use of pesticides was prohibited and the Marshes were designated as only suitable for low-impact grazing and an annual harvest of hay or silage. Halvergate Marshes was re-classified as a Site of Special Scientific Interest and later in the decade became Britain's first Environmentally Sensitive Area.

In 1981 The Wildlife and Countryside Act was implemented, in accordance with an EU directive, for the protection of rare and wild birds whose numbers had decreased sharply. The Act also added further protections to Sites of Special Scientific Interest, a jurisdiction first established in 1949 by the Nature Conservancy, and additional legislation for National Parks – the new laws introduced by the Act had no oversight of agricultural activity within the Parks. Farmers were instead offered compensation to encourage them not to develop or cultivate land further; while outside the National Parks more responsible farmers who had no intention of altering the landscape so dramatically received nothing.

For much of the 1980s the landscape of the South and West of England was emblematic of the recently increased prosperity in parts of the country. Agriculture was an industry participating in these boom years and southern landowners included some of the wealthiest members of society. Their arable holdings could be kept and farmed immaculately, and the visual effect of this new rural affluence was a re-creation of the conception of the countryside as an ageless idyll. Due to the use of pesticides and the introduction of subsidies, the low-lying panorama of England had rarely looked finer or so abundant during the century. Even if its appearance was a result of environmentally catastrophic chemicals, the land looked convincingly green and pleasant.

The renaissance of a pre-war Arcadia was introduced to many British living rooms at the start of the decade by the highly success-ful television adaptation of Evelyn Waugh's *Brideshead Revisited*, a programme that gained a significant audience due in part to the opu-lence in its depiction of the past. The end credits of each programme were shown against footage of Castle Howard, the show's location for the titular Brideshead. The stately home is set against a cloudless blue sky and its lawns are a perfect emerald green. The time of day may be either dawn or dusk, but the authority with which the sun-light dances on the architecture suggests the image is eternal.

It is in recollection of these immaculate grounds, and pushing the Bath chair of his friend Sebastian Flyte, then nursing a croquet injury, through kitchen gardens and hot houses during an endless, languid English summer, that the narrator Charles Ryder states he was 'very close to heaven'. If *Brideshead Revisited* succeeded in re-enchanting its considerable audience with the aristocratic landscape of the 1920s, the film *Chariots of Fire* re-established a similarly nostalgic patriotism. Its title taken from Blake's 'Jerusalem', the film was set in the same decade as *Brideshead*; its evocation of British underdog success at the 1924 Paris Olympics was a box-office tonic for a country that had just experienced the civil unrest of inner city riots.

In 1981, the year in which both *Chariots of Fire* and *Brideshead* were screened, the Environment Secretary Michael Heseltine published a consultation paper on the Organisation of Ancient Monuments and Historic Buildings in England, many of which might have been appropriate settings for either the television series or the film, or for the increasing number of titles set in the

Edwardian era made throughout the decade by the Merchant Ivory production company. In his introduction Heseltine wrote he was 'convinced that there is considerable scope for a more imaginative approach to promoting monuments without detracting in any way from their historical importance' and also of the need for 'a more commercially-minded approach'. A year later Heseltine oversaw the constitution of English Heritage, a new arms-length public body that would, in its management of historic buildings, eventually act as a curator, if not gatekeeper, of what it termed 'the story of England', one told with an application of nostalgia and aspiration similar to Granada Television's production of *Brideshead*.

Heseltine had imagined the National Trust as an operational model for English Heritage. The new agency was immediately subjected to the then relatively new processes of branding and management consultancy; its logo, considered brash by contemporary commentators, appeared on key rings and t-shirts. Of greater concern was that the same management consultants, not architectural historians, wrote several guides and brochures about the buildings now in English Heritage's care.

In the ensuing decades the organisation, first as a quango then as a charitable trust, found its curatorial voice, a soft patriotism with which it defined its 'story of England'. This was accompanied by a lively sense of the commercial opportunities of venue hire and heritage-as-commodity. The authority and remit of English Heritage grew exponentially to a point that, by the end of the twentieth century, it would be responsible for the management of the ancient site of Stonehenge.

Much of the countryside of the British imagination in the first half of the twentieth century now fell under some form of designation. The cracked landscapes painted by Paul Nash were now housed in a figurative frame; his beloved Wittenham Clumps fell within the North Wessex Downs Area of Outstanding Natural Beauty. The eeriness of the Avebury megaliths that so permeated his paintings, and in whose presence he had sought solace and inspiration, was now nullified by the presence of a supervisory body, in this case the National Trust. The argument frequently made in favour of rural spaces and sites being placed in curatorial custody was that such an arrangement allowed them to remain open to the public. Such access is our right.

Despite the information signs and insignia placed near them, the megaliths at Avebury and other landmarks that populate the county of Wiltshire still remained an atavistic and indefinable presence. The Ridgeway, the prehistoric track along which Rolf Gardiner had marched in the pale days of winter, has little sense of a definite beginning or end. It can be joined at the trailhead of Overton Hill. The Avebury stones are within sight of this starting point, as is the prehistoric Silbury Hill, the largest and certainly one of the most mysterious artificial constructions in Europe.

The energy Gardiner described experiencing there persists. Any time spent in contemplation at these spaces confirms that attempts by government agencies to explain or broker their significance into a national story are futile; even if the story is one of which Rolf Gardiner might have approved. The downs and flatlands through which the Ridgeway passes are home to sites of worship, such as the neolithic burial ground of Wayland's Smithy and the three-thousand-year-old White Horse at Uffington. The eighty-seven miles of the Ridgeway pass through the western Home Counties: Wiltshire, Berkshire, Oxfordshire, Buckinghamshire and Hertfordshire. In this heartland of wealth, power and orthodoxy the presence of an ancient past remains strong. In place of English Heritage this is England's Holy Land.

On the lower slopes of the White Horse is Dragon Hill, a small chalk mound. At its summit is a man-made plain, a flat top, a characteristic it shares with Silbury Hill. Dragon Hill takes its name from the legend of St George. The White Horse at Uffington is said to depict St George's charger, from where the blood of the slain dragon flowed down to the small plain below, leaving a barren white surface on which neither grass, nor any other fauna are able to grow. It was here on the summit of Dragon Hill that in 1985 Kate Bush filmed a video for the song 'Cloudbusting'.

At first glance the video features many of the contemporary signifiers of rural England in use by the middle of the decade: a cobalt blue sky that looms over a lustrous green hill; the fair isle cardigan Bush wears; the tweeds in which her co-star Donald Sutherland is dressed; the vintage car (in this instance a black 1934 Buick) driving along an empty A road. From the top of Dragon Hill the perfect square fields of arable Oxfordshire are radiant in the sunlight and extend to the horizon.

Despite these familiar tropes the video for 'Cloudbusting' is a far less orthodox evocation of the rural past than the ones with which television audiences had become familiar.

The song and short film are inspired by *A Book of Dreams*, written by Peter Reich about his relationship with his father, the psychoanalyst, author and inventor Wilhelm Reich, who among his other achievements coined the phrase 'the sexual revolution'.

The opening line of 'Cloudbusting', 'I still dream of Orgonon', with its faint but distinct echo of the first sentence of Daphne du Maurier's *Rebecca*, 'Last night I dreamt I went to Manderley again', refers to the house Reich constructed in Oregon in 1948. Orgonon was named for his discovery of 'orgone', a universal libidinal life force that Reich believed to be the controlling factor in people's health.

As well as affecting meteorological patterns such as producing the colour of the Northern Lights, Reich's research had demonstrated that orgone created gravity and was responsible for the emotional wellbeing of life on earth. To harness its potency Reich constructed orgone accumulators, his equivalent to a Faraday cage: wooden booths similar in scale to a church's confessional that were lined in metal and in which his patients were encouraged to sit naked and absorb orgone energy. His research led Reich to believe orgone radiation in the atmosphere was responsible for drought, which necessitated a device that could produce rain. Having built a house, observatory and laboratory at Orgonon, Reich then perfected a cloudbusting apparatus.

The construction of the machine involved a row of flexible metal tubes immersed in water attached to a series of fifteen-foot hollow aluminium pipes, mounted on a large rotatable plinth. These pipes were aimed at the sky like cannon, and depending on the required meteorological conditions were capable of either forming or dispersing clouds and had the ability to create or halt rainfall. Reich was wary of his machinery falling into the wrong hands, as he was convinced that a cloudbuster was sufficiently powerful to produce holes in the sky, generate endless downpours and summon tornadoes. A model of the machine, slightly larger in scale than Reich's original, features in Bush's video.

By the mid-1950s Reich was concerned about the presence of 'energy alphas', his term for the UFOs he was convinced were misusing orgone as part of a programme to destroy the earth. He and Peter visited Arizona and duly rented a property where they mounted cloudbusters onto a flatbed truck for use as 'space guns', to be aimed at the objects that Reich was convinced were flying across the desert.

Reich's methods and beliefs in the health benefits of orgone drew considerable media attention and also brought him to the notice of various government agencies, including the Food and Drug Administration, who instigated a campaign to cease the production and distribution of both orgone accumulators and cloudbusters. This culminated in the ransacking and destruction of the laboratory at Orgonon and, controversially, the burning of Reich's library and research papers. Upon receiving a two-year prison sentence Reich suffered a deterioration in his physical and mental health and he died in prison of a heart attack.

In the 'Cloudbusting' video rural Oxfordshire is recast as rural Oregon. The viewer sees Peter (Bush) and Wilhelm (Donald Sutherland) drag their cloudbuster to the summit of a hill; Peter has a premonition of his father's fate as Wilhelm walks towards the sunset;

G-men arrive at Orgonon and proceed to destroy Reich's life work before taking him into custody, unaware that Wilhelm is content in the knowledge Peter will prevail; as the son points the cloudbuster towards the clouds, sending shafts of orgone into the sky, an artificially created downpour of rain drenches the darkened landscape amid crashes of thunder and an electrical storm.

After Reich's death his reputation grew and his ideas about the need to overturn repressed emotions were an influence on anti-psychiatry and human potential movements of the 1960s. He would doubtless have approved of 'Cloudbusting' with its libidinal square dance rhythm and the ecstatic voices that rejoice in singing the refrain of 'yeahy-yeahy-yeahy-oohhh' as one.

Whoops and moans of untethered voices are a notable feature of *Hounds of Love*, the album from which 'Cloudbusting' was taken. Just as its video reconfigures the British countryside as the landscape in which Peter and Wilhelm Reich carried out their experiments in rain-making, the record draws on the resources of nature and processes them through the newly invented filter of digital sampling. Side A of the record is also titled 'Hounds of Love'. It depicts a landscape of hills, skies, clouds, trees and lakes, a setting of feral exhilaration. The suite of songs on Side B known as 'The Ninth Wave', replaces this breathlessness with near suffocation by drowning.

Bush was among the first musicians in Britain to own a Fairlight, a digital synthesizer, sampler and sequencer that opened a new field of recording and production to those who could not only afford the equipment, which in 1980 cost £12,000, but also had the patience and technical ability to master its complexities. A Fairlight was included in the recording process of Bush's 1980 album *Never for Ever*. On that record members of the band Landscape had assisted Bush with the Fairlight, but by the time of the *Hounds of Love* recording sessions she had mastered the instrument and was now one of only a handful of artists writing in the new digital space, created by a pitch-controlled keyboard, samples and computer-generated sounds.

Bush had commenced writing the album in the Kent countryside of her family home, Wickham Farm, near Welling, which included a barn she converted into a state -of-the-art 48-track recording studio she later described as idyllic. In the ensuing decade digital recording would become the orthodoxy, but for the creation of *Hounds of Love* Bush was in a position to use the new technology to amplify and shape her natural flair for innovation and experimentation. Throughout the album one of her most dramatic uses of the Fairlight was to pro-gramme voices, her own and others, into its sequencer function. In the album's first three numbers, all of which were released in the UK as singles, Bush multitracks her voice to use as a series of melodic and dramatic hooks: the 'yeah-yeah-yoh' of the opener, 'Running Up That Hill (A Deal with God)', the 'dooh-dooh-dooh' of the title track, and the series of mutated wails that can be heard throughout 'The Big Sky'.

On 'Running Up That Hill', a song about changing identity, Bush uses the Fairlight as a means with which to explore the idea; in its closing bars her sampled voice is played several octaves lower, suggest-ing that the 'deal with God' that would permit her to 'swap places' with her lover has been accepted.

The adult fear of being consumed by love is equated with the des-peration of being a child 'hiding in the dark', and both experiences are made to sound exhilarating on 'Hounds of Love', a song that compares the terrifying momentum of being chased by dogs with the acceptance of desire. The song's emotional peak occurs when Bush describes encountering a fox recovering from a similar fate. This is a natural world far removed from the woodland habitat of children's stories with which the animal is associated in British folklore. Instead it shares the same atmosphere of exaltation present in the film adaptation of Angela Carter's *The Company of Wolves*, released in 1984.

Few songs contain a detail so poignant as the beating, 'little' heart of the fox which Bush holds in her hand. Its presence within the rapture and urgency of the song makes the image all the more powerful.

In the track that follows, 'The Big Sky', Bush breaks off from singing to suggest 'that cloud looks like Ireland'. Throughout the song Bush sounds untethered by gravity, controlled instead by the energy of the air currents overhead. During one of the most exhilarating moments on the album Bush utters the phrase 'Tell me, sisters' and encourages a chorus of voices to join her singing. This sorority, comprised entirely of her multitracked self, then sings with an abandon that, even by the record's standards, is out of control. The song culminates in an ecstasy of groans, wails and ululations of what might be termed Albion throat singing.

The second side of *Hounds of Love* is set in a contrasting natural world. 'The Ninth Wave' takes its name from the nautical theory that waves arrive in groups of three and that the final, ninth wave is the most powerful, with the capacity to capsize or drown. In the sleeve notes of the album Bush included lines from the Tennyson poem 'Idylls of the King: The Coming of Arthur' that illustrate the phenomenon:

Wave after wave, each mightier than the last,
Till last, a ninth one, gathering half the deep
And full of voices, slowly rose and plunged
Roaring, and all the wave was in a flame . . .

'The Ninth Wave' is a suite of six songs whose subject is adrift in a dark sea, awaiting rescue following some undefined catastrophe, and is trapped between their waking nightmare and the dream state seduction of the loss of consciousness. It distilled many of Bush's recurring obsessions: water, witchcraft, death, the supernatural, the power of the senses, the frail line between reality and fantasy.

During this section of the record her use of the Fairlight includes programming an array of other voices, as well as her own: people talking, shouting, making indiscriminate accusations, often heard in conjunction with sounds Bush has sampled and treated such as helicopter blades, waves, whale song and an extract of Gregorian chant from Werner Herzog's *Nosferatu the Vampyre*.

On 'Waking the Witch' Bush samples her voice and uses it to chilling effect as it is played backwards to create the impression of voices speaking in tongues or casting spells. The accompanying digital surface noise and audio collage of demonic phrases culminates in massed voices repeatedly shouting 'Guilty!' – summoning the chaos of what may be the first computerised witch trial.

The vocal samples on 'Hello Earth' are taken from a radio transmission between the astronaut Daniel Brandenstein aboard the space shuttle *Columbia* and the NASA mission control centre at Houston. It introduces an out of body experience of someone who might be drowning and who achieves a form of astral projection, towards the cosmos where the minuteness of earth and its life forms, including that of the water-bound narrator, can be seen. The faint sound of sonar can be heard at the song's conclusion among a miasma of oceanic churn and siren voices urging sleep.

Hounds of Love concludes with 'Morning Fog', out of which come clarity and salvation. The song is the album's most minimal and prettiest track, concluding with the protagonist affirming her love, among one final chorus of Bush's multitracked voice, for their family and a declaration to 'kiss the ground'.

The second half of *Hounds of Love* might justifiably be described as a one-sided concept album. The record as a whole is a perfect synthesis of technology and experimental songwriting informed by Bush's familiarity, evident throughout her career, with the hills of Middle England and the secrets they contain, including the blood that flowed through the chalk lines from the White Horse down to Dragon Hill.

Hounds of Love remains Kate Bush's most successful studio album. Middle England took this music to its heart, as it did the music of the Penguin Cafe Orchestra. Their popularity proved there was a substantial audience for artistic risk and experimentation. These were recordings made in a decade of wealth and represent the era's commercial avant-garde, encased within cracked cassette cases found in its natural homes, the car door compartments and fruit bowls of mid-1980s Arcadia.

Members of the Greenham Common Women's Peace Camp, New Year's Day, 1983. Photograph by Raissa Page, a regular visitor to the camp who joined in the preparations of the trespass she documents in this picture. (Photofusion)

11 : The Temporary Shelter

In the decade of the televised *Brideshead Revisited* and increasing materialism, an experiment in an entirely different set of values was attempted on common land, deep in the heart of Wiltshire. 'Cutting Branches for a Temporary Shelter' is the fourth song on the *Penguin Cafe Orchestra* album and is based on 'Nhemamusasa', a traditional piece for the mbira, the African instrument often referred to in Britain as a kalimba or thumb piano. In 1981, the year in which *Penguin Cafe Orchestra* was released, the activity of cutting branches for a temporary shelter was a frequent, sometimes daily activity for the many thousand women establishing the Greenham Common Women's Peace Camp near Newbury, Berkshire. The temporary shelter the women constructed was usually a 'bender', a tent constructed from tied-together strips of hazel and willow. This meagre frame was covered with a tarpaulin, making it easy for belongings to be rescued in the face of oncoming bailiffs, policemen and military personnel.

I spoke with several women: family friends, distant relatives and passing acquaintances who had lived, visited or regularly participated at Greenham Common Women's Peace Camp, from its establishment in 1981 until its closure nineteen years later. Each person I talked to did so on the condition that her name was not mentioned in print. I understood their desire for anonymity as an assertion that, while every experience of Greenham Common was individual, the actions, activity and means of living at the Peace Camp were agreed collectively. Along with the wish for the earth to be rid of nuclear weapons, the defining characteristic of the Camp was its belief in leaderless, non-hierarchical, non-violent direct action.

The original impetus for the Peace Camp grew out of a march organised by 'Women for Life on Earth', a Welsh group whose members were drawn mainly from South Wales, including the Valleys. The march began in Cardiff in August 1981 and ended ten days later outside the main gate of RAF Greenham Common. A sign attached to the metal gate that read 'Home of the 501st Tactical Missile Wing, United States Airforce' left no doubt as to the current purpose of the base. The RAF station had been chosen as the site for ninety-six cruise missiles held under the direct command of the USAF. Their presence at Greenham had been agreed in secret in December 1979 at NATO headquarters, without being debated in Parliament or any other form of democratic oversight or accountability; as though a decision affecting the fate of the population of the United Kingdom had been decided for the country *in absentia*. This was a decision that brought the likelihood of a nuclear war significantly closer despite twenty-four years of protest by CND and widespread fear of a nuclear conflict.

I was told by someone who had participated in the march that 'the main reason it started was because women had children, and they were protesting against the fact that their children were going to be brought up facing nuclear war. The peace group in Cardiff wasn't a CND group; it was a women's peace group.'

The 'Women for Life on Earth' march took place during the dog days of summer in 1981 and consequently attracted very little attention from the media. Once at their destination the marchers met with the Base Commander at the perimeter of the base and presented him with a letter outlining their concerns and the reasons for their presence at Greenham Common. These included 'the future of all our children, and for the future of the living world, which is the basis of all life'. The Commander, an American flight officer, was blunt in his response: 'As far as I'm concerned you can stay here for as long as you like.'

The Commander's invitation unwittingly encouraged the marchers who, aware of the lack of attention their efforts had thus far received, duly established a base camp on the ground on which they stood. The Greenham Peace Camp would grow in scale, reduce, increase once more and become the site of what its occupants described as the 'continuous witness' against the ninety-six cruise missiles fitted with nuclear warheads, until their departure from Greenham a decade later and beyond.

Throughout its duration the Greenham Common Women's Peace Camp would attract the attention of the world's media, and the television news crews and documentary researchers would be continually frustrated at the Camp's lack of a spokesperson, figurehead or press liaison. The occupants' refusal to provide a running commentary to news agencies was but a single element of their policy of non-direct action. Their media reticence was eventually recognised, in tandem with many of the actions carried out by members and supporters of the Camp, as an innovative and powerful form of protest.

The Peace Camp was assembled around nine gates named for colours of the rainbow: the original camp at the main gate was Yellow Gate; Orange Gate was a Welsh gate; Blue Gate identified itself as New Age; Green Gate refused to have interaction with the population outside the Peace Camp, and Purple Gate was considered a spiritual space. One common factor the gates shared was the mutually agreed decision taken within six months of the Camp's formation that men were prohibited at Greenham. It is duly at first remove, and with the acknowledgement that I have very little authority to do so that I write about the Greenham Common Women's Peace Camp, a remarkable and, notably, successful act of resistance staged in Britain in the twentieth century and, for its re-imagining and repurposing of the landscape, one of the greatest. The history of the construction of new forms of rural communities in twentieth-century Britain is frequently a history of attempts to build utopia, modest as they may be. In its desire to protect, rather than create a perfect version of the world, the Greenham Common Women's Peace Camp was unique among these settlements. Instead of heading to the hills to escape urbanisation, or to live a romantic life of self-sufficiency away from the rat race, the occupants of the Greenham Peace Camp set up camp at the heart of the gravest possible threat to life. After the 1960s, the drift back to the land was often a rejection of conventional society accompanied by hedonism. For a community living in the open air Greenham was also remarkably free of sustained drug use.

The decision that the Camp should be a women-only environment was taken in early 1982. In the preceding few weeks Newbury District Council had served notice of their intention to evict the Camp from the common land it occupied and over which the Council insisted it had control. This was despite the fact that prior to the formation of the Peace Camp, Greenham Common had a rich history of arguments over its ownership and purpose. In 1941 the site was requisitioned for the war effort, then de-requisitioned in 1947, although its rights of common were not restored. In 1951, as the Cold War intensified, it was requisitioned once again, but this decision was met with resistance by over ten thousand signatories of a petition to conserve the Commons and reinstate its rights and liberties. The legal basis on which members of the Peace Camp might be evicted was inconclusive. Within a year the Newbury District Council revoked the common land bye-laws of Greenham Common, an action that was subsequently found to be illegal.

The activities and resolve of the Peace Camp continued despite the continual threats of eviction, and the Camp's philosophy of non-violent direct action was maintained by a series of events and gestures. The first major intervention was staged in December 1982 on the third anniversary of NATO's decision to house cruise missiles at Greenham Common. The action was given the name 'Embrace the Base' and involved over thirty thousand women surrounding the entire perimeter fence by linking hands. Thirty thousand is a speculative figure as the exact number of participants is unknown. Throughout its history Greenham had far greater support and higher visitor numbers than the official statistics show. These figures were collated by the police, who had been instructed to underestimate attendance at the Peace Camp, as they also had been when required to produce numbers taking part in previous anti-nuclear demonstrations.

The majority of those participating in Embrace the Base were among the regular attendees of the Peace Camp who arrived at weekends or during other moments of spare time to offer support, solidarity, food and clothing for the women in residence. In photographs of Embrace the Base there are women joining hands around the perimeter fence wearing overcoats or mackintoshes. There are bags over their shoulders and they have respectable haircuts. Instead of accentuating the contrast in appearance with the permanent residents of the Camp, their presence indicates the common strength of purpose and resolve on which the Peace Camp's ideals were founded. The disparity between the clothes of the weekend visitors and the necessarily basic and scruffy attire of those living in benders is an indication of how widely those ideals were shared.

A visitor who participated in Embrace the Base told me how women had brought items of clothing or soft toys belonging to their children to insert into the wire: 'When we embraced the base, we hung things on that fence that went for ten miles; every inch of that fence was covered in photographs, babies' jumpers, you name it, it was hung on that fence. It showed that women had power.'

And among the most powerful tools of disruption the women used was the human voice. Singing was a frequent communal action, and I was told that many of the songs sung at Greenham 'were very beautiful, very, very rousing songs' that soothed and restored the protestors. As well as providing solace and a sense of togetherness, the act of singing was a reminder to the authorities that the women were in occupation; their voices could be heard by the military personnel on the other side of the perimeter. To armed guards trained in crowd control, the sound of the beauty of the human voice being carried over a fence strung with razor wire was more unsettling than animated and angry shouting, particularly when the songs being sung included innocent nursery rhymes.

The majority of songs sung at the Camp were written by its occupants, they included 'We Are Gentle Angry Women', 'We Are Women', 'There's A Hole In Your Fence' (adapted from the nursery rhyme 'There's A Hole In My Bucket'), 'Brazen Hussies', 'Under The Full Moonlight We Dance', 'We Work For The Russians' and 'I Am A Witness To Your War Crimes'. Others were works in the public domain adapted to suit the context of Greenham. The lyrics of the 1975 feminist protest song by Naomi Littlebear Morena 'Like a Mountain' were modified by the Greenham Women and became known as 'You Can't Kill the Spirit', the Camp's unofficial anthem:

> You can't kill the spirit.
> She is like a mountain
> Old and strong

She goes on an on and on
She is like a mountain . . .

The pioneering folk singer and activist Peggy Seeger, wife of
Ewan McColl, wrote 'Carry Greenham Home' especially for the
Women's Peace Camp. As well as describing the 'singing voices
rising higher [that] weave a dove into the wire', the lyrics referred
to the status of Greenham Common in enabling the occupation:

Here we sit, here we stand
Here we claim the common land,
Nuclear arms shall not command,
Bring the message home.

Members of the Peace Camp also used their voices innovatively.
The sound of a wounded or dying animal keening was frequently
used as a tool of protest. These high-pitched ululations, eerie and
unearthly, became synonymous with the Camp, a reminder of the
continual threat of annihilation against which the women bore
witness.

On New Year's Day, 1983, one of the Peace Camp's most dramatic actions was staged as protestors crossed over the razor wire
and took their occupation within RAF Greenham Common itself.
Forty-four women climbed the perimeter and once inside the
base began to hold hands and dance on the top of one of the
six silos, the squat, grass-covered hangars that housed the artic-
ulated trucks on which the ninety-six cruise missiles, each fitted

with a warhead, were due to be positioned once the orders had been given to attack. A photograph taken of the women is one of the most powerful images of the decade and, indeed, of the Cold War. Two police squad cars are seen in the near distance; behind them, circles of razor wire are strung along the top of a fence with a regularity and efficiency suggestive of a threshing machine. A search tower is visible on the right, behind the fence on which two searchlights are stationed, the beams caught in what is either first light or dusk. The figures of the women, forming a circle, their hands joined together as if dancing around a Maypole, or in some other earth rite, are spread across the plateau of a silo. There is a suggestion of magic taking place on this earthwork, as there has been on man-made tumuli in Albion throughout the centuries. Whatever powers of destruction our ancestors attributed to their gods, their equivalents were contained within this artificial hill, and now this threat was recognised and momentarily neutralised by the act of forty or so women joining hands, singing and dancing above this site of terror.

'They danced and sang on the silo,' I was told, 'and we made music when we broke into the base: people played flutes and we sang loudly so they knew where we were, there was always lots of music.'

These instances of joyful, non-violent direct action were duly met with increasing hostility from the authorities. Within two months of the dances atop the missile silos a High Court Injunction was served to evict twenty-one women living at the Peace Camp. During the eviction, which was subsequently proved to have been illegal, bailiffs treated women with violence and a deliberate programme of humiliation. Eyewitnesses claim to have seen a pregnant protestor punched in the abdomen. The police and Ministry of Defence personnel regularly joined bailiffs in following women into bushes to watch them use the field lavatories they had improvised. Such intimidation was intended to demoralise protestors whose living conditions, during the back end of a harsh winter, were basic and often depleted.

The strain of life at Greenham Common ensured there were also instances of factionalism within the camp; certain gates held ideals which differed from those of their neighbours. I was told of instances of aggravated debate that tested the brittle constitution of a settlement established in the name of peace. And of protestors whose opinions were so strident they were unable to find accord with their fellow occupants: 'It felt very experimental. I can remember the police dropping off women who had mental health problems there, because they didn't know where else to take them or they couldn't be bothered, and they thought, "You can sort it out." So there were lots of women with severe mental health problems, being supported by those who lived in the camp, which wasn't easy.'

This form of decanting on the part of the state would increase throughout the decade, as New Age Traveller sites were evaluated as potential half-way houses and destinations for people facing eviction from social housing. Evidence has also subsequently been produced of police spies, posing as protestors, infiltrating the Camp.

Despite the hostility with which they were treated, the protestors continued to use warmth and humour as a tactic. On April Fool's Day, 1983, two hundred women dressed in furry animal costumes broke into the base and held a picnic. Two years earlier women dressed as soldiers had patrolled their side of the perimeter fence holding flowers in place of rifles. The lack of aggression in such tactics regularly worked in the Greenham women's favour. When mounted police attempted to disrupt a lie-in the protestors held at the Main Gate, during which hundreds of women joined hands and lay down together across the entrance to the airbase to prevent a training exercise, the officers were unable to clear the protest as instructed. With the protestors resting prone on the ground and offering no resistance or aggression, the horses felt no imperative to charge; they came to a standstill, and the police were forced to dismount in order to clear a path to the gate. What the police anticipated would be a swift, unsparing exercise in crowd control performed in front of newspaper cameramen was turned into a display of the strength of the protestors' strategy and their psychological intelligence.

One December evening, around the time of the shortest day when daylight is at a premium, over fifty thousand women assembled around the length of the perimeter and held mirrors directed towards the base. The armed guards and other personnel who stared impassively at the protestors saw their own faces and the grey-green contours of RAF Greenham Common reflected back. During this action, one of the most lyrical and imaginative undertaken by the protestors, the airbase staff were confronted with images of how the Greenham women and the rest of the world saw them and the missiles it was their duty to supervise and operate. The arrests that followed were in the hundreds.

This sense of continually creating new environments in which the exhibitionist and playful aspect of protest could flourish was kept alive at the Peace Camp through rigorous debates and planning sessions. 'There were always workshops about how you carry out an exercise followed by a review of what happened,' I was told; 'things like tying ourselves up in wool, clamping bicycle locks on the gates that they couldn't get off. I can remember that once we'd been arrested, the American soldiers weren't allowed to look at us, so we might start joking with them or saying things as we were trundling along in a truck being taken for processing, and they had to look away. They weren't allowed to answer you – and we just had a lot of fun, and they couldn't hack that at all.'

The authorities started to show signs of frustration with the tactics of the Peace Camp and the then Defence Secretary, Michael Heseltine, in an act of near-hysteria that demonstrated the flamboyance with which he approached the office, informed the House of Commons that anyone intruding at RAF Greenham Common now ran the risk of being shot. In recognition of the escalation in tone of the government's rhetoric, the protestors responded by using bolt cutters to begin the process of cutting down the perimeter fence. This culminated with an action on 4 July, American Independence Day, in 1984 that witnessed a co-ordinated attack on the fence. The decision to employ bolt cutters, with the inevitable consequence of renewed aggression from the authorities, was not taken lightly: 'If there was going to be a break-in, it was kept very quiet and various people would say they would break in and what the consequences of that would be. We were very competent as well as very moral about what we were doing. There was a huge debate around all the activities. It didn't seem like it was trivial at all. But, the media found it very easy to pick out whatever they wanted and distorted it.'

A large-scale eviction of the Peace Camp was duly ordered. The ensuing arrest of hundreds of protestors involved over four hundred members of Thames Valley Police, the Ministry of Defence and West Berkshire Council. The British constabulary were reinforced by members of USAF Police, and for a ten-week period the Peace Camp was surrounded and under the control of this specially convened taskforce.

The Thames Valley Police were eventually ordered to leave the site, as they were required to be redeployed for the Miners' Strike, which in the summer of 1984 was heading towards confrontation. In contrast to the non-violence of the Peace Camp, the paramilitary aggression of the police at the Battle of Orgreave saw them employ tactics unavailable to them at Greenham. Against the miners, the mounted police were ordered not to hold back but to charge.

Such was the government's desperation at their inability to close down the Greenham Peace Camp that Parliament rushed through a specific set of RAF Greenham bye-laws in 1985 with the purpose of making trespass a criminal offence. Members of the Camp immediately contravened the bye-laws by staging a mass trespass involving over fifty thousand women. Although this resulted in a great many arrests, the protest had been arranged under the correct assumption that such a swift and opportunistic piece of law-making by the government might be subject to appeal, especially as the land in question was a Common. For the next three years the police registered over eight hundred instances of trespass, together with the arrests, evictions and harassment by bailiffs, which inevitably followed while the Greenham women continued to challenge the legality of the bye-laws. In 1988 the Law Lords, the highest holders of legal office in the land, ruled in favour of the Peace Camp, judging the MoD bye-laws to be invalid. The women's convictions were quashed on appeal, and the Lords prohibited the creation of any further legislation that might 'take away or prejudicially affect any rights of Common' and stated that the Ministry of Defence had an obligation to inform Parliament of any intention it had to extinguish commoners' rights and to make such intentions overt rather than use 'the secretive dissembling of bye-laws'.

The policy of Glasnost initiated by Mikhail Gorbachev after his election in 1985 had begun to take effect. As the scale of the USSR and the West's nuclear arsenals was gradually reduced, a proportion of the warheads stored at Greenham were removed for decommissioning. It was at this moment that the Peace Camp suffered a tragedy when one of its members, Helen Thomas, died in a traffic accident near Yellow Gate in August 1989, just three months prior to the fall of the Berlin Wall, the symbolic ending of the Cold War.

Within two years, a decade after the establishment of the Peace Camp, the final Cruise missiles departed from RAF Greenham Common. Women maintained an occupational presence at the site until 2000.

At the turn of this century cattle grazed once more on Greenham Common. Public access had been granted and commoners' rights were enacted, which had been prohibited since the outbreak of the Second World War. While the land returned to public use, the experience of the Peace Camp continued to affect those who had participated in its occupation.

'After Greenham, people didn't go away and do nothing,' I was told. 'People went away and became much more involved in their communities and the planet. Ecological issues became extremely important, and they found you couldn't separate them, you can't separate all the things that people were there for, really: it was a huge, global phenomenon, it was everything, really.'

I visited Greenham on the day of the winter solstice. I had found the image of the women dancing on the silos in the attenuated December daylight extraordinarily powerful, as had so many others, and the thought of making a pilgrimage to the site on that day, when many of the surrounding area's landmarks such as Avebury and Stonehenge were considered to be charged with midwinter energy, seemed fitting. That day's conditions of strong winds, biting cold and little opportunity for shelter felt equally appropriate.

English Heritage now conserves the six missile silos as monuments to the Cold War. On my journey I had visited a motorway service station. Above the entrance was a garish LED display on which English Heritage encouraged people to visit 'YOUR STONEHENGE'. I doubted they would erect a similar notice for the former site of RAF Greenham Common. On my arrival at Greenham I reflected on the irony that English Heritage was the creation of Michael Heseltine. In his later capacity as Defence Secretary he would pass a bye-law criminalising trespass on the ground on which I stood and would furthermore suggest intruders be threatened with summary execution.

If the winter solstice has a power to renew the darkness, then surely its embodiment was here, in this former landscape of death now reseeded and revitalised by the co-consciousness of women aware of the invisible threads between people. The unfathomable power of endurance shown by those who had lived here, under the harshest of circumstances, felt palpable as I approached the site of what had been the perimeter fence.

In Wales, in my family and I'm sure many others, the shortest day is known as *cam ceiliog*. Roughly translated, *cam ceiliog* is the length of a cockerel's step. It describes the distance by which the daylight starts to extend as we walk away from the winter's depths. From this moment, every day grows a little, and the light returns, by the length of a cockerel's footstep. *Cam ceiliog* suggests a moment of quiet reflection, a wisp of a day that vanishes just as soon as it appears; a day to wander around the mind's interior for a few moments of thought, before it is concluded.

There would be celebrations a few miles down the road at Avebury and, a little further along the A road, at Stonehenge. Druids would be present at both sites. A sense of the eternal and unknowable might easily be summoned as the sun set among the stones of the ancient spaces. The view in front of me seemed equally historic. I stared and squinted at the missile silos, these strange, grassed-over, man-made tumuli. Their shape and contours, the entirety of their overall appearance, was similar to that of Silbury Hill, the large mound whose reason for existing remains impenetrable. Silbury neighbours Avebury and the Ridgeway, forming a nexus of Ancient Albion, the English Holy Land.

As I pictured the forty-four women dancing on a silo in the half-light I could think of no image more powerful or mysterious to represent the solstice. Whatever those present at Avebury or Stonehenge were experiencing on this Midwinter's Day, I doubted whether it was as overwhelming as the energy I felt circulating around these small, abandoned hummocks. The women's dancing was an act of protest and also a summoning of the spirit felt by those of a previous age who had taken to the commons to express themselves. I thought of the Esperance Morris performing a centuries-old dance together, in a demonstration of the change that had occurred in their social conditions. The light of this shortest day was sufficient to illuminate the memory of the Greenham women, their belief in non-violence and that each action they had taken was a step towards a world where there was less darkness.

I was reminded of another phrase heard in my family, of places that seemed or felt 'thin'. The thinness refers to the width between the physical and spiritual properties of a place and of how narrow this difference feels at certain locations. I have often heard Tintern Abbey described as being thin; its particular 'thinness' is the ease of psychological access it offers towards the age in which it was built. Today Greenham Common was a thin place. By placing a hand on the railings of what had once been Green Gate I was immediately connected with the terror that had shrouded the recent past.

I wandered along the rough shrub path that had once been the longest runway in Europe. In the early 1990s Newbury Council had removed the tarmac and reused it in the construction of the town's controversial bypass. This nine-mile stretch of dual carriageway required the clearing of over 360 acres of land, including woodland and tens of thousands of mature trees. The protest that accompanied its year-long completion may have been the largest ever held in Britain against the development of a road. Thus the raw materials of RAF Greenham Common were moved to another site of confrontation in the Royal County of Berkshire.

The phrase 'nuclear winter' was popularised by the American scientist Carl Sagan to describe the ecological conditions that would follow a holocaust. Now, as I walked, the grey sky over Greenham extended as far as I could see down the former runway, and the wind rose again and felt sharper. The planet had survived the threat of nuclear winter and in comparison to such a fate these conditions, now temporarily harsh against my face, were a source of comfort; they did, though, provide a fleeting sense of how close to intolerable the living standards must have been for many of the occupants of the Peace Camp. I had reached the end of the former runway and as I turned around to make my way back along the perimeter fence, I paused for one more glance at the silos and gathered my thoughts. The Common had almost become an everyday sort of place. Other than myself and a few dog walkers, their heads pointed down against the wind as they followed a familiar route along the open space as part of a daily routine, Greenham was deserted.

There is surely no adequate means with which to mark the history and significance of the Women's Peace Camp, although the poignancy of the Greenham Common Peace Garden, a quiet enclave of the common, situated near where Yellow Gate had stood, is undeniable.

The site consists of a small circle of seven standing stones, carved from Welsh bluestone, among which wildflowers have become established and an oak sapling recovered from the construction of the Newbury Bypass has taken root. They enclose a rust-red, metal, flame-shaped sculpture, which symbolises a campfire. Nearby is another sculpture, a squat spiral of steel and carved stone, and at its base is an engraving: 'Women's Peace Camp 1981–2000 – You Can't Kill the Spirit'. Within a small, formal planting nearby there is a stone memorial to Helen Thomas, the only fatality of the Peace Camp and the only woman named at this Commemorative Site. As I stood there in the midwinter stillness I was overcome by the lack of colour in the endless, empty sky.

As I made my way to the exit towards the car park, I was reminded of the song 'Final Day' by Young Marble Giants. It lasts little over a minute and forty seconds and is the most chilling evocation of nuclear war, made almost unlistenable by the disaffected but mellifluous voice of the band's singer Alison Statton, who sounds as though she is resigned to the moment, after 'too much noise' and 'too much heat', when 'the final day falls into the night / there is peace outside in the narrow light'.

The song is all the more terrifying for its brevity, and it felt appropriate that I found myself humming its melody on my departure from Greenham Common on this short day in the narrow light.

'Final Day' was released in 1980 on Rough Trade, a label sympathetic to many of the ideas explored at the Peace Camp such as independence, collectivism, feminism and the rejection of the authoritarianism of the New Right. I stood for one final moment at the entrance at what had been Yellow Gate, looking at the ground where thousands of women had lain down and linked arms. The sound of the industrial diesel engines of the trucks carrying warheads back into the base must have been deafening.

The actions of the women came from a determination beyond mere bravery. Their existence at Greenham was once described as 'living through one another'. The phrase was derived from a passage in *A Room of One's Own* by Virginia Woolf, in which the author describes the legacy of Shakespeare's imaginary sister:

> Now my belief is that this poet who never wrote a
> word and was buried at the crossroads still lives. She
> lives in you and in me, and in many other women who
> are not here tonight, for they are washing up the dishes

and putting the children to bed. But she lives; for great poets do not die; they are continuing presences; they need only the opportunity to walk among us in the flesh.

Another Rough Trade record from the era suggested itself as the soundtrack to this indefinable place. The thirteenth album on the label was *Odyshape* by the Raincoats, released in the year that the Peace Camp was established. Like its contemporary, *Penguin Cafe Orchestra*, it explored the use of the kalimba and other instruments. If *Penguin Cafe Orchestra* was a music that sought inspiration from all corners of the globe to create music for a global, imaginary folklore, *Odyshape* used similar sources as a means of expressing enclosed, private moments of the self.

In the 1980s, as a band of entirely female members, the Raincoats were in a minority. As a result of the attritional ethos of the times, the sound of *Odyshape* is exploratory and antagonistic. Many of the groups associated with Rough Trade played benefit concerts for CND, Rock Against Racism and other pressing causes. On *Odyshape* the Raincoats went further than merely participating in fundraising and explored the fractious social energy of the early 1980s in abstract terms. The album is a recording of lived music, music as a temporary structure. Certainly the Women's Peace Camp idea of 'co-consciousness' seems an apt explanation of its unique atmosphere. *Odyshape* was written in considerably more comfortable conditions than at Greenham, but they were nevertheless communal conditions of occupancy; members of the band squatted in a mildewed west London terrace with exceptionally rudimentary amenities. The recording engineer on the album was Adam Kidron, whose sister Beeban co-directed the 1983 film *Carry Greenham Home*. The documentary of the Peace Camp was made with the co-operation of the protestors, several of whom Beeban Kidron knew, as did members of the band.

As much as the Raincoats had a direct connection to Greenham Common, it is the sentiment of the final song of *Odyshape* that captures the spirit and resolution of the Peace Camp. 'Go Away' is one of the few songs in the Raincoats canon that might justifiably be described as violent, both in the careening nature of the music and in the lyrics sung by Ana da Silva, who uses a sharp, almost wailing voice rarely heard in their other material: 'Go away, go away, I feel insane / you know they've killed the fool / crushed her soul / I've seen them crushing the soul / they've killed her soul.'

The music that accompanies these words is played by people who sound as though they are at the edges of themselves. The song threatens collapse and uncertainty but is held together by a ferocious sense of purpose. Later in the song there is a contrasting moment of optimism: 'Rejoice, because this landscape is alive!'

As I finally left Greenham Common it was a line from 'Go Away' that stuck in my mind. It occurs in a momentary pause in the song's turbulence, da Silva sings clearly: 'She tried to fulfil her space.'

To fulfil space, to bear witness, to live through one another: the achievements of the Greenham Common Women's Peace Camp have yet to be sufficiently acknowledged. This is unsurprising.

How might the authorities explain their defeat at the hands of non-violent protestors, that by holding hands in the twilight, on a common near Newbury, women prevented ecological catastrophe? At Greenham the raising of consciousness proved more powerful than aggression. And a spirit of such strength can never be extinguished.

'Stonehenge. All June.' Free festivals handbill, including an animal rights protest at Porton Down and Women's Full Moon Festival at Avebury, 1984.

12 : Trilithon Britain

Greenham Common was not alone as a location of rural civil unrest during the 1980s. At the mid-point of the decade, one of the most contentious and still under-acknowledged confrontations between members of the public and Britain's increasingly autonomous police forces occurred forty miles from the Peace Camp, a short distance from Stonehenge, at what became known as the Battle of the Beanfield.

On 1 June 1985 a convoy of some six to seven hundred New Age Travellers drove from the forest of Savernake to Stonehenge for the now decade-old annual free festival held at the ancient site either side of the summer solstice. Before the end of their twenty-five-mile journey the Travellers were met by a police operation that included numerous roadblocks, over 1,200 police in riot gear, a helicopter and attack dogs. The ensuing hostilities resulted in bloodshed, a deliberate attempt at the wholesale destruction of a way of life and the largest mass arrest in Britain since the Second World War; arrests that subsequently resulted in the acquittal of each individual charged.

The idea of a free festival at Stonehenge had developed from the original week-long gatherings held at Windsor Great Park in the early 1970s, among the first purposefully free-to-the public festivals held in the country that century. The first Windsor event of 1972 was organised by members of London's squatting and rent-striking communities who had chosen the location in a deliberate anti-monarchist gesture. Their non-hierarchical leader was Philip Russell, a lifelong libertarian who had changed his name to Wally Hope by the time his plans for the inaugural Stonehenge free festival of 1974 had been put into practice.

The photographer, journalist, activist and filmmaker Alan Lodge, known within the Travelling community as Tash, established a Travellers Welfare Trust and has spent his life tirelessly campaigning against the injustices they suffered. Lodge was a young man among the thousands in attendance at the third, final Windsor Festival in 1974. The event had been planned as a ten-day celebration and included the August Bank Holiday.

'My first outing was Windsor Great Park 1974, over the August Bank Holiday,' Tash told me. 'I think I might have been at '73. But '74 was the first time that I'd experienced police action, when Thames Valley Police cleared us out of the Queen's back garden. I was about seventeen or eighteen, sitting on a log with a cup of tea, talking to my mates, then a line of six hundred coppers came over the hill at dawn. I expected them to say, "Come on, finish your tea," but no words were exchanged. This geezer walked up to me with a stick, hit me round the side of the head, I spilt me tea, fell off the log. No "Move along, now" or anything like that, he just hit me, and I've been militant ever since that day, 28 August 1974. I was an accident ambulance man in the London Ambulance Service and because of my background in public service, I eventually became involved with the festivals, offering my help and support to people that otherwise weren't getting any.'

Alan's interest in festivals was born of his love of the possibilities they afforded: a peripatetic life without the restraints of materialism, the sense of freedom engendered by living outside the boundaries of society, and the strong feelings of fellowship that many who adopted the Travelling way of life experienced. While living nomadically, Lodge simultaneously developed his career as a photographer and journalist. 'I think I started photography in about 1979, 1980,' he told me, 'but by the eighties I was doing it seriously and following the route.'

His exhaustive archive of pictures resonates with an authority, veracity and sense of trust. There are no faces staring at his camera in defiance at being treated as a sociological subject by a visiting press photographer, a feature common to many contemporary images of free festivals and Travellers; Alan was a member of the community he was documenting.

After the clampdown on the Windsor events an itinerary of free festivals was established that was by its nature piecemeal and unpredictable. Attempts to hold them were frequently met with resistance from the police, local residents or more usually both. Several festivals were miraculously held at the same site over successive years, including the Deeply Vale Festival near Bury between 1976 and 1979, an event that represented a departure from the musical conventions of free festivals in the late seventies, such as they were, by including punk acts in their line-up, and the Inglestone Common Free Festival (1980–3) in Gloucestershire. Given their improvised nature and the equally improvised Traveller life, the annual solstice festival at Stonehenge had grown in significance as a meeting point and place of celebration.

Stonehenge is built on an earthwork. It consists of the remains of an outer and inner circle of stones. The outer ring is constructed of large upright sarsens on which were placed lintels; the inner circle is a ring of much smaller upright stones. These circles surround a horseshoe, which is the tallest construction of the monument and comprised of trilithons. Each trilithon consists of two upright stones capped by a horizontal lintel. At the apex of the horseshoe stands a single stone that now rests on the ground, called the Altar Stone. An avenue runs from the stone circle across the earthwork, and near to the point at which the avenue meets the perimeter of the earthworks rests a solitary, large upright, the Heel Stone.

In 1882, when legislation to protect historic monuments was first successfully introduced in Britain, Stonehenge was classified as a legally protected Scheduled Ancient Monument. Druids of various orders and denominations had worshipped among the stones during the summer solstice since their great renaissance of the late eighteenth century, when the antiquarian Iolo Morganwg revived the Bardic tradition of the Gorsedd, which placed an emphasis on the supernatural properties of stone circles. Their celebrations were led and illuminated by the manner in which the sun projected its light across the standing stones.

The Druids observed that on midsummer's morning the horseshoe faced in the direction of the sun, which rose directly over the Heel Stone. Of equal significance was that during the winter solstice the sun set directly between the two upright stones of the great trilithon. These powerful demonstrations of alignment provided the

Druids with sufficient assurance that Stonehenge had been deliberately constructed on the axis of the solstice. No one will ever be in a position to state the reason for the construction of Stonehenge with any authority, but by establishing the stones' relationship to the longest and shortest days, the Druids provided a seductive and plausible explanation for its existence.

In the early 1900s the Druids came into conflict with the new owner of Stonehenge, Sir Edmund Antrobus, who had inherited the stones as part of his family's estate and was the fourth member of the Antrobus baronetcy to take their possession. One of Antrobus's first acts as owner of Stonehenge was to erect a fence around the stones to enable him to charge an admission fee for access. He also re-erected the tallest trilithon and began a restoration of the site. At the 1901 solstice, the first of his tenancy, Sir Edmund requested that the police intervene and force the Druids to leave.

Antrobus lost his son during the First World War and died soon after its conclusion. Another Baron, Cecil Chubb of Salisbury, purchased Stonehenge at the auction that followed. The new owner viewed the druidic fascination with the site with more sympathy than his predecessor. Within three years Chubb took the decision to gift the stones to the nation and suggested the Druids should be permitted to observe the solstice at Stonehenge in perpetuity. In 1927, with Stonehenge now in public ownership, the National Trust began a successful appeal to acquire a substantial acreage of pasture surrounding the monument, in order to prevent any development near the region of the site.

By the mid-1970s the purpose of this ring of prehistoric standing stones was being increasingly disputed. The revival of interest in pagan rituals, Celtic mysticism and Earth Mysteries that developed from the mid-1960s onwards ensured that the site, which by that time had been determined to be standing over several ley lines, was ascribed a renewed significance as a holy or sacred space by the counterculture's mystics. A new generation of Druids who worshipped at Stonehenge maintained the belief in the stones as a place of spiritual and magical authority. This was a belief shared by the New Age Travellers and esotericists who visited Stonehenge and attended the free festival, held every year from 1974. It was a belief that went unrecognised by the authorities. The increase in reported UFO sightings and the growing number of people who attended the solstice celebrations only increased the scepticism with which the local council, the National Trust and various government agencies and departments viewed the activities that took place around the stones.

For those who had chosen to live outside conventional society such as Alan Lodge, part of the significance of Stonehenge lay in its ability to provide nomadic people with a place of congregation. Many of those who made an annual pilgrimage to the site believed that Stonehenge had been constructed for such a purpose, and identified with the stones as a symbol that confirmed their way of life.

'Stonehenge was considered central to absolutely everything up to this point, because it was the hippies' AGM for what we decided we were doing the rest of the year,' Lodge told me. 'On the August Bank Holiday, we were generally in the south-east of England; on the May Bank Holiday, we were generally in the south-west of England; and in some parts of July and August, we'd go up north.'

A flyer from June 1984, drawn by hand in psychedelic style featuring tipis and the cosmic rays of a sunrise, set in the mind's eye of what might be an Inca god, is a testament to how far the festival circuit had developed by the middle of the decade. It lists six events taking place over that summer and early autumn: 'Stonehenge', 'Norwich Peaceful Green Fair June 29 / July', 'Porton Down Freedom for Animals Protest from July 1st', 'Cumbria Silvermoon Fair Aug 10–12', 'Avebury Full Moon Aug 10–12 Women's Festival', 'Mushrooms, Hay-on-Wye and Elsewhere Sept–Oct', and in small lettering at the base of the flyer: 'and all the rest'.

The participants at the early Stonehenge Festivals held from 1974 onwards numbered no more than a few hundred. By 1984 the figure had grown to almost thirty thousand, when the occupancy of Stonehenge lasted for over six weeks and significantly greater numbers than those present for the Solstice celebrations passed through the site. This flow of people was often travelling either to or from the nearby Glastonbury Festival, also hosted at midsummer. Alan Lodge remains convinced that the movement of people around the West Country in the weeks preceding or following the longest day was substantial enough to cause the authorities genuine concern. 'I reckon it was something like a quarter of a million people who came through, even though it was only twenty-five or thirty thousand in the field at a time. Our way of life had become attractive to an awful lot of people, young and old.'

The notion of an alternative, transient life had grown increasingly appealing to large numbers of people in Britain by the mid-1980s. The previously lax attitude of successive governments towards squatting in inner cities had been substituted with legislation in the Criminal Law

Act of 1977. The new law penalised 'unauthorised entry or remaining on premises in certain circumstances'. After the new Housing Act of 1985 anyone found squatting in an empty building could be legally challenged; homes created in Bedford vans and repurposed ambulances and buses became an increasingly common site at the edge of urban areas.

As well as enacting the centuries-old tradition of living nomadically according to the seasons, the Travelling life of the road represented an opportunity to substitute urban squatting with a rural equivalent. The convoluted and often arcane system of bye-laws and rights that determined access to the more remote and quiet areas of the countryside ensured that, even while disbelief and hostility would be a regular response to the choices they had made, this growing mobile population could broadly maintain an impecunious life on its own terms. In the absence of any available land, the Travellers were attempting a rootless form of self-sufficiency. For this transient and dispossessed people safe spaces such as free festivals took on a significance beyond mere hedonism.

After decades of vilification from a media that insisted New Age Travellers were the latest incarnation of folk devils, to hear Alan Lodge talk of the set of principles, which he understood the majority of Travellers abided by, is to be reminded of a more innocent age.

'I've got a code by which I live, and I expect others around me to operate on the same sort of wavelength, and if they don't, then perhaps I don't want anything to do with them,' he told me. 'So when we had problems on the site, you don't have to pick up the phone and call the police and get somebody arrested. Eighteen of you get together and make it clear to the individuals that are causing a wave that it's not acceptable, and would they like to leave? It was self-policing.'

This first generation of New Age Travellers found themselves the subject of constant harassment by local authorities concerned that their regulations were being broken and, more gradually, by the country's police forces. Members of the community, including Lodge, found their time was increasingly taken up with studying the law and understanding the finer points of new legislation increasingly introduced to hinder, if not criminalise their way of life. Travellers also became experts on specific rights of common land usage; the continually changing number of vehicles that constituted an assembly and the number of weeks it took for bailiffs to arrive to remove anyone occupying land owned by a public utility, typically six.

A more pressing legal technicality would bring events to a head at the Stonehenge free festival of 1985. If the festival were to be held that year it would have taken place for twelve consecutive years. This was the length of time required to provide legal precedent for a Stonehenge free festival to be staged in perpetuity. The gathering of 1984 had vividly demonstrated that the observance of the solstice was no longer a small event drawing on the spiritual power of the stones and ley lines of High Albion. The druidic interest in paganism of the early 1970s remained, but Stonehenge was now a site of opposition and occupation as well as celebration.

The band Hawkwind had been a mainstay of the free festival movement since their inception in the ferment of squatting and countercultural street activism of late 1960s Ladbroke Grove in west London. The group had started by playing free concerts under the

Westway overpass and remained committed to performing at unlicensed events, as well as habitually setting up their equipment on stages outside the perimeter fences of ticketed festivals to play for anyone unable or unwilling to pay the admission price.

Hawkwind played to a large audience twice during the solstice at Stonehenge in 1984. The festival site was an autonomous space unencumbered by security, hierarchy or, indeed, organisation. In previous years the entrance had been hung with a sign stating 'You Are Now Entering a Liberated Zone'. For the duration of the solstice the national monument of Stonehenge was unencumbered by the curation of the heritage industry and, in the minds of those in attendance, restored to its original purpose. The festival stage was constructed on a field close to the stone circle owned by the National Trust. It was appropriated without the institution's permission in the weeks preceding the solstice and hosted the kinds of behaviour that were anathema to their principles.

The first Hawkwind set concluded in darkness, and the band then returned at dawn just as the Heel Stone aligned with the rising sun. For forty minutes or so as day broke the band played a drone in their customary space rock style. A small group of white-robed members of the Secular Order of Druids, a gorsedd convened in the mid-1970s, sat deep in repose close to the stones, on which a handful of people had chosen to climb. The long drone continued on stage as a pagan ceremony was enacted. Women dressed in white held branches around the band members as a high priestess figure in black writhed dramatically. At first light on Solstice morning a concentrated sense of ritual dominated the atmosphere at Stonehenge.

When watching archive footage of day breaking at Stonehenge on this Midsummer Day it is evident the charged air owes something to narcosis. Handmade signs advertising various drugs are clearly visible. Few members of the onlooking crowd resemble the free festival cliché of hippy waifs. Many have a derelict, leather-jacketed toughness and a palpable air of disaffectedness. The prevalence of army fatigues on the site adds to the sense of attrition. To witness the dawn ceremony while on a strong dose of LSD must have been a powerful experience; watching a scratchy video of the ceremony decades later, the intensity of the occasion is unmistakable. The audience clearly believes a transmission is occurring between the stage and the standing stones and, whatever the form of this imperceptible exchange, it is one that draws its energy from an ancient source. In our age of designated access it seems extraordinary that this rite could be enacted deep in the English countryside, in the presence of tens of thousands of people, without any licence, supervision or administrative control.

The artist Joe Rush was in attendance and watched the performance. As a founder of the Mutoid Waste Company, a performance art and sculpture collective based in the bohemian, squatting and activist community Frestonia, west London, a stone's throw from Hawkwind's original mission control, he considered himself to be of a different generation to the band, but had been drawn to the sense of unfettered hedonism at Stonehenge in his teens.

'I think 1978 was the first time I went,' he told me. 'Myself and a friend called Willy X were the first two punks to go to the Stonehenge Free Festival, and I watched it change from a really optimistic, hopeful, inclusive, loving thing, to this really aggressive situation. By 1984 there was heroin being sold on the main drag. There was a mafia of people dealing drugs. Parts of the Convoy were being used as cover to carry drugs around. In a way Stonehenge probably needed stopping by that point, because it had become its antithesis.'

At the earlier festivals Rush had witnessed the atmosphere of tolerance and welcome that its founders and early attendees such as Alan Lodge understood to be its ethos. In particular, Rush had made the acquaintance of a man in early middle age who was in the process of selling two shoe shops, one in Yeovil, the other in Salisbury, which ensured he travelled frequently past Stonehenge. 'One day he thought, "Fuck it," stopped his car and came up and someone had built a bonfire. He sat there feeling a bit awkward, but as we got talking he got more and more into it. Then he used to come there more and more regularly and, the next thing, he had his little tent. At Stonehenge you could see the tension fall away from people, and you could see them become more beautiful, relaxed and happy. It was good to watch in those early days, because it was like a dream. But the dream ran into the cold, hard reality of the real world, which was the Beanfield and heroin and that free love doesn't work; instead people go and hit each other with sticks.'

By 1985, as a consequence of its length, activities and audience, some form of confrontation over the right to hold the Stonehenge Free Festival seemed inevitable. That year the standing stones were added to the portfolio of sites managed by English Heritage, which meant that Stonehenge was now under the auspices of an organisation established to enhance the commercial opportunities of the country's historic buildings. Such apparent contradiction highlighted the inherent tension that continued to dominate discussions of what role Stonehenge served as a national monument and who was best placed to interpret its significance. The stone circles were regarded as a place of worship by a minority of people, but owned by the state, which demurred from defining or classifying Stonehenge as anything other than an 'ancient monument'. The stones had become symbolic of the decade's social retrenchment. It is rare for national agencies to take such a deliberately secular position. English Heritage were prepared to classify the ruin as a monument, but not to offer any explanation of why it may have been constructed.

Aside from newly made archaeological discoveries, ancient monuments such as burial chambers and standing stones seldom draw attention in public life. By the mid-1980s Stonehenge had come to symbolise the conflicting ideas of whose set of values constituted a national definition of heritage. The contradictions found in Frank Newbould's poster of the South Downs, produced near the start of the Second World War, were now evident in the stewardship of Stonehenge. A place of natural beauty was presented to the public as belonging to the nation, but the terms of this ownership were ambiguous and confused. An additional source of tension was whether marginal religious practices such as druidism and their desire to worship at the stones were worthy of recognition as part of the site's function. By admitting to the significance of the solstices in the construction of Stonehenge, the authorities would effectively have been granting a licence for the longest and shortest days to be celebrated there.

The ancient landmark, older than Britain itself, continued to be a powerful and inscrutable presence in the Wiltshire landscape.

Once the Stonehenge festival of 1982 had concluded at the end of June, an estimated one hundred and fifty vehicles drove from the site to the Women's Peace Camp at Greenham Common. The *Daily Mail* reported the incident and christened the procession of Bedford vans, repurposed ambulances and trucks a 'Peace Convoy'. Once at the Peace Camp the presence of so many vehicles became a subject of much debate.

Members of the Convoy cut through the perimeter fence and set up camp on an isolated part of the common located at a distance from the main gate of the airbase. A small festival attended by fewer than two thousand people took place over the ensuing three weeks. It was marked by a series of drug overdoses and an outbreak of fighting and tension between the festival-goers and members of the Peace Camp, alongside the usual features of a festival: music, partying and reflection – and even a temporary sauna.

The act of destroying part of the airbase's perimeter proved to be an early example of how the behaviour of members of the Peace Convoy could be described as 'anarchic' by those wishing to denigrate them. Their presence at Greenham, where many of their number acted with autonomy, also earned the Convoy the reputation as troublemakers.

'I thought Greenham was a woman's protest,' Joe Rush told me. 'To start tearing fences down was missing the entire point of it. It was a place of female passive resistance, not male aggression. Aggression was why we'd got into the mess of having nuclear bombs in the first place.'

Rush had also noticed a fissure developing between those who considered themselves to be hardened members of what became known as the Peace Convoy and those, such as Alan Lodge, who lived as Travellers drifting from one destination to another across the circuit of Britain's free festivals.

> By 1985, Stonehenge Free Festival and the Convoy were not really the same thing to my mind. The Convoy was a mixture of the hippie ethos and the post-punk ethos. It was young men who may have had a taste of power from overturning police cars who had convinced themselves they were Jack the Lad. There was a lot of that. Once the Convoy arrived on the scene people started to earn a living from the circuit. The people who came to free festivals suddenly started to be called punters and that sense of difference between the Convoy people and the people who came to the festival was new and helped ruin everything.

After the visible demonstrations of lawlessness at Stonehenge and other free festivals, the police now deemed the events anarchic and dissolute rather than naive or idealistic. There was a sense of inevitability about a confrontation between the Traveller community and the authorities. According to Joe Rush a clampdown was already in the planning stages.

'The police drove past the Convoy in minibuses on their way to Greenham Common,' Joe Rush told me, 'and some of them had handwritten posters in the back window saying "YOU'RE NEXT!"'

Of great irritation to the Establishment was the regularity with which New Age Travellers made their temporary settlements in the heartland of Southern England. 'It's county, isn't it, everywhere from Wiltshire, Hampshire, Dorset, going up to Royal Berkshire. So we're in the Queen's back garden, and we've been there since Windsor Great Park,' Alan Lodge told me.

The Peace Convoy favoured an area in the Savernake Forest near Marlborough, Salisbury, not far from the spiritual sites of Stonehenge and Avebury with plentiful areas of sheltered country, byways and green lanes which allowed them to live without breaking the law, as did the fact that Savernake was the only privately owned forest in the country. Whatever the legal status of their presence, much to the indignation of the locals, the fact remained that the great unwashed and unemployed were continually in occupancy in a cherished district of shire Tory England.

Alan Lodge had registered an escalation in police tactics during the miners' strike and anticipated that the Travellers' way of life would soon be under consideration for new forms of legislation. His attention to detail and recollection of the decisions that enabled the authorities to plan for the Battle of the Beanfield are testament to the diligence with which he has continually fought such injustices.

The miners' strike was the first time that British police forces have operated as a unitary set. Because of the national nature of the strike and the flying pickets, the county police force system wasn't working, and so they invented a thing called the National Reporting Centre, which operated from the fifth floor at Scotland Yard, where a number of chief officers got together and formed a committee where it made them generals of an army, essentially. But basically, it ended up as a military unit to take this head-on, and operating under political direction rather than legal direction, which is another deviation from the way that we've carried on in this country. And after the defeat of the miners, they didn't instantly disband it. I mean, it was there, it was costing money, and I think somebody high up in the Cabinet Office looked at this and thought, "We've got other irritants out there; we could use the same method here for them.'"

In contrast to the tens of thousands of miners who at least had the benefit of union co-ordination and a voluntary national support structure, the assemblage of adapted and dilapidated vehicles that drove from Savernake Forest to Stonehenge in June 1985 contained a few hundred families: men, women and children, their dogs and few belongings. The large majority of them had chosen their way of life as a means of avoiding confrontation.

'The difference between heavy-duty, twenty-stone, sixteen-pint miners and mild-mannered weedy hippies is significant,' Lodge told me. 'The same tools were applied to us as on the miners. And consequently when it came to the Beanfield it was no contest, we were sitting ducks.'

Stonehenge under a barricade of barbed wire during the police operation that led to the Battle of the Beanfield, 1985. (Alan 'Tash' Lodge)

13 : The Story of England

'Stonehenge Riot – Dramatic Picture!'
Western Daily Press headline, June 1985

In April 1985 English Heritage, the National Trust and seventeen other plaintiffs successfully applied for an injunction against eighty-three named individuals who they believed to be the co-ordinators of the Stonehenge free festival. At the end of May, Wiltshire County Council established an exclusion zone that extended for four miles around the boundary of Stonehenge. The zone included roadblocks, several tonnes of tipped gravel piled into large intimidating mounds, and layers of razor wire. Metres of the latter were wound into a temporary hedgerow along the perimeter of the site. Such a high-handed and expensive deployment of resources was emblematic of the extent to which Stonehenge was now a contested landscape; and few images provided a better metaphor for the argument over its purpose than the sight of the stones being barricaded by razor wire. The spending of public monies to temporarily convert a public monument into a paramilitary zone reflected the symbolic value the government attributed to Stonehenge despite its reluctance to define what function the monument served.

The police operation was undertaken to deliberately exclude a section of the population from a site which the law states we are all permitted, if not encouraged, to consider part of our heritage. By creating an exclusion zone and therefore the likelihood of a confrontation of such scale, the police were able to demonstrate their belief that the Convoy presented a danger to the public; while another interpretation of the authorities' actions might be that the heritage industry had unilaterally taken the decision to save Stonehenge from itself.

The fact the site sits so deeply in the heart of England's patchwork of landed estates and safe Tory seats makes Stonehenge's central position in this landscape an anomaly. It was the conservative values of Wiltshire, in contrast to the fellowship, mystery and companionship represented by the passing of the summer solstice, that provided justification for the passing of bye-laws and further legislation to enable the state to intervene on such a scale.

Before it had a chance to enter the newly established exclusion zone, the Peace Convoy that had set out from Savernake Forest was met with riot police armed with dogs. 'People who had gathered in Savernake just knew the general direction from there to Stonehenge. And somebody up front had turned left onto a minor road to get onto the A303 and it completely nonplussed 1,600 coppers, because it was almost as though we were trying to outflank them. We'd come at them from four miles in the wrong direction.'

The police assumed that this inadvertent circumventing of the roadblock was deliberate and proved the Convoy was spoiling for a fight. The bus in which Alan was travelling was positioned in the middle of the retinue of gimcrack vehicles; he was therefore unable to see the melée that now unfolded at the front of the procession. 'There was lots of shuffling about and much movement across fields.

I think they'd approached us as though we were a real threat, because of this accidental outflanking manoeuvre, and that's why so many of them exceeded themselves, because they were all hyped up.'

Notice of the new bye-laws in operation was given to the Travellers, whose response was an attempt to negotiate. After a short impasse between the two sides, the commanding officer, Assistant Chief Constable Lionel Grundy, ordered his men to arrest every member of the Convoy.

Unedited footage of what followed over the next few hours eventually came to light over a decade later. It is difficult to watch. A police helicopter flies overhead as riot police with truncheons routinely smash every window of the Travellers' vehicles, several of which were occupied by women with small children whose terrified screams, despite the presence of the helicopter and a police loudhailer, are often the loudest sound on the film. Police dogs, vigorously encouraged by their handlers, chase those attempting to disembark from their vehicles and flee the breaking glass. The police subsequently set many of the empty vehicles on fire as the Travellers are manhandled with a vigour that appears to be entirely unnecessary. The men are not only assailed unnecessarily while being arrested, but humiliated by being made to kneel or lie in supplication by the police, who have covered up their identification badges and outnumbered the Convoy members by almost four to one. In an attempt to escape the violence some Travellers tear down the fences to nearby fields and take refuge in a bean field, from which the confrontation was to take its name.

The sight of some officers urging their colleagues to show restraint is perhaps the most chilling testimony to the pathology running through many of the police. An operation to prevent a free festival had escalated into a gratuitous attack on a community, one that those in authority clearly regarded as unworthy of being treated with human decency.

'The idea that this is two opposing armies having a pitched battle in a field in medieval style is completely false – this was an ambush that happened on a small, mild-mannered bunch of hippies,' Alan told me. In the midst of the destruction one moment from the day in particular has lodged in his memory. 'There were these two pregnant ladies the police dragged out of the broken windscreens by their hair. Their screams are with me now.'

In the tabloid press in particular, interest in New Age Travellers was sensationalist. A group of people who have chosen to reject, ignore or circumvent the conventions and strictures of society are never likely to receive sympathy or have much agency within the media. News crews were present throughout the bean field confrontation and the footage that eventually emerged reveals the extent to which the events were distorted to present the Convoy in a worse light than the authorities. This editorial manipulation was against the wishes of the few journalists present.

'There was a reporter called Kim Sabado, who worked for ITN, and he'd been in war zones, and you could see he was completely nonplussed,' Alan said. Sabado's on-air statement included his assertion that at the bean field he had seen 'some of the most brutal police treatment of people that I have witnessed in my entire career as a journalist'.

Nick Davies, the investigative journalist who decades later would break the phone-hacking scandal at the *News of the World*, covered the story for the *Observer*. His report highlighted 'glass breaking, people screaming, black smoke towering out of burning caravans' and 'men, women and children led away, shivering, swearing, crying, bleeding, leaving their homes in pieces'.

Davies's report was left unsupported by any visual evidence, as the *Observer*'s photographer Ben Gibson was arrested for obstruction. The charges were dropped later on the day of the confrontation, but the police had succeeded in preventing images of their activities appearing in the more liberal newspapers.

A BBC camera crew had also been present earlier at the edge of the exclusion zone, but had been advised by the police not to cross its barriers. 'They were asked to leave by the police and left the field when told to do so,' Alan said, on the only occasion during our conversation when the pace at which he spoke increased. 'I haven't forgiven them for that, and I mention it every time I talk to them.'

The occasions when Alan engages with the BBC are rare, however, as he regularly refuses their invitations to commemorate the anniversaries of the events he experienced. 'They'll always want a retired senior police officer or judge on to appear with me "for balance",' he said. 'I didn't see much balance in what happened to us that day.'

Once the police finished their operation sixteen travellers had been admitted to hospital, several with head injuries, one of whom was treated for a cracked skull. The police had made 520 arrests, a figure that accounted for the majority of the Peace Convoy and constituted the largest mass detainment in Britain since the outbreak of the Second World War. The charges were for unlawful assembly (these were immediately dropped), obstruction of the highway and obstruction of the police. The latter charge included testimonials that officers had come under attack from Travellers throwing wood, stones, fire extinguishers and petrol bombs, testimonials that were demonstrably false and absent when the charges were presented in court.

'The only way the police had of stopping the free festival was by beating people senseless, and you can't do that without arresting them,' Lodge said. 'You've got to accuse them of something and prove what you're doing is defending the law, hence the Affray, Unlawful Assembly and Assaulting. I was charged with Unlawful Assembly, which is a serious matter.' The space available in local police stations for the charging procedures to take place was limited. The arrested Travellers were shuttled across the country as far away from Wiltshire as the Midlands and the North, and consequently several children were separated from their mothers.

'I spent three days being trawled around the South-West of England because they didn't know where to put us all, and eventually ending up in Salisbury Magistrates Court, and bailed,' Alan continued, 'and of course that then means that you can't gather together again, as we would have expected to.'

Joe Rush of the Mutoid Waste Company had put the finishing touches to a new sculpture, a school bus he and his colleagues had converted into the company's signature vehicle, a futuristic desert transporter with sawn-off roof that brought to mind the dystopia policed by Judge Dredd in the pages of *2000 AD*. Rush had planned to drive the machine on its maiden journey to Stonehenge before the news from Wiltshire made him reconsider his destination.

'Somebody had given me this old school bus. It was all burned out, somebody had been living in it but it still ran. So I built the front into this big fibreglass skull with a big rib cage over the back with the idea to drive it to the Stonehenge festival, but by the time we were ready to leave, we were getting bad reports of what was going on at the Beanfield and by the time we actually got out the gate with this thing, middle England was in lock-down. We thought, "Fuck it, we'll go to Glastonbury."'

Once at Worthy Farm, Rush found many of those intending to travel to Stonehenge as usual had taken a similar decision and, thanks to the magnanimity of Michael Eavis, found refuge at the festival, where members of the shell-shocked and now destitute members of the Convoy who had fled arrest were also present. 'Michael was really supportive,' Rush told me, 'especially straight after the Beanfield, when the police were looking to find them and attack them again. All their trucks were gone and their dogs had been stolen or put down; they were like refugees, and Michael let them in and he supported them. He didn't get thanked much for it, because they were so angry.'

Another benefactor to the Convoy was the Earl of Cardigan, David Brudenell-Bruce, the then secretary of Marlborough Conservative Association and the owner of both Savernake Forest and of the Beanfield itself. 'Cardigan had always let everyone stay in his woods,' Joe continued, 'and a few people had escaped back there. The police basically said, "Can we come in and finish the job?" and he went, "No you fucking can't."'

Once the arrests proceeded to Crown Court there were substantial gaps in video and radio evidence submitted by the police, including the alteration of communication logbooks. Due to the removal of their badge numbers and other forms of identification the officers avoided prosecution apart from one, a sergeant, who was found guilty of causing actual bodily harm. The Earl of Cardigan testified against the police, an action that contributed greatly to the charges against the Travellers being dropped. The right-leaning press consequently vilified the Earl, an editorial in *The Times* concluding that, as one of his ancestors had ordered the charge of the Light Brigade, the condition of being 'barking mad' was 'probably hereditary' in the Cardigan genealogy.

The editor of the *Daily Telegraph*, W. F. Deedes, accused the Earl of behaving like a 'class traitor' in print. Cardigan took both newspapers, along with three tabloids, to court, was successful and won considerable damages. Speaking a decade later he recalled, 'I hadn't realised that I would be considered a class traitor. If I see a policeman repeatedly truncheoning a very pregnant woman over the head from behind I do feel I'm entitled to say, "That's a terrible thing you're doing, Officer." I went along, saw a dreadful episode in British police history, and simply reported what I saw.'

A week after the confrontation at the Beanfield, *Police Review*, a trade journal for the constabulary, had reported on the success of the Stonehenge operation and included a reference to the fact the exercise 'had been planned for several months and lessons in rapid deployment learned from the miners' strike were implemented'. There was no mention of the cost of the exercise, or of isolating Stonehenge with razor-wire barricades for months, although accounts show the budget ran to millions of pounds. As an example in extreme authoritarianism on the part of the British government it remains unparalleled.

Over the next five years Alan Lodge and twenty-three other members of the Convoy took the Wiltshire Police to court for wrongful arrest, assault and criminal damage.

'The interesting thing about Alan Lodge,' Joe Rush told me, 'apart from being the great documenter of the whole thing, was he was the one who went to court and out of ten points of law, he won nine and the police won one, which was whether the police could believe that they were in physical danger or not, and they found in favour of the police on that one, because a couple had ended up in hospital; otherwise, they found everything else in favour of the Travellers.'

Despite their victory the Travellers received no compensation. In one final act of Establishment retribution the presiding judge declined to award Lodge or his fellow plaintiffs legal costs, as was often the convention. Instead the meagre amount of damages they received, a thousand pounds each, was instructed to be absorbed into the costs of the proceedings. Even in victory the Travellers were treated with gratuitous cruelty. Nor was a public inquiry ever held into what had essentially been, under the bright blue skies of a burnished June day in rural Wiltshire, a police riot.

The lack of any contrition on the part of the authorities was a signal of their intentions. The operation at Stonehenge proved to be the first stage of a concerted effort to criminalise, in all but name, the itinerant life of New Age Travellers and to dismantle the black, or blag, economy by which they functioned.

In 1986, twelve months after the Battle of the Beanfield, a dawn raid was mounted on 1 June against a Traveller settlement at Stoney Cross in Hampshire that had gathered for the solstice celebrations. The presence there of the media, now more alert to the injustices Travellers experienced, resulted in a significant reduction in violence. However the effect of the raid was the same as before.

'When it came to Stoney Cross a year later, kids were taken away from people, homes were removed and John Duke, the chief constable of Wiltshire, attempted to call it the decommissioning of the convoy, i.e. it was an attempt to finish unfinished business and to remove the potential to carry on this lifestyle,' Alan said.

The police were assisted in their wish by the passing of a new law by the Home Secretary Douglas Hurd who, two days after the police operation at Stoney Cross, gave a speech to the House in which he stated: 'Hon. Members from the West Country will be aware of the immense policing difficulties created by the Peace Convoy; it is anything but peaceful. Indeed, it resembles nothing more than a band of medieval brigands who have no respect for the law or the rights of others.'

He was encouraged in making such an assertion by the Prime Minister. In a statement ripe with the prurient obsession for discipline she regularly displayed in her enduring post-Falklands War imperial phrase, Margaret Thatcher told the House her government would be 'only too delighted to do anything we can to make life difficult for such things as hippy convoys'.

The obvious and malevolent disdain successive governments felt towards the Travellers was not limited to the Conservatives. Within two years of New Labour attaining power the Home Secretary Jack Straw made a succession of inflammatory remarks about 'so-called travellers' and included members of their community as examples of the need for his proposed Antisocial Behaviour laws.

At Glastonbury 1987 the Mutoid Waste Company fabricated a bespoke version of the standing stones at the festival, named 'Car Henge'. The focal point was a trilithon constructed of three cars, a trilithon made from detritus, which proved to be as stimulating an attraction as the monument it replicated, if more dystopian, as the sun rose over Worthy Farm. That year Michael Eavis had reached an accommodation with the Convoy, now in effect permanently prohibited from Stonehenge at the time of the solstice. During the weeks either side of Glastonbury the Travellers were welcome to set up their own encampment in fields adjacent to the festival for free. They could stage their own celebrations there on condition that the area was left as they had found it. This arrangement continued until 1990, by which time 'Convoy' had become a catch-all term to describe the thousands of people in Britain who identified themselves as New Age Travellers when they congregated together.

'Car Henge' furthered the reputation of the Mutoid Waste Company for hosting increasingly lawless parties. These were regularly held at their Kings Cross headquarters, an abandoned bus depot they had decorated in their apocalyptic house style. The events were hedonistic sessions that lasted till first light with a soundtrack that included hip-hop, dub, electro, the few 12-inch records then available recognised as house music. To accompany these American imports were the handful of releases by London groups such as Renegade Soundwave and World Domination Enterprises. The latter were friends of Mutoid Waste and regularly played at their parties. Their sound was the Mutoid aesthetic in audio: a rough collision of samples, trashy noise and modified aggression. Many of the revellers present wore elaborate costumes and face paint that glowed amid the pyrotechnic displays and animated welded sculptures. For some it was the perfect environment to experience a new drug, Ecstasy.

Whatever energy levels the new drug brought to its contemporary version, for Alan Lodge the life he had lived for over a decade had now been destroyed. 'Basically, the festival circuit was broken; and, I mean, sometimes, you might sit round fires with people, having a conversation, you're then dispersed, and you don't find people until two or three years later, and I always thought it hilarious that we could pick up the conversation where we left off! But that had ended.'

Lodge had nevertheless noticed a potential loophole in the new Public Order Act that proved serendipitous with the arrival of Ecstasy and the new form of hedonism that accompanied its use. 'It might have just worked out by accident that the new style of enjoying yourself and whatever was going on in the cities and in London at the time, but it's reasonable to hypothesise that there was a bunch of thinkers sat round a fire thinking. And they came up with "How are we going to get round this new Act?" – it was operated from 1 April 1987 – and the answer was "I know, we won't reside there." And having not resided there, you just go there, give it one and run away again, and you've still got an event, haven't you?'

The free festivals subsequently transformed into the much more condensed free parties, where the issue of residence was inapplicable. The first generation of warehouse parties, which featured those held by the Mutoid Waste Company at their converted bus depot, duly started to thrive.

'It was way before the big Orbital parties around London really started,' Rush told me. 'We could get six hundred people into a place without the police sussing it. They wouldn't turn us all onto the street, because they'd have a fight and then they would have six hundred pissed-off people in the street. What was extraordinary about it was you'd see all sorts of people there; somebody you last saw sitting round a camp fire, drinking Special Brew, wearing rags, would be in trainers, bouncing up and down, waving his arms about like the years had dropped off him. And there was a moment where the entire country, from all the different class structures, regional structures, age structures, were all totally in harmony, and the music was totally in harmony, and it was an extraordinary, extraordinary moment.'

Lodge was only party to this moment at first remove. Although he continued to live as a Traveller, the events of the Battle of the Beanfield two years earlier had had a fatal impact on the spirit of the Peace Convoy and the nomadic life of freedom and optimism that represented a detachment from society without vilification.

'An awful lot of hope went that day. There was an influx of bad drugs that hadn't been allowed before. Suddenly people succumbed. They sold bits of their bus that had been broken. Vehicles were in a low state of maintenance because of police action, and there was a certain amount of "fuck everything" attitude. Heroin use and Special Brew use increased dramatically; to my mind those people are casualties of war.'

Before we ended our conversation I asked Alan what I realised would be a hard question for him to answer. And tellingly, from someone as quick-witted and garrulous as him, it was the first moment of silence since we had spoken.

'What is our legacy?' he said, repeating my enquiry. There was the softest of cracks discernible in his voice. 'We scared the bejaysus out of the authorities, and my principles have stayed the same,' he said with a laugh before turning silent again . . . 'but in the end they won.'

———————————

In the years following the Beanfield, the Peace Convoy was informally reconstituted as the popularity of the Travelling life grew significantly. At the time the people I knew who had chosen to live in this manner often talked of how much the community they felt part of was like any other: full of people going about their lives, many of whom had jobs, but had elected to live in a vehicle or caravan as it was a solution to the country's enduring housing crisis; but peopled as well by an above average number of individuals who had fled difficult domestic situations. They also suggested that among their number there was perhaps a greater concentration of people with mental health issues than would be found in more orthodox parts of society. Given the then contemporary proliferation and growing use of Prozac and other SSI medications across the professional classes, such a consideration might seem less melodramatic than it once did.

A thread of the nihilism Alan Lodge mentioned was easy to discern in an element of the Convoy. In particular groups of men known as the Brew Crew gained a reputation for the continual consumption of Special Brew, which for some of their number was combined with hard drug use and a rejection of the unstated moralism and understanding Alan Lodge and Joe Rush had experienced in the Travelling community prior to the Battle of the Beanfield.

At the Glastonbury Festival of 1990 I was told it was members of the Brew Crew that I saw spitting at the back of a police horse, until it was almost covered in mucus. The police, who were present at the festival for only their second year, as a condition of the licence, refused to engage with the provocation. Given the extent to which they were outnumbered this was presumably their only logical, or safe, course of action. The image of the horse's gelatinous-looking back stayed with me throughout the weekend and seemed to illustrate the extreme polarisation that had occurred between some of the Convoy and the police as a consequence of the Battle of the Beanfield. I had met Travellers who experienced very little harassment or even attention from the authorities. They were a regular presence at festivals and especially in the lay-bys of the A and B roads of the West Country throughout the first years of the 1990s. I also knew members of their community whose experience of the police had been far more fraught and intimidating, but their violence at the Beanfield five years earlier had created an antipathy so visceral that, even in one of the most tolerant and joyful festivals in Europe, a horse could be the victim of such unwarranted denigration.

For many people in attendance, certainly myself, that year's Glastonbury Festival was their first experience of dancing together en masse under the stars. At nightfall traders closed their stalls and many substituted their wares for basic sound systems as much of the site transformed itself into a free party. In the adjacent site which Michael Eavis had donated to the Convoy, the music kept to its own timetable and continued long after the main attractions had reached their curfew. Throughout the long weekend these enclaves some distance away from the Pyramid stage were a destination, for music and for what was on offer to ensure people could continue dancing. To any visitor present in the early hours of the morning the multitude of painted ambulances, repurposed buses and Bedford vans made a vivid impression, as did the small cordoned-off area of a field restricted to horse-drawn vehicles in which a row of gypsy caravans had been neatly parked. If one wandered through these fields in an altered state of mind it was possible to imagine the encampment as a free festival village show, one without any particular focal point but instead a series of areas where activities were underway at their own pace and rhythm, occasionally to the accompaniment of a sound system. The Tonka Sound System, which pioneered the idea of a collective that played house and techno at festivals and free parties, was present in that year in the Travellers Field and contributed to the sense of liberation many have felt at Glastonbury; of being in a community encamped together on a ley line connecting Stonehenge to St Michael's Mount in Cornwall and drawing on its energy.

Alan Lodge told stories of meeting strangers around the campfire at free festivals, bonding over its duration, dispersing, then resuming the same conversation a year later in a similar environment. Whether or not the fireside chats I witnessed wandering dazed around the Travellers Field were a consequence of similar encounters, the sense of otherness I experienced there was marked. I had rarely encountered such a chaotic, warm, but intimidating atmosphere, part of which may have been due to the presence of so many dogs. The Travellers Field was a rich complement to the rest of the festival; the unrestrained behaviour there infected the rest of the festival, as though it were encouraging everyone present to allow themselves to go further, or higher.

On the Monday afternoon, Glastonbury 1990 ended in a confrontation between members of the Convoy and a private security team Eavis had hired. After days of lack of sleep and over-stimulation on both sides, the fractious relationship they shared due to past encounters at other festivals was likely to break. Eyewitnesses reported a truck being driven into a fence, an over-eager response from members of the security team who took advantage of the incident as an opportunity to lash out, and a small pitched battle ensued between security guards and Travellers. In the news reports that followed it was suggested members of the security team, who ended the confrontation in retreat, had gone as far as throwing petrol bombs at the Convoy. The Travellers prevailed although their reputation for trouble and chaos was again enhanced. 'It was 1990,' Joe Rush told me, 'when the Travellers kicked off against the security who were taking the piss badly, and they were attacking people, bullying people, robbing people and there were rumours of far worse. And everyone had had enough, basically, and some members of the Convoy tooled up, just went for them, and that was that.'

Eavis had been supportive of Travellers since the Battle of Beanfield. From 1986 he had provided a set of fields for them to settle and stage their own free festival in parallel to his own, and he had proved adept and patient at negotiating with the Convoy, which when parked together at Glastonbury now numbered almost five hundred vehicles, and earned their trust. Joe Rush, who continued and continues to work with the Eavis family and Glastonbury every year it is held, witnessed the tact with which the festival's owner negotiated with the Convoy. 'Michael could see they were going to turn up anyway and gave money to this bloke called Spider, who was connected with all the Convoy lot, and let them all in at the back of the festival basically,' he told me.

In 1987 disturbances broke out between some of the Travellers and more hardened, organised drug dealers and the festival was cancelled for the following year, during which acid house took hold in the United Kingdom. Glastonbury festival returned in 1989 and for the following year, until it was once again abandoned in 1991. Upon its resumption in 1992, a newly constructed ten-foot fence surrounded the festival site. An exclusion zone had replaced the Travellers Field, and many members of the Convoy found themselves unable to gain access. Eavis continued to work with Travellers, several of whom were involved in the construction of the site, but there would be no repetition of the Convoy's festival and its seductive, unlicensed mix of ad hoc sound systems, drugs and unpredictability, which had allowed people to experience free parties within the safe space of the Vale of Avalon.

Ultramarine and Robert Wyatt, around the time of the recording of *United Kingdoms*, 1993. Left to right: Paul Hammond, Robert Wyatt, Ian Cooper. (Phil Nicholls)

14 : Acid House Pooh Corner

'I had to dance, to relieve myself of the whole of
western culture ... to see if there is such a thing
as truth I wanted it now. I wanted to experience it
I wanted it in this body in this lifetime, not some
other day some other time I wanted it now.'

Gabrielle Roth, sampled on Ultramarine, 'Stella'

A phenomenon that penetrated rural Britain, from the well-appointed farms of Buckinghamshire to the slate quarries of Bradford, was born in an underground cellar in south London. In the South East of England the momentum behind the new moral panic of acid house had flourished from the kernel of Shoom, a club held overnight on Saturdays at a gym in Southwark. From its opening night in December 1987 those attending Shoom experienced a powerful epiphany. For the first six months of the club these feelings were largely confined among its regular crowd, which consisted of three hundred people familiar to its promoters Jenni Rampling and her DJ husband Danny.

Among the Shoom audience were Andrew Weatherall, Terry Farley and Cymon Eckel; together they had started what became the first acid house lifestyle fanzine, *Boy's Own*. The modest publication documented the euphoria experienced by dancing on Ecstasy as it spread outwards from the initiates of Shoom across the strata of street culture.

At its inception in 1986 *Boy's Own* had concentrated on terrace style, record reviews, in-jokes and disparaging commentary on contemporary tastes from a character called Millwall, a football hooligan dog with notable prejudices.

The latter feature was written by Weatherall, who as a child had witnessed the first Windsor Free Festival, having been taken there by his parents on what he termed 'hippie safari'. The proximity of Windsor to the immaculately kept stretches of green space of its Great Park meant that in their youth he and Eckel, who both hailed from the Berkshire town, regularly found themselves in the outdoors. By the mid-1980s the pair's appetite for music and music-related pleasure-seeking was firmly established. 'We were out every weekend and two or three nights a week at gigs or parties before acid house,' Eckel told me. This desire for new experiences included the happenings at Mutoid Waste Company's Kings Cross warehouse, where in attendance were other notable figures of the forthcoming rave movement, including Alex Paterson of The Orb, whose brother was a member of the Company, and Phil Hartnoll of Orbital.

Eckel had first encountered Mutoid Waste Company at the Car Henge installation at Glastonbury the previous year, where the aura of unregulated behaviour was pronounced. The degree of open drug use in plain view and the energy of the black market economy in operation was a revelation to many present, including Eckel and Weatherall.

'It was as though every tent we'd walk past would have a sign scrawled together on cardboard advertising their wares. You could buy yellow or blue microdots, hash cakes and lines of speed. It felt as though everyone was retailing drugs out of their tents or vehicles,' Eckel continued. 'The overriding emotion was, "I can do what I want," and the excitement of seeing people being free, breaking rules, not worrying about anything, was an incredible experience that never left me.'

For Eckel the emotions Glastonbury stirred were enhanced by the intensity of attending Shoom, where profound friendships were forged as the first wave of Ecstasy washed through the small clientele. The regularity of the club ensured those undergoing the experience grew evangelical about the possibilities that music, Ecstasy and togetherness might realise in the near future; the potential for an openness in which people concentrated on the positive aspects in one another was now evident at the end of a decade that had promoted individualism. But as he and his friends' personalities started to undergo this transformation, Eckel suffered a tragedy.

'I had an industrial accident on the fifth of May 1988,' he told me. 'Right in the supernova of Shoom I cut my fingers off and was sent to a specialist hospital in East Grinstead.'

The quiet town in West Sussex would develop an almost mystical significance for Eckel in the ensuing year. Upon admission into a ward for acute hand injuries he made the acquaintance of 'an anarcho-hippie type, called Peter'. The two men bonded through their shared tastes in music and drugs; to such an extent they began stockpiling their four-hourly medication in order to self-administer their prescription in one substantial, late-night dose. 'We'd double-drop our valiums and they gave us a liquid paracetamol developed in the Second World War for severe burns.'

Undeterred by his injuries, Eckel lost none of his zeal for acid house or his belief in the potential for a communal understanding. In hospital, his new friend Peter received a regular set of visitors, including the owner of a rural recording studio, with whom Eckel discussed the possibility of hosting an outdoors acid house party, to which the studio owner proved amenable. 'He didn't really charge us anything,' Eckel continued, 'and it was a five-bedroom house with a large barn at the bottom where he had his studio.'

Once discharged from hospital Eckel began organising the event. The few hundred tickets were sold to members and associates of the *Boy's Own* network. The guests arrived on coaches from London that had been specifically chartered for the party, which according to many in attendance was the very first outdoor rave in Britain, in the early autumn of 1988.

'None of us at that period did anything purposefully or consciously,' Eckel said. 'We went with the emotion of the time. It was a very simple resolution: "I found a great place, he's got a sound system there, he's up for it, can you believe it, we can have an all-night party. Let's hope it doesn't rain." It caused a little bit of tension because it was on a Saturday night and Shoom was still running. But by then, people felt that if you're flying on Ecstasy or acid you want to be out in the open. You need a bit of space.'

The success of the first party inspired Eckel to consider repeating the event, but as late summer turned to autumn, then winter, the need to find a suitable location felt less urgent. No longer merely a fanzine, *Boy's Own* now had a record label and a growing reputation, one sufficiently large within the acid house underground that Eckel,

Farley and Weatherall sensed it would only be a matter of time before the perfect site for the next party would reveal itself. Then, as Eckel recalled, 'A guy who owned a clothes shop in Windsor said, "You've got to go and meet such-and-such. He does paintball, he rents fields and forests, so he's quite in with the farmers in Sussex."'

Over the course of the ensuing three or four years, as the popularity of acid house grew exponentially, rave events in rural areas would be presented in the media as intrusive and illegal and as the latest threat to the sustained peace of the countryside. As Eckel's experiment in promoting an outdoor party demonstrated, many landowners were happy to participate in the culture's illegal business practices by leasing a site to promoters and party organisers. This was hardly surprising. Such cash-in-hand, fly-by-night deals were second nature to anyone earning a living in agriculture, for whom a new style of overnight parties in isolated areas presented further opportunity.

The Sussex location suggested to Eckel was close to East Grinstead. He duly found himself returning to the town where he had been hospitalised, to negotiate with the owner of an ad hoc paintballing business. 'He had one leg that he'd lost in a motorcycle accident and he was a really effervescent character. We drove through East Grinstead, over the hill, and then ended up at a magical field opposite Weir Wood Reservoir. I asked him, "Do you think I can do a party here, really?" and he said, "Yeah, yeah." And we agreed a deal, and the deal for him was that he would do the barbecue.' Any doubts Eckel felt about the formality of the arrangements he had made were absolved by the beauty and seclusion of the site.

'There was a field at the top of a hill where everybody parked. Then you walked through a dingly dell, down a descending passageway that was entirely green, covered in leaves, and came out into a field in a concave shape that sloped down to the water's edge of Weir Wood Reservoir.'

There Eckel erected two traditional canvas marquees replete with woven guy ropes and wooden fastenings; into one he installed a dance floor, sound system and lighting rig; into the other, a bar. The production of the rave took place during a day Eckel remembered as 'baking hot'.

Over the course of the party Eckel would visit the local filling station five times for fuel for the generators that supplied power to the PA and lights. On each occasion he would fill a set of industrial petrol tanks to capacity, only to have to return a few hours later to repeat the process.

'The generators were actually hand-cranked by me, all night, taking Ecstasy. They were in their own little straw enclosure we'd built. As soon as we put the sound system up we constructed sound barriers with big circular hay bales and made a curved wall from them, which went up behind the speakers. Not that it actually did anything, because there's no density in hay.'

The preparation, attention to detail and acquisition of such a unique location would be rewarded in a manner the *Boy's Own* organisers or their cognoscenti could not have anticipated. After several hours of dancing through the night, dawn broke on the Weir Wood Reservoir water at five o'clock to reveal a deep layer of mist on its surface. The change in conditions provided the tiring revellers with a new source of energy as the beauty of the surroundings were revealed in the new morning sunlight.

'There was this moment when the sun rose over the water,' Eckel continued. 'Everyone had been there, dancing through the night, and then it was like, "Nature!" Everybody reconnected with the setting at sun-up, and I could feel this energy. I could see as well as hear the hum spreading across everyone.' The hum of a summer sunrise, the sound of insect activity in the grass following the dawn chorus had been present in its human form at Stonehenge, Glastonbury Tor and wherever anyone had consciously made the decision to witness a new day begin. While taking their first dose of MDMA on Ibiza two years earlier, the organisers of Shoom and their friends had experienced a powerful first light epiphany. They had founded the London club on the strength of their experiences on the Spanish island, and now Eckel, Weatherall and their friends had created a small, perfectly judged Albion Ibiza.

Eckel's *Boy's Own* partner Terry Farley would later talk of seeing a flock of geese descend from the sky to make a perfect landing at the water's edge. And here in the early hours of a perfect English summer's day five hundred people sitting, or collapsed, on hay bales, grew energised by the dawn and looked out onto the water of Weir Wood Reservoir that borders Ashdown Forest, the location that inspired A. A. Milne's '100 Aker Wood', and the haven Eckel and his friends had created was experienced by all those present as their private Acid House Pooh Corner. Their serenity was periodically interrupted by the arrival of a pantomime cow. The costume was worn by Barry Mooncult of the band Flowered Up, who had hired it especially for the occasion. Other revellers then attempted to climb a ladder that led only to morning-fresh air.

The smiles and evident happiness in the few pictures that exist of the East Grinstead rave may have been chemically enhanced, but the sense of bucolic reverie is undeniable. Several people who were present had rarely, if ever, encountered such a setting before. The social group that *Boy's Own* introduced to the countryside for twenty-four hours was one seldom encountered in rural Britain: people open about their chosen sexual orientation, people of colour and people who earned their living in new creative fields that had yet to be clearly defined; all of whom exhibited the vigour of youth and had joined together at an unlicensed event without doormen, security or regulated permissions. The unwritten behavioural codes of acid house that had been established at Shoom were enough to ensure the party would be a success.

Although the *Boy's Own* party was exceptionally low key, the authorities had become familiar and in some cases helped facilitate a tabloid Acid House Scare. Eckel received visits from the local force throughout the evening: 'The police came down about three or four times. Our explanation was that it was a magazine launch party, but they put me through it. "Where's the tickets? You haven't numbered the tickets; these are going to be easy to counterfeit. Are there any drugs here?"

'After the party finished at about eight o'clock in the morning I finally got the majority of people off site and at that point they almost ran me out of town. As I got in my car with my friend Steve Mayes and my girlfriend Lisa, we drove out, and a police car followed me out of the county. They just wanted to see me leave their patch and then I was no longer their problem.'

The police would find their resources increasingly stretched throughout 1989 as larger raves were staged throughout the South East and the North West of England. Almost simultaneously with the *Boy's Own* party at East Grinstead, the Sunrise company started organising large outdoor raves in the 'English Countryside 20 miles from Central London', as it stated on its flyers. Sunrise sold tickets and gave details of their party's locations through the innovative use of an anonymous phone bank that allowed callers to hear the relevant information for a limited period of time. This system enabled them to produce events on a far larger scale than *Boy's Own*, but to Eckel and his friends, whose evangelical, if not spiritual, commitment to the possibilities of Ecstasy and dance that had been initiated at Shoom, such extravagances represented a break with the connection they had felt under the drug's influence.

'Some people do say "Boys' Own wankers were elitist" – we were never, ever trying to be elitist; we just didn't want to do three, five, ten thousand-people parties. Boys' Own was never a career. The one Orbital party I tried, the police stopped us. And then I went to Beckton Gasworks, which was one of the original Sunrises, but on the whole my close friends and I shunned it.'

Such subtle shifts in perception and experience are fundamental to any youth culture. The entrepreneurial flair demonstrated by the organisers of Sunrise, and other M25 Orbital parties that followed, provided its customers with an experience of Acid House on a far greater scale than that of Shoom. For some who had been present at the club these larger events were redolent of an opportunism that indicated acid house had begun the inevitable process of commercialism.

'As soon as the Orbital raves started, it was done,' Eckel said. 'Corruption creeps in and suddenly parties had a value. Then promoters in London realised, "This is incredible, look at the amount of people converting overnight, let's do a party for five thousand," and that was complete anathema to the whole idea of what it was. You can't deny those people having a moment of togetherness, but once you go up to that scale, there's too much money for something to be innocent.'

For Eckel and his associates the purity of the acid house experience had culminated in staring at the early morning geese in a quiet patch of rural Sussex. The event they held was a forerunner, by almost twenty years, of the boutique festival, where audiences immerse themselves in music and well-appointed surroundings, with details such as wooden tent pegs, hay bales and the romanticism of open skies and weathered awnings, and do so at no little cost. The sense of being outdoors together in the communal experience *Boy's Own* had created at East Grinstead was born of a wonder they and their friends had felt at the effects of Ecstasy and the desire to concentrate its potential in the most pleasant situation imaginable.

'I remember my first night at Shoom,' Eckel recalled, 'going back to someone's house and lying there thinking, "Wow, this is incredible, imagine what you can do with this energy and this power," and I was thinking along a sort of socio-political level, but it soon became very apparent that there wasn't going to be socio-political level. There was a social revolution, but it had no politics really applied to it.'

Eckel shared one final thought with me. 'It was a soft revolution,' he said. 'It was a soft revolution, wasn't it?'

The extent to which rave and free party culture had penetrated the national psyche is evident during the opening track on *Adventures Beyond the Ultraworld*, the debut album by The Orb, released in 1991. The voice of the Radio 4 presenter John Waite introduces a documentary on the new phenomena then taking place under the night skies of rural Britain: 'Over the past few years, to the traditional sounds of an English summer, the droning of lawnmowers, the smack of leather on willow, has been added a new noise . . .'

The sample provided the intro for 'Little Fluffy Clouds', The Orb's breakthrough hit, and a song that established the genre of ambient house and the popularity of music associated with dancing. There had been no rave tunes for *Boy's Own* to play at East Grinstead, or Shoom, where Weatherall frequently included tracks by Penguin Cafe Orchestra in his set, but now music tailor made for the purpose of raving outdoors was filtering into the mainstream.

A sample from the same Radio 4 documentary appears on the track 'Pansy' by the band Ultramarine. A learned voice states those participating in the events are seekers 'looking for spiritual reasons, they're looking for something more than this world can offer'. The song is taken from the album *Every Man and Woman Is a Star*, one of the most distinctive electronic records of the era, released during the euphoric mid-point between the increased popularity of raves and its repudiation at Castlemorton.

The duo of Paul Hammond and Ian Cooper that comprised

Ultramarine's core membership had been friends since their boyhood in semi-rural Maldon in Essex. The name Ultramarine was taken from the title of the one album recorded by their earlier group, A Primary Industry, whose late 1980s sound had been simultaneously industrial and ethereal. In contrast Ultramarine's debut album *Folk* made use of accordion, handclaps and acoustic instruments that Hammond and Cooper paired with rhythm loops. *Folk* was released on Les Disques du Crépuscule, a Belgian label based in Brussels where Hammond briefly worked, which had a reputation for esoteric, frequently instrumental records housed in sophisticated artwork suggestive of the ennui, as well as the bonhomie, of pavement cafes.

The recording sessions for the duo's next record *Every Man and Woman Is a Star* started in a Brussels studio. Rather than these urban surroundings, the album was informed by the availability of new technology, which provided Hammond and Cooper with the means to capture longer and more complex samples and sequence them in a manner that allowed them to become part of the duo's writing process.

As source material Hammond and Cooper frequently chose records by the Canterbury groups of the early 1970s, music with a distinct, if sometimes obscure air of Englishness: Soft Machine, Caravan and Kevin Ayers and The Whole World. These groups had placed an emphasis on musicianship that ensured their albums were rich in samples of well-played instrumental breaks and phrases. There was an additional reason for using the Canterbury groups as source material; if found in a second-hand record shop their releases were rarely expensive. The esoteric and somewhat whimsical albums made by these artists were almost entirely out of favour in 1991.

Ultramarine blue is suggestive of a calm, meditative sky. The optimism heard in much of the new decade's music was also an influence on the duo. Hammond and Cooper found inspiration in the studio innovations of the hip hop trio De La Soul and their producer Prince Paul on *3 Feet High and Rising*, and in the positive energy expressed in *Club Classics Vol. One* by Soul II Soul. Where Prince Paul had included a snippet of Otis Redding whistling on De La Soul's 'Eye Know', Hammond and Cooper were inspired to similarly introduce a bar of Robert Wyatt's distinctive scat singing on the *Every Man and Woman Is a Star* track 'Saratoga'. The duo had determined that the album should be a standalone piece of work, and chose to ignore the then prevailing trend in electronic music of collecting together a series of previously released 12-inch singles. This decision, along with their approach in the studio, combining analogue instruments with the technology of a sampler, proved inventive and would later become formalised over the course of the decade into the genre of electronica.

On the back sleeve of *Every Man and Woman Is a Star* Cooper and Hammond included a dedication to Dewey Bunnell, the lead singer of the soft-rock trio America, who had achieved significant success in the early 1970s with their songs 'A Horse with No Name' and 'Ventura Highway'. The dedication was accompanied by a fictitious anecdote about Ultramarine visiting the singer in rural Arkansas. While they were in his presence Bunnell had imparted to Cooper and Hammond some rough-hewn advice concerning a canoe trip as a metaphor for mental travel and the essential truth that there is 'music for the body *and* for the mind'.

Whatever the motive for including such flights of fancy, the sleeve notes established *Every Man and Woman Is a Star* as a record that might be a suitable soundtrack to inner journeys. This was despite Hammond and Cooper having never attended a rave and eschewing Ecstasy or other stimulants, particularly in the recording studio. Such behaviour came as a shock to the many listeners who found themselves immersed in the album's glistening currents and the seemingly expertly sequenced songs of high summer airiness.

Every Man and Woman Is a Star opens with a sample, the voice of a Native American elder discussing 'the same ceremony' that took place 'every year' at a location 'up in the mountains', which was attended by 'everyone from miles around . . . cousins, aunts, uncles and the kids, grandmothers, grandfathers, everyone,' and the listener is positioned in a head space of familiarity and discovery – the word which Hammond and Cooper used as the title of the piece.

The lightness of the album's sound is partly due to the duo's wish to make a listening album rather than concentrate on the heavy bass line and breakbeat dynamics of rave. Their choice of spoken word samples that feature voices imparting quasi-mystical life lessons adds to the atmosphere of outdoor consciousness-raising and evokes the intensity of daybreak conversations in sun-dappled fields.

On the track 'Stella', a female American voice asserts her need to dance: 'I had to dance, to relieve myself of the whole of western culture . . . to see if there is such a thing as truth I wanted it now. I wanted to experience it I wanted it in this body in this lifetime, not some other day some other time I wanted it now.'

The voice belonged to Gabrielle Roth, a shamanic dance teacher and therapist who had practised at the Esalen Institute at Big Sur. Hammond and Cooper had recorded her appearance on *The New Age*, a Channel 4 round table discussion programme, and subsequently approached Roth about using parts of her contribution. In combination with the lightly disorientating music to which the duo set her voice, the insistency and authority of her words are a perfect audio replication of the overwhelming now of the high being experienced by increasing numbers of people in the first years of the decade. The ethos of self-discovery-through-dance Roth espoused is echoed in several of the album's song titles: 'Gravity', 'Lights in My Brain', 'Skyclad'; although observers of rave culture not participants, Hammond and Cooper had intended to make a record that filtered the positivity and communal energy of the times.

Throughout the creation of *Every Man and Woman Is a Star* Hammond and Cooper felt as though the recording process had developed a momentum over which they had only partial control. 'Lights in My Brain' contains one of the record's most delicate and shimmering melodies. Its vocal sample is taken from 'Lullabye Letter', a track on Soft Machine's self-titled debut album. The phrase evokes perfectly the sensation of dancing outdoors at night, either under a lighting rig or with eyes shut underneath the stars.

The album concludes with 'Skyclad' and a voice repeating, 'We were just into a space trip.' The music is influenced by the sleek, processed beat of Detroit techno and shares the genre's same sense of purpose and momentum. With the addition of echoing woodwind the track represents a very English form of electronic *motorik*, one that exchanges the interstates around Detroit for the undulations of an empty and familiar rural A road at night. This was the setting in which many listeners first encountered the charms of *Every Man and Woman Is a Star* – on the journey home from a rural rave. To some the use of the phrase 'British Summertime' as a song title may have suggested the record was a concept album about the new experiences they were having. Few records have ever captured the dewy freshness and optimism of a new culture enfolding, or of a new summer's day.

On their following album, *United Kingdoms*, Ultramarine consciously decided to make an overtly English record that paid homage to the Canterbury music of the early 1970s and to explore a strain of national history found in forgotten protest songs. Now signed to a major label, Cooper and Hammond spent part of their recording advance on travelling to Majorca, where in the village of Deià, the bohemian colony founded and watched over by Robert Graves, they hoped to encounter Kevin Ayers, the charismatic singer-songwriter whose disregard for the record industry and his personal health ensured his considerable talents remained under-appreciated. A portrait of Ayers had previously graced the cover of Ultramarine's double A-side single 'Weird Gear', the lyrics of which included verses of Ayers' song 'Butterfly Dance'. On the reverse, the song 'British Summertime' was illustrated by a photograph of a circle of people joining hands as they danced around Stonehenge.

Although Hammond and Cooper were unable to locate Ayers in Deià, the duo ran into June Campbell Cramer or Lady June, the heiress, painter and bohemian and intimate of Soft Machine, of which Ayers had been a founding member. His former band-mate Robert Wyatt appears twice on *United Kingdoms*. Unlike on *Every Man and Woman Is a Star* where his distinctive voice was sampled, Hammond and Cooper visited Wyatt at his home in Lincolnshire and recorded his performances, which are among his best of the decade, at a nearby studio the singer used regularly.

The lead melody on 'Kingdom', the first song on which Wyatt appears, is played on the flute by the multi-instrumentalist Jimmy Hastings, another Canterbury alumnus who Ultramarine had tracked down, and who had been a regular presence on 1970s albums by Caravan and Soft Machine. 'Kingdom' is adapted from a Chartist song that Hammond had discovered through the English Folk Dance and Song Society. He had been inspired to visit Cecil Sharp House by listening to the album *John Barleycorn Must Die* by Traffic and having been made aware of their working method of scouring the manuscripts in the library there for suitable traditional songs to cover. Within a decade folk music would undergo a significant revival and several artists would continue this tradition of visiting the library at Cecil Sharp House to seek inspiration. For Hammond and Cooper to make this pilgrimage in 1991 and marry their discoveries with technology was as innovative as it was anachronistic.

Their choice of material for Wyatt could not have been more apposite. The lyrics lament the position of working people and were adapted by the duo to include a reference to the Poll Tax:

We're low – we're low – mere rabble, we know / But, at
our plastic power / The mould at the lording's feet will
grow / Into palace and church and tower / Then prostrate
fall – in the rich man's hall / And cringe at the rich man's
door / We're not too low to build the wall / But too low
to tread the floor . . .
And whenever he lacks – upon our backs / Fresh loads
he designs to lay / We're far too low to vote the tax / But
not too low to pay.

The duo had prepared the backing track for Wyatt's distinctive
vocal range especially. This remarkable voice, which had so often
been used to lament iniquity and injustice, was heard in what was
then one of the few examples within electronic music of a protest
song.

In the accompanying video, filmed in Lincolnshire near Wyatt's
home, the duo and some friends are dressed as medieval peasants,
of a sort, with Wyatt in the role of their liege. In the obligatory
sun-dappled footage that accompanied dance music promos of
the time, a river flows brightly and trees shine in the morning sun.
Although the video is now the most dated aspect of their collaboration, it evokes the innocence of its age. 'Happy Land', the second
song that Wyatt sings, was a Victorian song which Hammond and
Cooper once more adapted for their age:

Happy land! happy land! Thy fame resounds shore to shore
Happy land! where 'tis a crime, they tell us, to be poor.

If you shelter cannot find, of you they'll soon take care:
Most likely send you to grind wind – For sleeping in the
air.
Happy land! happy land! To praise thee, who will cease?
To guard us, pray, now ain't we got a precious New
Police? A passport we shall soon require, which by them
must be scanned, If we to take a walk desire – Oh, ain't
this happy land?

The partnership between Ultramarine and Robert Wyatt produced a contemporary folk music as languid and sophisticated as its
Canterbury forbears. It now has an additional sense of melancholy,
as the age of communal raving and re-appropriating the countryside
was drawing to a prompt end. After one final gathering, punitive
changes to the law and to policing would once again reconfigure the
country's relationship to its land.

The banks of Loch Lomond, site of the Pure summer solstice rave, 1991–92.

15 : In a Beautiful Place out in the Country

For the first three years of the 1980s Inglestone Common in South Gloucestershire had been a regular destination on the free festival circuit. In 1989 the Common was reintroduced as the venue for the Avon Free Festival, a gathering that took place at an agreed site in the county across the final weekend of May. This was a date that coincided with the month's second bank holiday, traditionally a time of early summer debauchery in Britain; the location was usually confirmed mere hours before the festival began. The free festivals of the 1980s had now been transformed and, in the view of many participants, revived as free parties a decade later. The Avon Free Festival was again held at Inglestone Common in 1990, although a significantly larger police presence there that year ensured a new site would be needed for the festival in 1991, when Sodbury Common, near Chipping Sodbury, was chosen as a suitable destination. That year the Avon Free Festival was attended by an estimated fifteen thousand people and demonstrated the free party version of raving was capable of attracting as many numbers as its legal, commercial equivalent.

With the gradual conversion of free festivals from an environment where music was provided by bands playing live, to parties hosted by sound systems, their popularity had increased substantially. The Avon Free Festival of 1990 had attracted sufficiently large numbers for the Avon and Somerset Police to launch an ongoing surveillance and intelligence-gathering procedure known as Operation Nomad. During the 1991 festival the force executed a stop and search policy on the main roads leading to Sodbury Common that resulted in over fifty arrests during the course of the weekend.

By the spring of 1992 the various police forces of the West Country and South West had anticipated and planned for an event on a similar scale to take place over that year's second May Bank Holiday weekend. The peripatetic nature of the Avon Free Festival meant that the police's ability to prohibit the party from taking place was limited; an injunction cannot be granted for an event whose location or date is unknown. Instead consecutive forces deployed the similar tactic of requesting that anyone they suspected of living like Travellers, or of being prospective free party-goers, disperse from their respective perimeters. The result was a mass herding operation conducted across the West and South West of Britain, which enabled each of the relevant constabularies to clear its county lines of potential troublemakers. By the Thursday of the bank holiday weekend, with the weather set fair, vehicles had started to gather at Castlemorton Common in Worcestershire in significant numbers. The constant flow of Travellers and ravers that had been directed away from various rural counties added to the sense of a critical mass developing at the foot of the Malvern Hills. Opinion is divided as to whether Castlemorton had previously been agreed as the site for that weekend's festival by the owners of the various sound systems and anyone else involved in making such a decision, or whether the police had concluded the expansive common in Worcestershire was of a sufficiently large scale to accommodate the thousands of people they had suspected as potential attendees of the Avon Free Festival. If the latter was the reason that year's festival was staged at Castlemorton, it was due to the encouragement of local authorities, MPs and police chiefs that tens of thousands travelled towards a destination set securely in the heart of Middle England.

Whichever argument is to be trusted, throughout the following week the largest illegal party ever witnessed in Britain took place. Attendance is estimated to have been between twenty-five and forty thousand people, with a concentration of numbers over the long weekend. That such a high volume of party-goers decided to travel to Castlemorton is unsurprising as the festival received ongoing coverage on local news programmes throughout the bank holiday. These reports functioned as an impromptu advertisement for anyone looking forward to spending the long weekend in a hedonistic fashion. The fact that the Glastonbury festival had not taken place the previous year ensured that, during a fine weekend in late May, which often signals the arrival of summer, a significant number of people in the country were prepared to vigorously enjoy themselves.

The festival had attracted all the major autonomous sound systems. Each set up equipment in their own dedicated space; it was probably the one and only occasion when Adrenalin, DiY, Spiral Tribe, Techno Travellers, Bedlam, Circus Warp and others gathered together under the same sky to broadcast their hardcore version of techno. The music was a distant but relentless audio backdrop to the television news bulletins, which by the Saturday all included interviews with the police.

Senior officers were interviewed on their respective local channels (a feature on Television South West charmingly referred to the mass illegal rave as a 'pop concert'; the station would lose its broadcast franchise by the end of the year). In each instance they rehearsed the lack of options available to them to safeguard the public: the policing of such a large amount of people required an amount of officers unavailable to them; Castlemorton was common rather than private land; it was uncertain that the existing bye-laws concerning congregation or noise pollution could be applied to the type of event into which the free festival had developed; as they were unable to prove those in attendance were residing at the site, the regulatory powers available to the police were redundant.

What was also doubtless a matter of serious, if unspoken, concern to the police was the ability of those gathered at the free festival to self-govern. The footage of harried residents of the nearby village and frustrated MPs and other dignitaries looking out over the mass of trucks, buses, tents, people and dogs supported the narrative that the organisers and festivalgoers had lost control of events. The air quality around the site had also become noticeably different. Although seasoned Travellers always carried a shovel with which to attend to their personal needs, many of the weekend ravers present were less prepared.

Once the Castlemorton Festival had reached its natural conclusion, with the police having made a scant fifty arrests, elements of the national media immediately determined that the case for new legislation against free festivals, convoys and raves had rarely been clearer. Their editorials amplified the voices in Parliament speaking in favour of altering the law to make sure an event such as Castlemorton could never be repeated. The Home Secretary Michael Howard, who was of a more heavy-handed temperament than his predecessor Douglas Hurd and who had held the position for little more than a year, undertook the process of preparing the Criminal Justice and Public Order Act. In less than two years after Castlemorton, Parliament passed the Act now widely perceived to be one of the most draconian pieces of legislation placed before the House.

At the time of its approval, the 'anti rave clauses' featured in the Act drew the most significant attention. The ramifications of the Act have outlived the phenomena of raves and free parties. They include the criminalisation and suppression of non-violent protest, the creation of a police DNA database that held information about members of the public who had never committed a criminal offence, and the introduction of 'precautionary' arrests.

Part V of the Bill was titled 'Public Order: Collective Trespass or Nuisance on Land'. It contained seven sections (61–7), each with numerous subsections and clauses, relating to 'Powers to remove persons attending or preparing for a rave', which was defined as a 'gathering of more than 100 people'.

Due to its clumsy legalese and the awkward, if not pompous manner with which the government had struggled in its attempt to define 'music', one particular piece of text in Section 63 grew into a *cause célèbre.* Subsection 1 clause b stated that music 'includes sounds wholly or predominantly characterised by the emission of a succession of repetitive beats'. Thus the Home Office equated the sound of an illegal rave with that of an Evangelical Christian Service in which members of the congregation were encouraged to clap and sing along.

While that clause became a subject of ridicule and helped galvanise widespread opposition to the Bill, Section 63 included over ten subsections replete with qualifiers and clauses that suggested a need on the part of the government to preclude any form of disturbance, regardless of type. One of the most disturbing sections stated: (8) A constable in uniform who reasonably suspects that a person is committing an offence under this section may arrest him without a warrant. To widespread surprise the Bill had passed its final reading unopposed by the Labour Shadow Home Secretary, Tony Blair.

A number of free parties were staged in protest against the Bill, including a mass rally at Hyde Park that led to confrontations between police and public. Once the Bill had been approved, the new laws of Section 63 were enacted and over the ensuing three or four years the free party movement and Convoy were substantially reduced in scale.

The changes forced upon this community were hard to endure and the comedown that followed was severe. Life as part of the Convoy had always been basic, austere and fraught with difficulties. It had nevertheless afforded a genuine sense of freedom and an alternative to the difficult conditions from which many participating in the Traveller life had escaped. An intense experience of liberty, amplified by dancing to music in open spaces while on drugs such as MDMA and LSD, was a defining characteristic of free parties, and some of those no longer able to achieve such profound highs sought solace in the hopelessness of harder drugs.

The fact that government had passed a law that specifically addressed the legality of raves was the subject of much outcry in the music and entertainment media. In these accounts the Bill was regularly abbreviated to the Criminal Justice Bill or CJB, which overshadowed and underestimated the full significance of other new laws the Act implemented. The full title, Criminal Justice and Public Order Act 1994, gave a better illustration of the regressive nature of much of the legislation. Within the same Section that addressed the culture of raves were contained a number of changes to the legal definition of trespass, including a highly symbolic offence of 'Aggravated Trespass'.

Anyone suspected of this new crime could face arrest and, if convicted, a prison sentence of three months. Under the previous law trespass had been considered a civil, never a criminal offence. Those accused might now be forcibly removed by a landowner or a person in a position of responsibility such as a gamekeeper and appear before the magistrate, or even a judge as Benny Rothman and his friends had done sixty years earlier, after walking up Kinder Scout. The new definition of trespass as set out in the 1994 Public Order Act was now a matter for the police:

> Trespass(ing) on land in the open air and, in relation to
> any lawful activity which persons are engaging in or are
> about to engage in on that or adjoining land in the open
> air, does there anything which is intended by him to have
> the effect (a) of intimidating those persons or any of

them so as to deter them or any of them from engaging in that activity, (b) of obstructing that activity, or (c) of disrupting that activity.

Legal experts assumed part of the motivation for this change in definition was to criminalise the practice of hunt sabotage. The first arrests made under the new law in November 1994 were duly three saboteurs, who intended to disrupt a meet in Northamptonshire.

Nevertheless, within weeks of the law passing into the statute book the new Public Order section was being enacted in a subtler, perhaps less anticipated manner.

Members of the Ramblers Association reported encountering new signs appearing on familiar footpaths. In the Scottish Highlands a group of walkers were met with a notice reading: 'Keep Out. Deer stalking in progress. You may be arrested under the Criminal Justice Act.'

The Head of the Mountaineering Council of Scotland made public his concerns that landowners were interpreting the law as they saw fit. 'Anyone could be charged with this offence if a landowner believes they have affected some estate activity, whether intentionally or not.'

In addition Kate Ashbrook, the chair of the Ramblers' Association and a lifelong campaigner for access, was leading a group across the Pennines when she found their route obstructed by barbed wire and notices stating 'Keep Out'. The Ramblers' Association raised its concerns, citing the example that by walking along a field as sheep were being rounded up they could be accused of disrupting a lawful action, without any prior knowledge or intention of doing so. The acts of taking photographs of the countryside, singing, even birdwatching all risked selective legal interpretation. Common sense largely prevailed.

What was certain was authority once more resided with landowners. In the intervening years between the mass trespass of 1932 and the passing of the Criminal Justice and Public Order Act 1994 a new relationship between the people of a country and its land had been established. Now it had reached its conclusion.

During those years, rural Britain witnessed exceptional change and also a significant change in its use. Attempts were made at new methods of farming, of living from or simply existing on the land. Few were entirely successful but the energy and spirit in which they were undertaken affected the public's consciousness of and connection to the landscape. The few areas of Britain under national ownership witnessed an alteration in our perception and use of natural spaces; of how we might preserve their beauty while recognising them as our own.

So little of the United Kingdom is open land. Unless one is fortunate, to go in search of nature is to seek a form of permission or to abide by a designated set of behaviours. A people are nothing without the ability to congregate together in the outdoors, under the sky. In the twentieth century this need was demonstrated in terms of survival, protest, hedonism and the search for personal freedom. And where people congregate there is invariably music. Whenever the landscape acquiesced to these demands and desires, its custodians proved more resistant. In contrast, the larks overhead ascended in their approval.

To the uninitiated the distance between the city centre of Glasgow and the banks of Loch Lomond is almost unnerving. By car the journey lasts less than an hour; in light traffic it can be made in forty-five minutes. In comparison to most British cities there is little gradation in the built environment. Instead there is a dizzying sensation of transportation, as the metropolitan energy of the city is exchanged for the expansive wilderness of the Loch Lomond and The Trossachs National Park. These are two distinct worlds, but travelling between them the thought occurs that their proximity sustains the independence and authority of each.

Once past the small town of Balloch at the southern end of Loch Lomond the visitor can choose to drive along its twenty-two miles on either the east or west bank. A few miles north, on the western side, is an inconspicuous set of buildings that constitute the outdoor premises of a University of Glasgow research faculty. The small compound includes a beach, from where there is an expansive view of the loch including the looming presence of Ben Lomond on its eastern bank.

It was on this secluded beach that Keith McIvor, the DJ and promoter of Pure, the Edinburgh club night, held a secret rave on the summer solstice of 1991.

McIvor, who would go on to have a career as an international DJ and found the highly influential Optimo club in Glasgow, had been offered the location by a friend whose father worked at the university and from whom he had surreptitiously borrowed a key to the gates of the research faculty. Two or three hundred people attended the rave and danced as the gentle tide rippled on the small beach and the sun rose over Ben Lomond in the distance. McIvor once described the moment of the early hours on this solstice morning to me as 'quite shamanic'.

Pure was the first club in Scotland to play techno. The club's sound and lighting systems were unusually powerful and created an intense environment for the audience, which included a regular weekly coach party from Glasgow. The club-goers were members of the incipient rave community in Central Scotland. Free parties were held at similar beach locations to Loch Lomond, or in abandoned farm buildings in the Pentland Hills south of Edinburgh and, notably, in a disused quarry in the city's well-appointed area of Blackford. Among the weekly audience at Pure were two brothers, Michael Sandison and Marcus Eoin, who like McIvor hailed from the village of Balerno in the Edinburgh suburbs.

For several years during this era of raves, parties and the weekly Pure night, Sandison and Eoin experimented with tapes and treated recordings before releasing their debut twelve-inch 'Twoism' as Boards of Canada in 1994.

It is uncertain whether the brothers were in attendance at the Pure raves held over the summer solstice on the banks of Loch Lomond, although the material on their debut album *Music Has the Right to Children* is suggestive of a similar environment; where the shared experience of music in a rural setting is had under the influence of the landscape as well as stimulants. Upon its release in 1998 the consistently slower pace of *Music Has the Right to Children* represented a departure from the prevailing currents in electronic music. Since its development in the late 1980s electronic music had maintained a trajectory towards the future. Its momentum was upheld by the increase in tempo registered by each progressive micro-shift in the genre. By the middle of the 1990s the accelerated pace of drum and bass and Gabber, the latter a style especially popular in Scotland, had condensed music and rhythm into a relentless propulsion.

The sense of entering a hermetic space for the course of *Music Has the Right to Children*'s hour-long duration was further enhanced by the introduction of an element that had been rarely been a presence within the genre: the past. The cover of the record is a family portrait, which in its backdrop and composition suggests a holiday photograph. The cut of the clothes place the picture in the 1970s, but the other hallmarks of age and wear appear more artificial. The faces in the photograph have been digitally erased and in contrast to the sepia tones associated with faded Kodachrome prints the colouration is a greenish turquoise.

The seventeen tracks on the album vary in length; a handful last for over six minutes, while seven pieces are of roughly a minute's duration. Several of the shorter tracks, notably the opener, 'Wildlife Analysis', 'Kaini Industries' and 'Olson', contain the album's prettiest melodies. These have echoes of the music used in public information or documentary films from the era of the album's cover artwork. The duo took their name from the National Film Board of Canada, and their childhood recollections of watching the company's nature documentaries informed their music's aesthetic. Reflecting on these experiences from the past was also presumably what led Sandison and Eoin to include the children's voices that are heard with varying degrees of clarity throughout the album. Much of *Music Has the Right to Children* is the sound of, if not memories, then the more subtle, uncontrollable impulses by which memory works.

The past is also physically present in the sound of the album. The duo had amassed a large personal library of cassettes that contained recordings from television and other sources with which they had experimented since their inception. The average fidelity of these recordings and the passage of time had given them an aural patina similar to the effects of colouration suggested by the album's artwork. Sandison and Eoin mixed short passages of voices, incidental music and celluloid ambience from their tape archive into their own recordings. These snatched fragments of laughter from long ago, adrift in the fog of simple, childhood melodies, contribute greatly to the record's atmosphere of disconcerting numbness.

A recording of wind that runs throughout 'Triangles & Rhombuses' is one of the most audible examples of the influence of the natural world on this album, echoed in song titles such as 'Wildlife Analysis', 'An Eagle in Your Mind' and 'Turquoise Hexagon Sun'. The latter is a name the duo used for their home studio in the Pentland Hills. It is also a vivid description of how the first light of morning might look during a shamanic rave in rural Scotland.

Standing on the small shore next to the University of Glasgow premises where McIvor and his friends had danced at the start of that decade, it is easy to imagine the landscape imprinting itself on the disorientated minds that witnessed the solstice here together. There are eagles in the sky, and once the generators had been switched off in the morning and the music had ended, the hypnotic sound of the tide must have sounded calm and powerful.

Music Has the Right to Children was released near the end of a century. Through word of mouth the record found a large constituency beyond electronic music purists; its disconcerting combination of reflection and psychological intensity registered with the times. For a listener in a certain mood, the reflective ambience, ghostly voices and the presence of the outdoors in the music represented an elegy for the rave years.

The symbolism of a new century provided the opportunity for an evaluation of the manner in which the British landscape should be managed. A repurposing of the Common Agricultural Policy was announced for the end of the millennium. From 1999 farmers were increasingly paid more for the stewardship of the land than for their produce, stock or harvest. The subsidies they received were assigned around environmental needs and measures, as the effects of a fifty-year preoccupation with intensive farming became visible in a topography denuded of native species and experiencing the desolation of climate change. Payments to farmers were made according to the scale of the land they farmed and no longer took into consideration the yield the land provided in stock or crops. The benefits to the countryside of a subsidy system that discouraged overproduction were quickly seen in a more diverse landscape and in the planting of native species such as willow, birch and beech. This new system once more introduced an economy of scale that ensured farms with the highest acreage, which in Britain consistently means the wealthiest, received the largest payments.

A decisive alteration in the country's relationship to the land was brought into being by the CROW (Countryside and Rights of Way) Act of 2000, which introduced the 'Right to Roam' in open country such as moors, heaths and mountainside. The Act allowed ramblers and birdwatchers increased access to hinterlands and a further sense of identification with the landscape; but meanwhile, for all the miles of this newly opened space, the criminal act of Aggravated Trespass introduced in 1994 remained on the statute book.

Within a year of such significant changes the British countryside experienced the crisis of the 2001 foot-and-mouth disease epidemic. The disease was vigorous and had been absent from the United Kingdom since 1967; the measures in place to manage an outbreak had failed to anticipate the changes in farming methods, and contamination was active for almost nine months. The source of the contagion was never officially named, but a pig farm in Northumberland whose owner regularly fed catering waste to his animals was frequently claimed to be the source, while there was also speculation he may have been scapegoated due to having a poor record of husbandry that included past offences.

From its outbreak in February 2001 over two thousand cases of the disease were recorded during the year. The culling that accompanied its proliferation was necessarily brutal: over six million cattle, sheep and pigs were destroyed. The images of fields of burning livestock created a nightmarish vision of rural Britain in a state of emergency. A sense of systemic collapse was reinforced by the application of exclusion zones throughout the countryside, which for many months experienced the eeriness and lifelessness that accompanies moments of great change. The acrid smell of incinerated livestock lingered in the air.

Rob St John and the author, Pendle Hill, child summit of Kinder Scout, 2017.

Epilogue

Within a year of the foot-and-mouth epidemic I had moved to Radnorshire, a district of the county of Powys in Mid Wales. It is among the least populous places of the British Isles, and the regularity with which the Milky Way is visible is testament to the area's lack of light pollution. As a lingering preventative measure against the disease, which had finally been contained, buckets and troughs of disinfectant remained secured to sties and the entrance posts of footpaths. Signs instructing walkers to immerse their boots in the liquid were positioned above them. The sense of crisis and life continuing under emergency measures was palpable.

For almost two decades my home has been within this deep countryside. Despite being one of the country's poorest counties Powys was recorded in a recent census as being one of its happiest. This was a result met with disbelief by many of my nearest neighbours, all of whom except one, a clergyman, are farmers or earn their livelihood from agriculture.

My neighbours regularly talk with the stoicism, bordering on complaint, which is the lingua franca of farming. Whether they are right to be so subdued, at times despondent, about their lot only they can answer, as farming is ultimately an individual profession.

Their companionship has inculcated in me the habit of regarding the countryside and the landscape as a working environment. However life-affirming the view of month-old lambs gambolling together that signals the arrival of spring, or however beautiful the sunset across a harvested field in late summer, I instinctively experience these sights as carefully managed constituent elements of the farming year, rather than as some natural ordering of the countryside.

Rob St John is, among his other roles as a musician and writer, a sound artist whose works regularly explore our contemporary relationship with nature. The house he shares with his family in the Trough of Bowland in Lancashire is one of the few I have stayed in that rests in a location as isolated as my own. I asked Rob if I might visit him in order to spend a day together walking up Pendle Hill, a child summit of the Kinder Scout National Nature Reserve, which is situated not far from his home.

We met fell runners, fellow walkers and other members of the public taking the refreshing weekday air on Pendle as we made our way along its trail. Once we had broken the back of our hike the fells flattened a little, and as we approached the summit Rob indicated a wire fence. In an experiment he had once attached contact microphones to its posts to record the environment.

The towns of Burnley, Colne and Nelson all sit near the base of Pendle Hill. While listening to the results of his research Rob mentioned hearing the sound of their daily activity in his headphones. From the valleys below, everyday noise of traffic and voices had soared upwards in the wind and along the fell to this point near its peak. I was struck by the way Rob had demonstrated what little separation there is between these two worlds and the extent to which places such as Pendle and its surrounding fells are now part of our lives. We have learned how to inhabit these locations without being present in them. Rob and I discussed how bird numbers had fallen drastically in the short few years since his contact microphone experiments, and he listed the species no longer regularly seen. Our visit felt like something of a re-enactment. Perhaps every walk in rural Britain is now a form of elegy, one made in recognition of what the landscape has lost; each footstep an act of remembrance of all we have destroyed.

Our final destination was the trig point at the top of Pendle Hill, and once there Rob and I rested. We looked out over the moors and the former mill towns that add a utilitarian inflection to this view over an Area of Outstanding Natural Beauty. Soon we were joined by a group of five or six ramblers, men in late middle age whose carefree demeanour suggested they might have been enjoying retirement. Our occupation of the trig point had lasted sufficiently long and Rob gestured to them that we were moving away and the view was theirs. 'Always clear a trig point we will,' one of them said, 'we're well known for it.'

We made our descent along the Nick of Pendle and arrived above the village of Sabden. It was a calm day in early October and there to meet us were three or four young men wearing sweatshirts whose hoods were pulled over their heads. They were staring intently at the ground as they shuffled slowly across the moorland. Occasionally one of their number reached down to gather the thin stalk of a psilocybin mushroom. We exchanged impassive smiles and carried on our way. Although it is a common assertion that as a country we are losing our connection with the environment, the bond this particular group of men felt with the natural world was likely to endure.

We paused and I asked Rob in which direction we should look to see if the peak of Kinder Scout was visible. The autumn air had the fleeting thickness that lasts for the few weeks between the end of summer and the first ground frosts. It had filled in the middle distance. Beyond the mist, some miles ahead, lay the highest point in the Peak District, the site of an act of civil disobedience whose legacy was enacted by the presence of everyone we had encountered on the moors that day.

Rob suggested we drive to two local landmarks. We visited a derelict mill situated in the steep, secluded valley of Jumble Hole Clough. The rapid stream that had supplied the mill still flows through the valley towards the River Calder. Rob had previously carried out a number of recordings in this water, including soaking tapes and encouraging their erosion by algae and other stream life and placing hydrophones beneath the surface of the water, a process he likened to 'fishing for sound'. He would develop these methods on the book and album *Surface Tension*, a project drawn from field recordings made in the water and on the banks of the River Lea in East London, during which his working methods resembled a cross between an artist's installation and an environmental field study.

The temperature had started to drop as we drove a few miles to our final destination, the Bridestones, a set of distinctive grit rock and boulders that cluster together on a dramatic area of moorland near the town of Todmorden. The largest of them, the Great Bride Stone, has the gravity-defying appearance of an upturned bottle. In the dying light of the day the presence of the rocks was especially powerful.

As we turned to make our departure, the sky above had suddenly filled with larks. Rob smiled; aware of the proposed title of my book, he mentioned that he had arranged the display especially.

From the small road where we had parked a man walked towards us. He gave the impression of rather a careworn individual. There was a hunched awkwardness to his gait that he offset with a fixed, rueful smile. His hands clasped a duffle bag tightly as he spoke to us without stopping.

'Excuse me,' he said in the same accent we had heard throughout our walk on the fells. 'Do you know what all those birds up there are?'

I assumed that Rob, who has a thorough knowledge of birds, knew the collective noun for larks is an 'exaltation', but neither he nor I felt the need to demonstrate such learning; to do so would have ruined the atmosphere of the day.

'They're larks', Rob said in his calm, assuring way.

'Larks, righto,' said the stranger, walking off in the sunset towards the Bridestones and the moorland beyond. And as he did so the entire landscape was his alone.

Discography

The titles listed below are shown in the format of their original release. In some cases they may more easily be heard in other versions or reissues, for which the website www.discogs.com is an excellent resource.

Out of the exhaustive catalogue of recordings of *The Lark Ascending* I have chosen the one made by Iona Brown and Sir Neville Marriner in 1972; a popular interpretation, it seems to especially capture the mystery, spaciousness and poignancy of Vaughan Williams' composition. This is also the recording with which I have become most familiar, having first heard it during childhood and which provided the source and inspiration for this book.

Prologue

Laurie Spiegel: *The Expanding Universe* (Philo, 1980)
Steve Reich: *Six Pianos* (Deutsche Gramophon, 1974)
        Music For 18 Musicians (ECM, 1978)
        Octet (ECM, 1980)
        Sextet (Nonesuch, 1986)

Boards of Canada: *Twoism* (Music70, 1995)

Jim O'Rourke: *Bad Timing* (Drag City, 1997)

I'm Happy, And I'm Singing, And A 1, 2, 3, 4 (Mego, 2001)

Aphex Twin: *Selected Ambient Works Volume II* (Warp, 1994)

John Fahey: *The Voice of The Turtle* (Takoma, 1968)

The Yellow Princess (Vanguard, 1968)

Robbie Basho: *The Seal of the Blue Lotus* (Takoma, 1965)

Chapter One

Ralph Vaughan Williams, Academy Of St. Martin-in-the-Fields, Director: Neville Marriner: *Fantasia On A Theme By Thomas Tallis / The Lark Ascending / Five Variants Of Dives And Lazarus / Fantasia On Greensleeves* (Argo, 1972)

Chapter Two

Ewan MacColl & Peggy Seeger: *The World Of Ewan MacColl & Peggy Seeger* (Argo, 1970)

Ralph Vaughan Williams, Sir Adrian Boult conducting The London Philharmonic Orchestra: *A Pastoral Symphony* (Decca, 1953)

Ralph Vaughan Williams: Sir Adrian Boult, conducting The Philharmonic Promenade Orchestra: *Norfolk Rhapsody / English Folk Song Suite / Fantasia On A Theme Of Tallis / Fantasia On 'Greensleeves'* (Westminster, 1954)

Chapter Three

Stan Tracey: *Jazz Suite (Inspired By Dylan Thomas' 'Under Milk Wood')* (Columbia, 1965)

Bobby Wellins, Scottish National Jazz Orchestra: *Culloden Moor Suite* (Spartacus Records, 2014)

The New Departures Quartet: *The New Departures Quartet* (Transatlantic Records, 1964)

Chapter Five

The Byrds: 'Turn! Turn! Turn! (To Everything There Is A Season)/ She Don't Care About Time', 7" (Columbia, 1965)

Nick Drake: *Five Leaves Left* (Island, 1969)
          Bryter Layter (Island, 1970)
          Pink Moon (Island, 1972)
          Time of No Reply (Hannibal, 1986)

Chapter Six

John Cameron: *Kes* (Trunk, 2001)

Harold McNair: 'Indecision/The Hipster', 7" (RCA Victor, 1968)

Donovan: *Mellow Yellow* (Epic, 1967)
      A Gift From A Flower To A Garden (Pye, 1967)
      Donovan In Concert (Pye, 1968)
      Barabajagal (Epic, 1969)

The Incredible String Band: *The Hangman's Beautiful Daughter* (Elektra, 1968)

Pink Floyd: *The Piper At The Gates of Dawn* (EMI Columbia, 1967)

The Beatles: *The Beatles* (Apple, 1968)

Vashti Bunyan: *Just Another Diamond Day* (Phillips, 1970)

Traffic: *Mr. Fantasy* (Island, 1967)
      Traffic (Island, 1968)
      John Barleycorn Must Die (Island, 1970)

The Small Faces: 'The Universal /Donkey Rides, A Penny A Glass', 7" (Immediate, 1968)

Paul & Linda McCartney: *Ram* (Apple, 1971)

Chapter Eight

Traffic: *When The Eagle Flies* (Island, 1974)

Wings: 'Mull of Kintyre/Girls School', 7" (MPL, 1977)

Chapter Nine

Gavin Bryars: *The Sinking of The Titanic* (Obscure, 1975)

The Portsmouth Sinfonia: 'William Tell Overture' one-sided Flexi-disc
    (no label, 1970)
            Plays The Popular Classics (Transatlantic, 1973)
            Hallelujah (Transatlantic, 1974)

Brian Eno: *Discreet Music* (Obscure, 1975)

Michael Nyman: *Decay Music* (Obscure, 1978)

Chapter Ten

Penguin Cafe Orchestra, Simon Jeffes, performed by Members of the Penguin Cafe: *Music From The Penguin Cafe* (Obscure, 1976)

Penguin Cafe Orchestra: *Penguin Cafe Orchestra* (Editions EG, 1981)
Broadcasting From Home (Editions EG, 1984)
Signs of Life (Editions EG, 1987)

Kate Bush: *The Dreaming* (EMI, 1982)
The Hounds of Love (EMI, 1985)

Chapter Eleven

The Raincoats: *Odyshape* (Rough Trade, 1981)

Young Marble Giants: 'Final Day/Radio Silents/Cakewalking/ Colossal Youth', 7" (Rough Trade, 1980)

Chapter Twelve

Hawkwind: *Space Ritual* (United Artists, 1973)
Hall of the Mountain Grill (United Artists, 1974)
Warrior on the Edge of Time (United Artists, 1975)

Chapter Fourteen

Ultramarine: *Folk* (Les Disques Du Crépuscule, 1990)

Every Man And Woman Is A Star (Brainiak, 1991)
United Kingdoms (Blanco Y Negro, 1993)

Soft Machine: *The Soft Machine* (Probe, 1968)
Volume 2 (Probe, 1968)
Third (CBS, 1970)

Kevin Ayers: *Joy of a Toy* (Harvest, 1969)

Kevin Ayers And The Whole World: *Shooting at the Moon* (Harvest, 1970)

Boards of Canada: *Twoism* (Music70, 1995)
Music Has The Right To Children (Warp/Skam, 1998)
In A Beautiful Place Out In The Country (Warp, 2000)

Epilogue

Rob St John: *Surface Tension* (Pattern & Process Press, 2015)

Select Bibliography

Anderson, J. R. L. and Godwin, Fay, *The Oldest Road: An Exploration of The Ridgeway* (Farnham: Ashgate Publishing, 1975)

Barrie, J. M., *Peter Pan* (London: Hodder & Stoughton, 1911)

Betjeman, John, *Collected Poems* (London: John Murray, 1958)

Blunden, John and Curry, Nigel, *The Changing Countryside* (Beckenham; Helm/The Open University, 1985)

Blunden, John and Curry, Nigel, *A Future For Our Countryside* (Oxford: Blackwell, 1988)

Blythe, Ronald, *Akenfield: Portrait of an English Village* (London: Viking, 1969)

Blythe, Ronald, *The Time by the Sea* (London: Faber & Faber, 2013)

Brand, Stewart (ed.), *The Last Whole Earth Catalog* (Menlo Park, The Portola Institute, 1972)

Brooks, Alan (ed.), *Woodlands* (Wallingford: British Trust for Conservation Volunteers, 1980)

Brooks, Alan (ed.), *Hedging* (Wallingford: British Trust for Conservation Volunteers, 1980)

Burnett, Frances Hodgson, *The Secret Garden* (London: William Heinemann, 1911)

Carr, J. L., *A Month In The Country* (Brighton: Harvester Press, 1981)

Carroll, Lewis, *Alice's Adventures In Wonderland* (London: Macmillan, 1865)

Carroll, Lewis, *Through The looking Glass* (London: Macmillan, 1871)

Carson, Rachel L., *Silent Spring* (Boston: Houghton Mifflin, 1962)

Carson, Rachel L., 'Undersea' (*The Atlantic*, 1937)

Carson, Rachel L., *Under The Sea Wind* (London: Staples Press, 1952)

Chambers, Emma (ed.), *Paul Nash* (London: Tate, 2016)

Gantz, Jeffrey (trans.), *The Mabinogion* (London: Penguin Classics, 1976)

Gardiner, Rolf, *Water Springing From the Ground* (Fontmell Magna: Springhead, 1972)

Gardiner, Rolf, *England Herself: Ventures in Rural Restoration* (London: Faber & Faber, 1944)

Grahame, Kenneth, *The Wind In The Willows* (London: Methuen, 1908)

Graves, Robert, *Good-Bye to All That* (London: Anchor, 1929)

Grigson, Geoffrey; Gentleman, David; Branfield, Peter *The Shell Book Of Roads* (London: Ebury, 1964)

Hargrave, John, *The Wigwam Papers* (London: Pearson, 1916)

Hargrave, John, *The Totem Talks* (London: Pearson, 1918)

Hargrave, John, *Tribal Training* (London: Pearson, 1919)

Hargrave, John, *The Great War Brings It Home: The Natural Reconstruction of the Unnatural Existence* (London: Constable, 1919)

Hargrave, John, *The Confession of the Kibbo Kift: A Declaration & General Exposition of the Work of the Kindred* (London: Duckworth, 1927)

Hargrave, John, *Kibbo Kift* (London: The Kin Press, 1931)

Hargrave, John, *The Imitation Man* (London: Victor Gollancz, 1931)

Hargrave, John, *Summer Time Ends* (London: Constable, 1935)

Heaney, Seamus, *The Redress of Poetry* (London: Faber & Faber, 1990)

Hines, Barry, *A Kestrel for A Knave* (London: Michael Joseph, 1968)

Hipperson, Sarah, *Greenham, Non-Violent Women vs The Crown Perogative* (London: Greenham Publications, 2005)

Hobsbawn, Eric, *The Age of Extremes: The Short Twentieth Century, 1914–1991* (London, Michael Joseph, 1994)

Horovitz, Michael, *Children of Albion: Poetry of the Underground in Britain* (London, New Departures 1-24, Penguin,1969)

Ishiguro, Kazuo, *The Remains of the Day* (London: Faber & Faber, 1989)

Kennedy, Michael, *The Works of Ralph Vaughan Williams* (London: Oxford University Press, 1964)

Kennedy, Michael, *A Catalogue of the Works of Ralph Vaughan Williams* (London; Oxford University Press, 1983)

Kumar, Satish, (ed.), *Resurgence* (Crymych: Resurgence, 1977)

Larkin, Philip, *Collected Poems* (London: Faber & Faber, 1988)

Leslie, Paul, *The Living Hedge* (London: Faber and Faber, 1946)

Leslie, Paul, *Angry Young Man* (London: Faber and Faber, 1951)

Lymington, Viscount, *Famine In England* (London: H. F. & G. Witherby, 1938)

Lymington, Viscount, *Alternative to Death the Relationship Between Soil, Family and Community* (London: Faber & Faber, 1944)

Massingham, H. J., *The English Countryside* (London: Batsford, 1951)

Massingham, H. J., *Chiltern Country* (London: Batsford, 1940)

Massingham, H. J., *Cotswold Country* (London: Batsford, 1942)

Nash, Paul, *Outline, An Autobiography* (London: Faber & Faber, 1949)

Newby, Howard, *Green And Pleasant Land? Social Change in Rural England* (London; Pelican, 1980)

Newby, Howard, *Country Life, A Social History of Rural England* (London; Weidenfeld & Nicolson, 1987)

Newby, Howard, *The Countryside In Question* (London; Haper Collins, 1988)

Pollen, Annebella, *The Kindred of the Kibbo Kift: Intellectual Barbarians* (London: Donlon Books, 2016)

Ross, Cathy, *Designing Utopia: John Hargrave and the Kibbo Kift* & Bennett, Olive (London: Philip Wilson Publishers, 2015)

Sassoon, Siegfried, *Memoirs of a Fox-Hunting Man* (London: Faber & Faber, 1928)

Seymour, John, *On My Own Terms* (London: Faber & Faber, 1963)

Seymour, John, *The Complete Book of Self Sufficiency* (London: Dorling Kindersley, 1976)

Seymour, John and Sally (ill.), *The Fat of the Land* (London: Faber & Faber, 1961)

Seymour, John and Sally (ill.), *Self-Sufficiency* (London: Faber & Faber, 1973)

Seymour, John & Sally (ill.), *The Countryside Explained* (London: Faber & Faber, 1977)

Seymour, John & Sally (ill.), *I'm A Stranger Here Myself: The Story of a Welsh Farm* (London: Faber & Faber, 1978)

Street, Sean, *Radio Waves: Poems Celebrating the Wireless* (London, Enitharmon Press, 2004)

Thomas, Dylan, *Under Milk Wood* (London: J. M. Dent & Sons Ltd, 1954)

Thomas, Dylan, *The Collected Poems* (New York: New Directions, 1953)

Thompson, E. P., *The Making of the English Working Class* (London: Victor Gollancz, 1963)

Waugh, Evelyn, *Brideshead Revisited, The Sacred & Profane Memories of Captain Charles Ryder* (London: Chapman and Hall, 1945)

Williams, Raymond, *The Country And The City* (London: Chatto and Windus, 1973)

Wodehouse, P. G., *Summer Lightning* (London: Herbert Jenkins, 1929)

Wodehouse, P. G., *Heavy Weather* (London: Herbert Jenkins, 1933)

Woolf, Virginia, *Jacob's Room* (London: Hogarth Press, 1922)

Woolf, Virginia, *Mrs Dalloway* (London: Hogarth Press, 1925)

Woolf, Virginia, *To The Lighthouse* (London: Hogarth Press, 1927)

Woolf, Virginia, *A Room of One's Own* (London: Hogarth Press, 1929)

Vaughan Williams, Ralph, *Letters of Ralph Vaughan Williams, 1895–1958* (London; Oxford University Press, 2008)

Vaughan Williams, Ralph, *National Music* (London; Oxford University Press, 1934)

Vaughan Williams, Ralph, *The Penguin Book of English Folk Songs* (London; Lloyd, A. L., Penguin, 1959)

Vaughan Williams, Ralph, Leather, E. M. and Palmer, R. (ed.), *Twelve Traditional Carols from Herefordshire* (London: Stainer & Bell, 1920)

Vaughan Williams, Ralph and Deamner, P. (ed.), *The English Hymnal* (London; Oxford University Press; Dearmer, Percy, 1906)

Yarnall, Williams, *The Dome Builder's* Handbook (Philadelphia: Running Press, 1973)

Sources

The source of all Public General Acts and Private Acts of Parliament, Secondary and Delegated Legislation and Ministerial Statements is Hansard: https://hansard.parliament.uk/

The Hansard Archive: www.hansard-archive.parliament.uk/

The Agricultural statistics stated are drawn from the Ministry of Agriculture, Fisheries and Food: Statistics (Census and Prices) Division: Agricultural and Horticultural Census Datasets at The National Archives, the syllabus of *The Changing Countryside* Postgraduate Course, produced by The Open University in association with the Countryside Commission (1983–91), the archives of *Farmers Weekly* and *New Scientist* (Vols 91–105, 1981), *Agriculture from 1945* in The National Archive and CAP Payments, UK DEFRA.

Bearman, C. J., *The Sorcerer's Apprentice: Mary Neal and Rolf Gardiner* (The Morris Ring, vol. 4, I, 2009)

Craven, John Francis Charles, *Redskins in Epping Forest: John Hargrave, The Kibbo Kift And The Woodcraft Experience* (Thesis submitted for PHD, UCL, 1998)

English, Penny, *Disputing Stonehenge: Law and Access to a National Symbol* (*Entertainment Law*, vol. 1, no. 2 (London: Frank Cass, 2002)

Moore-Colyer, R. J., *Rolf Gardiner, English Patriot and the Council for the Church and Countryside* (*The Agricultural History Review*, vol. 49, II, 2001)

Stamp, Gavin, *The Debasement of Heritage* (*The Spectator*, i-iv-88)

The Papers of Henry Rolf Gardiner, Cambridge University Library
The John Hargrave Archive, Museum of London

Acknowledgements

I am grateful to staff at the British Library, the Museum of London, the National Trust, the Ralph Vaughan Williams Society, the National Farmers Union, the Imperial War Museum, English Heritage, the Department of Archives and Modern Manuscripts, Cambridge University Library, the Open University Archive, the Archive of Faber & Faber and the Letterpress Collective, Bristol.

My sincere thanks to the following for their generosity in agreeing to be interviewed:

Gavin Bryars, John Cameron, Ian Cooper, Cymon Eckle, Bill Hamblett, Paul Hammond, Richard Hines, Arthur Jeffes, Alan Lodge, Members of the Greenham Common Women's Peace Camp, Keith McIvor, Joe Rush, Rob St John, Anne Sears, David Sears, Matthew Smith, Carys Swanwick, Andrew Weatherall.

I am indebted to my editor Lee Brackstone for his dedication, energy and vision, and to my agent, Jonny Geller, for his counsel and patience.

Over the course of writing, the following people were kind enough to offer their encouragement, insight and expertise. My heartfelt thanks to them all:

Martin Orbach, Juliet Noble, James Lynch, Sian Tucker, Jackson Tucker Lynch, Robbie Tucker Lynch, Calder Tucker Lynch, Teifi Tucker Lynch, Harriet Hand, Nick Hand, Susannah Walker, Mark Pilkington, Owen Hatherley, Christine Hamlett, Christopher Hamlett, Patrick Keiller, Matt Sewell, Gruff Rhys, Robin Turner, Jeff Barrett, Dan Papps, Paul Baillie-Lane, Jesse Ingham, Georgiana Treasure-Evans, Jacqui Rice, Laurence Bell, John Wilcox, Barbara Wilcox, Rob Jones, Rob Tyler and the hill farming community of Llandeilo Graban, Chris Sharp, Jon Savage, Ben Thompson.

My enduring gratitude and love to Sarah Chilvers and Elijah King.

And to Ralph Vaughan Williams: *There never was a less typical 'typical Englishman'.*

Index

setting by Vaughan Williams, 69–70, 72–73

Donovan (Leitch, Donovan Philips), 110, 111–113
  drug use, 113, 115
  works, 115
    Barabajagal (alb), 111
    In Concert (alb), 113
    A Gift from a Flower to a Garden (alb), 111–112, 113, 115, 143, 154
    Isle of Islay, *102*, 103, 112–113
    Mellow Yellow, 111
    Poor Cow (songs for), 108

Dorman-Smith, Sir Reginald, 94

Dragon Hill, Oxfordshire (location for *Cloudbusting* (Bush)), 196, 203

Drake, Nick, 90–91

drugs, 116. *see also* psychedelic music
  alcohol, consumption by Travellers, 259–260, 261
  The Beatles' use of, 117
  Donovan's use of, 113, 115
  Ecstasy, 258, 267, 269. *see also* acid house music; acid house parties
  at Glastonbury Festival, 261, 262, 264–265, 268–269
  heroin, 54, 240, 260
  hippies' use of, Preseli Hills and Meigan Fayre, 140, 142–143
  marijuana (Preseli Hills), 142–143
  psychedelic mushrooms, 140, 143, 305
  at Stonehenge Festival, 239–240
  Travellers' use of, 239–240, 258–260, 292

Druids, 86, 221, 232–234, 238–239

Dylan, Bob, 119

East Grinstead, 'Acid House Pooh Corner', 271–274

Eavis, Michael, 253, 262, 263, 264. *see also* Glastonbury Festival

Eckel, Cymon, 267, 268–273, 275, 276. *see also Boy's Own* fanzine and label

eco-housing, 152

Ecstasy, 258, 267, 269. *see also* acid house music; acid house parties; drugs

electronic music. *see also* Boards of Canada; Ultramarine
  Bush as pioneer in, 199–200, 202–203

electronica, as suitable accompaniment to walking, 2

Elgar, Edward, 3
  The Enigma Variations, 3
  The Fringes of the Fleet, 3
  Pageant of Empire, 3
  Pomp and Circumstance Marches, 3, 159
  'Elgar Country', 3
  threatening of, by Castlemorton Common rave, 4–6

English Array, 96–97
  Quarterly Gazette of the English Array, 96

English Folk Dance Society, 67
  Cecil Sharp House library, as source material, 283
  conflict with Gardiner, 73–74, 95–96
  Neal's opinions of, 75

English Heritage
  formation, 194
  Stonehenge, 194, 220, 240–242, 247. *see also* Stonehenge

English Mistery, 94–96

Eno, Brian
  involvement with Portsmouth Sinfonia, 170, 171
  work on generative music, 175–176
  work with Bryers in experimental music, 171–175
  work with David Bowie, 176
  works, 187
    Discreet Music (alb), 175–176
    Three Variations on the Canon in D Major by Johann Pachelbel, 175–176

environmental organisations
  Council for Clean Rivers, 47
  CPRE. *see* Council for the Preservation of Rural England (CPRE)
  Ferguson's Gang, 33–34
  Friends of the Earth, 132
  National Trust. *see* National Trust

Smoke Abatement Society, 47
Environmentally Sensitive Areas, 192
Eoin, Marcus, 297. *see also* Boards of
  Canada
Espérance Club, 75–76, 80
Esperance Morris, 75
estates, large. *see also* landowners
  field sports. *see* field sports
  forestation post-WWI, 30–31
  housing developments post-WWI,
    31–32
  loss of workforce post-WWI, 10–11, 31
  preservation by National Trust, 36
eugenics, increased consideration of in
  1920s England, 81
experimental music, 170, 171–172. *see also*
  Bryars, Gavin; Obscure Records label
  generative music, 171–172, 175–176

Fahey, John, as suitable accompaniment to
  walking, 2
Fairport Convention, 114, 118
  Liege and Leif (alb), 91
falconry
  Hines' passion for, 104, 105–106,
    107–108
  Kes. see Kes (Loach)
  The Treatise of Hawkes and Hawking
    (Bert), 105–106
farmers and farming. *see* agriculture
fascism. *see also* anti-Semitism
  in 1930s Britain, 61–63, 93–95, 97
  in 1930s-1940s Germany, 62–63, 93. *see
    also* Hitler Youth
  'blood and soil' ideology, 62, 64, 67, 77,
    87, 93
  British Union of Fascists, 61–63, 65,
    93–94
  Darré, 62, 65, 93
  English Array, 96–97
  English Mistery, 94–96
  Fuller, 94
  Hess, 93
  influence on Gardiner and Springhead
    Ring, 90, 93, 99

Ferguson's Gang, 33–34
fertiliser use, post-WWII, 126, 127. *see also*
  intensive agriculture
festivals, *228*, 235, 287–288. *see also* raves;
  warehouse parties
  Aldeburgh Festival, 29
  Avon Free Festival, 287–288
  boutique festivals, 276
  Castlemorton Common. *see*
    Castlemorton Common rave
  Deeply Vale Festival, 231
  dissolution of festival circuit, 258
  Glastonbury Festival. *see* Glastonbury
    Festival
  Inglestone Common Free Festival,
    231–232, 287
  media coverage, 263–264, 289, 290, 291
  Meigan Fayre, *136*, 143, 144–146
  Pembrokeshire, 125
  policing, 230–231, 261, 287–288,
    290–291
  as 'safe spaces' for Travellers, 236
  Stonehenge Festival. *see* Stonehenge
    Festival
  Windsor Festival, 230–231, 268
feudalism, advocated by Sanderson and
  English Mistery, 95
field sports, 6–7, 11
  conserving, role of CPRE, 33
  hunt sabotage, as Aggravated Trespass,
    294
fishing, ii, 158
Flowered Up, 273. *see also* Mooncult,
  Barry
folk dance
  English Folk Dance Society. *see* English
    Folk Dance Society
  Gardiner's obsession with, 65–66, 67,
    73–74, 96
  in Germany, Deutsche Freischar youth
    organisation, 67
  Morris dancing, 65, 67, 68, 75–77
    Esperance Morris, 75
    Travelling Morrice, 67, 73
    as white or black magic, Neal's
      questioning, 76–77

People's Budget 1910, 10
pesticides
    creating 'convincingly green and
        pleasant' land during 1980s, 192
    DDT, 132–135
    impact on biodiversity, 107, 132–135
    prohibited, in Halvergate Marshes,
        Norfolk Broads, 191–192
Pethick-Lawrence, Emmeline, 75, 80
Pink Floyd
    The Piper at the Gates of Dawn (alb),
        115–116
    See Emily Play, 180
Pitt-Rivers, George, 97
Portsmouth Sinfonia, 168–171
    Also Sprach Zarathustra (Strauss), 171
    *Portsmouth Sinfonia Plays the Popular
        Classics*, 170–171
    William Tell Overture, 169
post-traumatic stress disorder ('shell
    shock')
    depiction in literature, 18–19
    Sassoon's experience of, 19–20
    Williamson's experience of, 62
Powys, i–ii, 303–304
Prebble, John, *Culloden*, 54
    The Culloden Moor Suite (Wellins),
        54–55
Preseli Hills region, Pembrokeshire,
    122–126, 129–131, 137, 138–139,
    140–147
    Meigan Fayre, *136*, 143, 144–146
Primary Industry, A, 278
Proms, Last Night of the, 4, 159
protest songs
    at Greenham Common Women's Peace
        Camp, 211–212
    use of folk songs and music, 91,
        282–285
psychedelic mushrooms, 140, 143, 305
psychedelic music. *see also* Beatles, The;
    Donovan (Leitch, Donovan Philips);
    Pink Floyd; Traffic; Zorch
    drawing from children's literature,
        115–116
Public Order Act 1986, 258–259

Pure, 296–297. *see also* McIvor, Keith

RAF Greenham Common. *see* Greenham
    Common (RAF base)
ragas, as suitable accompaniment to
    walking, 2
Raincoats, 225–226
    Go Away, 226
    Odyshape (alb), 225–227
Rambler's Association
    founding, 7, 38
    Dalton as chair, 50
rambling. *see also* walks and walking
    mass trespass of Kinder Scout, 6–7, 8,
        37–39
    National Council of Ramblers
        Federations, 37
    as 'political activity', 37
    rambling clubs, 1920s, 37
    'Right to Roam' under CROW Act
        2000, 300–301
raves, 268, 271, 274–276. *see also* acid house
    parties; festivals
    Castlemorton Common, 4–6, 288–291
    impact of Criminal Justice and Public
        Order Act 1994, 8–9, 291, 292, 293
    Loch Lomond, 296–297
Rawnsley, Canon Hardwicke, 35
Reich, Peter (son of Wilhelm)
    A Book of Dreams, 197
    depiction in *Cloudbusting* (Bush),
        198–199
Reich, Steve, as suitable accompaniment to
    walking, 2
Reich, Wilhelm, 197–199
    depiction in *Cloudbusting* (Bush),
        198–199
    Orgonon and cloudbusting apparatus,
        197–199
Resurgence (Journal of the Fourth World)
    (magazine), 137–139
ribbon housing development, 31–32
Ridgeway, The, 75, 195–196, 221
'Right to Roam' under CROW Act 2000,
    300–301
rights of way, landowner responsibilities, 7